THE CONSPIRATORS

THE CON

HARPER & BROTHERS PUBLISHERS NEW YOR

SPIRATORS

GEOFFREY BAILEY

To V., who knows

CONTENTS

A SECTION OF ILLUSTRATIONS WILL
BE FOUND FOLLOWING PAGE 86.

Author's Preface

This book is the story of certain events that took place in Russia and in Western Europe during the years of crisis between the end of World War I and the beginning of World War II, and of the individuals directly or indirectly involved in them. At first glance, some of the incidents described may appear of secondary importance or even trivial. Yet all of them were to lead eventually to, or merge with other, bigger events. And these have determined the course of our time.

For ours is an age not only of total war, but also of total diplomacy that shuns no means and neglects no factor in achieving its ends. As the tide of war, revolution and counter-revolution swept back and forth across Europe—and Asia—diplomacy at the highest level became often inextricably enmeshed with the crudest forms of espionage, subversion, police provocation and plain terrorism. While top-hatted envoys negotiated politely in the capitals of Europe or in the shoreside hotels of Switzerland and the Riviera, agents and counter-agents were everywhere. Some, such as those described by E. Phillips Oppenheim and W. Somerset Maugham, were mere pawns in the day-to-day game of power politics. Others, of the Eric Ambler type, played for subtler stakes, still others for the highest stake of all, their personal power and advancement. More than at any other period of history, relations between Russia and the Western powers were as much a story of cloak-and-dagger operations as an account of diplomatic negotiation and maneuver. Pitted with missing links, confused by conflicting facts and interpretations, masked behind the camouflage of state secrets, rendered dramatic by a small army of dead or missing persons, every episode can be viewed from a different angle. As for the inner thoughts, feelings and motivations of some of the principal protagonists, they will doubtless remain unknown to us even after the facts themselves are no longer secret. For most of them are dead, and their friends, enemies, employers and accomplices are dead also. And the few surviving eye-witnesses seem reluctant to talk—out of fear, or out of a lingering loyalty to the causes they once served, or because they have, on the contrary, long lost their faith, and would now rather forget . . . and be forgotten.

And yet despite the unbelievably complex and tangled scheme of action, large and small, and the general aura of mystery that char-acterizes this period, mystery need not become a fetish, pursued for its own sake and serving merely to obscure or distort further the picture of an unresolved dilemma. If much about the events de-scribed in the pages that follow has still to be deduced and con-jectured, a careful analysis of the existing documentation (periodicals, press reports, memoirs, government publications, trial accounts and the few obtainable eyewitness reports) does at least provide a first rough but coherent and *integrated* sketch of a patchwork of intrigue that may well be unparalleled in the history of mankind. This is the primary purpose of this book.

In my search for and study of this source material, I am above all indebted to the Library of Congress in Washington, D.C., the Hoover Library on War and Revolution at Stanford University, California, and the New York Public Library, the unfailing helpful-ness and courtesy of whose staffs did much to alleviate what could otherwise have well been a grueling task. I am particularly in-debted to Cass Canfield, Jr., whose encouragement, advice and as-sistance throughout the preparation of the manuscript were largely responsible for making this book possible.

G. BAILEY

London, Paris, New York
February 1956–December 1959

PART ONE

THE "TRUST"

1

THE GENTLEMAN
FROM REVEL

It all began one late summer day in 1921, when a bearded, middle-aged gentleman alighted from the Petrograd train as it steamed into Revel (soon to be rechristened Tallinn), capital of the newly established Baltic republic of Estonia.

Well-dressed, distinguished-looking, with an air of assurance bordering on arrogance, the gentleman could have been taken for a successful businessman or a civil servant of rank. In fact, Aleksander Aleksandrovich Yakushev was both. In Tsarist days he had held an important position in the Ministry of Communications; and when the Communists or Bolsheviki (as they were better known in those days) took over in the fall of 1917, he was one of the many technicians whom the then all-powerful Trotsky had cajoled or coerced into serving the new regime. He was now on his way to Oslo, to attend an international lumber conference. His stopover in Revel, however, was motivated, supposedly, by strictly personal considerations.

For Yakushev had been for some time on terms of close friendship with a lady whose husband had after the Revolution fled to Revel. He now hoped, allegedly, to persuade this gentleman (who will hereinafter be known as Captain X) to grant his wife a divorce.

This seemingly innocuous episode was to serve as the point of departure for one of the most ingenious, successful and far-reaching undercover operations of our time, one which brought about, among other things, the temporary neutralization of several Western intelligence services; the capture and death at the hands of the OGPU* of two such prominent anti-Communists as Boris Savinkov and Sydney Reilly; the sensational kidnaping in broad daylight in the streets of Paris of the two White Russian generals Kutyepov and Miller and, lastly, the dramatic Red Army purges of 1937-1938.

Yakushev had several talks with Captain X, in the course of which, apart from the immediate object of his visit (which seems to have soon been disposed of to their mutual satisfaction), they discussed many things. Then, in an outburst of candor, Yakushev presently admitted that although he served the new regime in Russia, he was himself unalterably opposed to Communism. Moreover, he added, he was not alone; countless other ex-Tsarist officials and officers, who had for one reason or another agreed to work for the Communists, remained at heart staunch foes of the regime. Indeed, the Soviet government apparatus and the Red Army were already so heavily infiltrated by those whom Lenin sarcastically referred to as "radishes"—outside Red and inside White—that, under their influence, Communist rule itself was undergoing a subtle change. And Yakushev went on to describe in vivid detail the new leaders of Russia (many of whom he claimed to know personally)—their individual qualities and frailties, their petty jealousies and intrigues.

All this—coming as it did from one so obviously familiar with the innermost workings of the Communist administration—was so unexpected, so exciting, indeed so heartening, that Captain X could barely wait until his visitor had proceeded on his way before sitting down to write a detailed report on their conversations to a friend in Berlin who, in his turn, promptly relayed the information to certain Russian *émigré* circles there.

This was, to say the least, imprudent. True, Captain X had taken

---

* For the sake of this narrative, the Soviet secret police—as distinct from the Intelligence Department of the Army, the famous GRU—will be referred to variously by its successive names of Cheka (until February, 1922), OGPU (from February, 1922, to July, 1934), and NKVD (after July, 1934).

what he regarded as an adequate precaution: he had omitted specific mention of Yakushev's name and had referred to him merely as "a high Soviet official." Actually this was no precaution at all, for not many "high Soviet officials" were traveling through Revel these days; moreover, the Soviet Cheka had by now its confidential agents in many White Russian groups. So that when eventually a summary, if not an actual photostatic copy, of Captain X's letter to his Berlin friend found its way to the desk of Commissar Kiakowski, of the Counter-Intelligence Department of the Cheka, the latter, presumably, did not have to go to too much trouble to discover the identity of the Captain's mysterious visitor.

Early in 1922 White Russian circles abroad became aware of the existence in the U.S.S.R. of an underground organization which, calling itself the "Monarchist Union of Central Russia," or MUCR for short, seemed eager to get in touch with the *émigré* monarchists.

The existence of such a monarchist underground in Russia was confirmed, presently, by yet another traveler from Moscow—one Kolesnikov, who, upon his arrival in Revel, immediately contacted Captain X, allegedly on behalf of his "good friend Aleksander Aleksandrovich Yakushev." At first Captain X was inclined to be wary of his new guest. The latter's barely perceptible Polish accent, which seemed to belie the authenticity of his Russian-sounding name; his pale, somewhat shifty eyes; his ingratiating manner—all these made Captain X feel somehow uneasy. But when Kolesnikov went on, presently, to describe in every detail their conversations with Yakushev of the preceding autumn, the Captain's misgivings were completely allayed.

Kolesnikov turned out to be even more sanguine about the situation in Soviet Russia than Yakushev had been. The monarchist movement, he said, was better organized than ever. In fact, at this point, the main problem was not so much Communism as such (which was on the way out, anyway) as the wildcat activities of certain White Russian secret agents who, operating as they did without any real knowledge of the ever changing situation and often at cross-purposes with the inside anti-Communist groups, might do more harm than good. And yet, Kolesnikov hastened to add, men of their resourcefulness and daring could be invaluable so long as their missions were planned in concert with the underground, which, "having its agents everywhere," alone was able to elude or frustrate the inevitable reprisals of the OGPU. Whereupon Kolesnikov went on to outline a detailed system of clandestine liaison between the MUCR and the *émigré* monarchists, complete with intricate security precautions against eventual *agents provocateurs* of the OGPU, which he urged Captain X to recommend for adoption to his White Russian friends. Shortly thereafter, he departed again for the U.S.S.R.

Toward the middle of November, 1922, Yakushev himself re-appeared, this time in Berlin, as the MUCR's appointed representative to an *émigré* monarchist congress that had recently convened in that city. He traveled now under a different name, as "Mr. Feodorov," and was able, presently, to establish personal contact with certain monarchist leaders.* They had a number of talks, in the course of which Yakushev confirmed most of what he himself and then Kolesnikov had told Captain X in Revel. Communism, he announced confidently, had failed in Russia. The recently proclaimed "New Economic Policy," or NEP, was a first concession of defeat on the part of the Kremlin, a first step toward Russia's "return to normalcy."† And he went on to describe the activities of the MUCR. The latter, he claimed, was already so powerful that it had even

---

* By now, the 1½ million White Russian *émigrés* scattered about the world could be grouped, broadly speaking, into two main categories: (a) those who had accepted—some reluctantly, others with enthusiasm—the first Revolution of February-March, 1917 (which overthrew Tsarism and established a democratic republic), but had opposed the Bolsheviki's seizure of power in October-November of that year; and (b) those who were opposed to the idea of *any* revolution. It is with this latter faction that Yakushev first made contact.

† In March, 1921, against a background of mass discontent and open revolt and despite violent opposition on the part of many of his followers, Lenin had proclaimed his "New Economic Policy": the system of forced grain requisitions was abolished and replaced by a new system of state purchases and a measure of private initiative was reintroduced in retail trade and light industry. Designed to provide Russia with a "breather," while she recovered from the untold havoc of war and revolution—an objective that was to be largely achieved—the NEP continued roughly until 1928-1929, when Stalin's First Five-Year Plan heralded the era of integral Socialism in Russia.

succeeded in infiltrating the secret police—which accounted, incidentally, for his being able to come, go and talk so freely! Indeed, at this point, what the anti-Bolshevik forces in Russia needed most of their friends abroad was not so much active assistance as moral and especially financial support. They themselves would take care of everything else.

He then went on to elaborate upon his friend Kolesnikov's suggested liaison system between the MUCR and the *émigré* monarchists. The former, he explained, was camouflaged at present as the "Moscow Municipal Credit Association," an officially recognized commercial firm which, under the new NEP dispensations, was able to engage in legitimate business abroad. It was these business activities, incidentally, which also provided the funds needed to run the underground organization. Nothing would be simpler, he asserted, than to use the firm's business correspondence as a code for passing secret messages in and out of the country. The MUCR itself would thus be referred to as the "Trust" and the various individuals and operations involved would be similarly camouflaged. As for the more important communications, they could be carried by hand, by special couriers whom he, Yakushev, would undertake to recruit and organize.

According to all available evidence, Yakushev produced an impression of great daring, energy and intelligence. Moreover, he had considerable charm, and though not a very good orator, he spoke with an utter lack of heroics and bravado, in an even, serene, indeed almost indifferent tone of voice and yet at the same time with obvious knowledge of what he was talking about and with absolute conviction. More important still, his patriotism seemed so genuine and what he said resembled so little the gloomy reports that had been his listeners' main diet since they fled their country; it was so hopeful and corresponded so completely to what they *wished* to hear, and what they *wished* to believe, that—human nature being what it is—he seems to have had little difficulty in convincing them that he was telling the truth.

For in those days only a few White Russians regarded their defeat as final. Granted, the White anti-Communist armies had been crushed and scattered and their erstwhile allies, after affording them grudging recognition and inadequate support, had left them to their fate and come to terms with the new regime. But then this was just one lost battle, one isolated episode in the continuing struggle against those "Forces of Darkness" (as the Bolsheviki were so often referred to in their enemies' speeches and publications) which had so suddenly, and as some thought so incomprehensibly, seized power in Russia. Once the Russian people had discovered—at their own expense—the real face of Communism, once they had learned that the freedom which the Revolution was supposed to bring them was in reality a servitude far greater than anything they had as yet experienced, they would surely rise up in arms against the Soviet regime; while the Western powers, having overcome their postwar weariness and having awakened to the reality of the threat which the continuing existence of a Communist Russia represented to the non-Communist world, would rush to their assistance. And in the recent mutiny of the Red Baltic fleet in Kronstadt, the continuing peasant risings in central Russia, the never-ending guerrilla warfare in the forests of Byelorussia and especially in the growing anti-Communist reaction abroad, they chose to see the turning of the tide and the first steps toward the confirmation of their dreams.

And at first Yakushev was as good as his word: throughout the winter of 1922-1923 a steady flow of information on a variety of subjects kept coming out of Russia via the Trust. The gist of it all: Russia was "stirring."

In the spring of 1923, however, there appeared all of a sudden a change in Yakushev's attitude toward those circles with which he had first made contact. They were, he complained, timid and ineffectual; their refusal to send an emissary into Russia, as he had suggested, had caused a deplorable impression there, etc., etc. At the same time he began to show an increasing interest in another, far more important group, namely the various White Army veterans' organizations centered about Generals Baron Wrangel and Kutyepov and their nominal chief, the Grand Duke Nicholas, the elderly but prestigeful ex-Tsarist Commander in Chief in World War I.

Baron Piotr Nikolayevich Wrangel is acknowledged even by Soviet historians to have been the most outstanding of the White leaders. "In the person of Wrangel and his army," writes Mikhail V. Frunze, a top Red Army commander in the Civil War and a later War Commissar, "our motherland had without doubt a very dangerous opponent indeed. . . . In the various operations [in which he participated] Wrangel demonstrated in most cases both outstanding energy and complete understanding of the situation."[1] * A brilliant cavalry general in the grand tradition, a gifted strategist and a born if exacting and even harsh leader of men, who would show just as little reluctance in hanging White deserters by the score as in shooting hundreds of captured Red officers, Wrangel combined good looks, a powerful personality, absolute fearlessness, complete integrity and a will of iron with an intelligence and breadth of vision all too rare in the average professional soldier. Moreover, though himself the typical guardsman-aristocrat and an avowed monarchist and conservative, he had proved to be the only White leader to have appreciated the significance and implications of the Revolution and to have drawn the appropriate conclusions. His appointment early in April, 1920, to the command of the defeated and war-weary Southern forty-thousand-man strong "Volunteer" Army had come too late for him to undertake anything but a holding action. Nevertheless, during his eight months' stand in the Crimea not only did he succeed in raising, through often ruthless measures, the combat effectiveness of his troops to a peak the White armies had never previously known, so that even the official Soviet history of the Civil War has to admit that "the Wrangel army . . . was the best combat force the Russian and international counter-revolution ever disposed of in its armed struggle against the Soviet republics";[2] but through his realistic foreign policy ("Even with the devil, but against the Bolsheviki!") and his so-called "leftist policies by rightist hands" (that included the legalization of the peasants' arbitrary land seizures), he

* Superior numbers refer to notes in a section beginning on p. 273.

provided the anti-Communist forces, for the first time since the start
of the Civil War, with allies and a constructive political program.
However, when in October, 1920, the victorious Poles, whom
Wrangel's last stand had helped save from Communist domination,
signed an armistice with the Soviet government, thus enabling the
bulk of the Red Army to be hurled against his tiny force, his doom
was sealed.

Shortly before his final defeat, Wrangel had negotiated with the
Allied governments an agreement under which all those who wished
to leave the territory under his control (some 145,000 men, women
and children all told) would be evacuated to the Gallipoli peninsula
and the island of Lemnos, where there still existed large encamp-
ments dating back to the days of the ill-fated Dardanelles campaign.
And here they remained, in conditions of considerable hardship,
until the fall of 1921, when they were shipped for final resettlement
to Yugoslavia and Bulgaria.

There the men were put to work building roads and mining coal
—in themselves morale-sapping chores. At first they remained in formation, uniformed, subject to military discipline and under the command of their own officers. But soon, what with the obstruction of
the leftist Stambulisky government in Bulgaria and growing Soviet
diplomatic pressure generally, it became clear that this situation
could not continue. Some other form of organization was required
in order to retain a solid nucleus of dedicated and combat-hardened
officers, N.C.O.'s and men, around which a new White Army could
be rebuilt at short notice if and when circumstances allowed, and
to provide them with material and psychological support during
the difficult period of their adaptation to civilian life.

On September 1, 1923, Wrangel announced the creation of a
"Russian Armed Services' Union" (*Russkii Obshche-Voyenskii Soyuz*),
or ROVS for short, which was gradually to absorb into its ranks
most ex-Tsarist and White Army veterans at present abroad.

Thereafter, wherever White Russian refugees happened to settle,
there presently appeared organized veterans' groups, in close permanent touch with one another and with Wrangel's headquarters
in Yugoslavia. Eventually, the sight of a White Russian coal miner

or factory hand in Belgium, Bulgaria or Yugoslavia or of a White Russian taxi driver in Paris, London or Berlin doffing his overalls at the end of a working day and changing into faded but carefully patched, laundered and pressed uniform for evening duty at his local veterans' post became as characteristic a phenomenon of Russian *émigré* life—at least in those early days—as the better-publicized gypsy night haunts on Montmartre, in Soho or off the Kurfürstendamm. In due course the ROVS set up its own military cadet schools for the sons of the White veterans, correspondence courses in military science for their fathers and even a war college for senior officers. It is also from the ranks of the ROVS that General Kutyepov, Wrangel's second-in-command and, after the Baron himself, the most dynamic of the White leaders, was to draw most of the members of his famed "Combat Organization."

For in March, 1924, Kutyepov was called to Paris by the Grand Duke Nicholas and put in charge of all underground political work inside Russia. Thereafter and for more than a decade following the triumph of Soviet rule, White agents would steal, singly or in groups, across the Soviet border, as one *émigré* author has put it, "through some snow-muffled fir forest, to potter about their native land in the various disguises worked out, oddly enough, by the socialist-revolutionaries of yore, and quietly bring back to the little café in Paris . . . or to the little *Kneipe* in Berlin . . . the kind of useful trifles which spies are supposed to bring back to their employers. . . ."[3]—and also to continue the armed struggle against Communism from within, through propaganda, subversion and, if need be, terror.

That the Soviet authorities, for one, were fully aware of the latent threat these White para-military groups represented in those days can be seen from the following admission of a high official of the OGPU, V. Triandafilov, who wrote in 1922 warning: "We are watching this second Russia and we assume that its armed forces will reappear somewhere on our borders and that we will have to resume the struggle."[4] From then on Wrangel, Kutyepov and the ROVS were to be the object of the Kremlin's constant solicitude."

A first contact with the White military leaders was established by the Trust in June, 1923, in Berlin, where General Evgheni E. Klimovich, Wrangel's Chief of Intelligence, arrived from Belgrade especially to confer with Yakushev. They had a number of talks, as a result of which Klimovich too was completely won over and reported back to Wrangel in glowing terms. But Wrangel was wary; to his closest friends he even confided that he suspected Yakushev of being an *agent provocateur* of the OGPU. Nevertheless—no doubt so as to probe his game further and although he personally refused to have anything to do with the organization—he instructed Klimovich to keep in touch with the Trust.

Presently Yakushev made an even more valuable contact in the person of General Nikolai A. von Monkewitz. The latter, despite a rather checkered past, had succeeded somehow in worming himself into the confidence of General Kutyepov. He now played a prominent part in the latter's Combat Organization, where he lurked, says one eyewitness, "like a huge, hulking, bloody spider."

Thereafter Klimovich and Von Monkewitz were to be Yakushev's most enthusiastic sponsors in White Russian circles.

Meanwhile, the liaison service which Yakushev had organized had reached such a peak of efficiency that dispatches from, say, Paris or Berlin to Moscow and back traveled faster than official Western diplomatic couriers—in little over a week. Moreover, this messenger service operated so smoothly that Kutyepov's Combat Organization found itself relying more and more on the Trust to ensure the safe passage of its own agents to and from the U.S.S.R.

Presently Yakushev also established contact—again, presumably, through generals Klimovich and Von Monkewitz—with certain Western intelligence services, and in time these too came to rely to a growing extent upon the information which the Trust so willingly supplied and which appeared to be so much more complete, more up-to-date, more reliable and—most important of all—so much easier to obtain than anything their own agents seemed able to produce. Eventually, special liaison officers were assigned to some of the Western legations in the border states of Finland, Estonia, Latvia, Poland and Rumania, whose sole function it was to process the Trust's dispatches. On a number of occasions, information from regular intelligence channels was rejected solely because another, different report had come in from the Trust. In turn the Trust appointed "resident representatives" in certain key cities abroad—to maintain contact with foreign intelligence headquarters and keep abreast of White Russian *émigré* politics generally, and roving ones to co-ordinate their activities.

For nearly three years, beginning in 1924 and through the spring of 1926, the Trust thus virtually monopolized all undercover contacts between the U.S.S.R. on the one hand and the White para-military organizations and their Western friends on the other. Encouraging one group, rebuking another, mediating between them and a third, Yakushev himself was by now *persona grata* in some of the most exclusive White Russian and Western circles. By 1924 he had gained such recognition that General Von Monkewitz was able to arrange for him to be received by the Grand Duke Nicholas himself.

And yet it was somehow not possible to escape the feeling that all was not well with the Trust, or rather that all was just a little *too* well. By now, the OGPU's reputation for efficiency and cunning was well established. Yet many of Yakushev's couriers proceeded about their business as if they hadn't a care in the world; in fact, their arrivals and departures were sometimes an open secret. True, the very nonchalance with which they performed their duties, vanishing from Moscow one day, allegedly on a business trip to the country, only to turn up in Berlin, London or Paris the day after, had about it a quality of romantic, Scarlet Pimpernel-like daring that predisposed one in their favor. Nevertheless, at a time when the movements of so-called "stateless" persons (to which category most White Russian *émigrés* in those days belonged) were often restricted by various passport formalities, the ease with which those who happened to work for the Trust went from country to country, at a moment's notice, seemed as enviable as it was odd. Of course, in his official capacity as Soviet representative to the annual Königsberg Trade Fair and Ost-Europa Institut, Yakushev himself could travel to and from the U.S.S.R. without arousing suspicion. But he was an exception; the others had to use so-called "windows" (as the clandestine crossing points along the Soviet frontier were known). And the

Polish frontier guards, for one, were constantly complaining about
the couriers' flagrant disregard of the most elementary rules of conspiracy. True, there just never seemed to be any Red patrols around
when they were on their way; but then this in itself was strange, to
say the least. Indeed, even the cover names sported by the Trust's
leaders in their so-called "business correspondence" sounded just a
trifle too flamboyant to be of much use in throwing the OGPU off
the scent. And then, although Yakushev kept deploring his organization's alleged financial difficulties—"We are poor as church mice!"
he would say—his people never seemed to lack funds.

Presently these dawning misgivings became even more serious
when two prominent anti-Communist agents, the veteran terrorist
Boris Savinkov and the Englishman Sydney Reilly (both of whom
were known to have worked closely with the Trust), returned to
Russia via Trust-operated "windows" and were never heard of again.

2

BORIS SAVINKOV AND
SYDNEY REILLY

Boris Savinkov remains a controversial figure to this day. Winston Churchill, who met him for the first time in 1922, was immediately fascinated. The portrait sketch he has left of "this strange and sinister man," as he calls him, is a masterpiece:

". . . Small of stature; moving as little as possible and that noise-lessly and with deliberation; with remarkable grey-green eyes in a face of almost deathly pallor; speaking in a calm, even voice, almost a monotone, Boris Savinkov [he writes] combined the wisdom of a statesman, the qualities of a commander, the courage of a hero and the endurance of a martyr. . . . His manner was at once confidential and dignified; a ready and ceremonious address, with a frozen but not a freezing composure; through all the sense of an unusual personality, of veiled power in strong restraint. . . . His features were agreeable, but though still only in his forties, his face was so lined and crow's-footed that the skin looked in places, and particularly around the eyes, as if it were crinkled parchment. From these impenetrable eyes there glowed a steady regard. The quality of this regard was detached and impersonal and it seemed to me laden with doom and fate. . . . Boris Savinkov's whole life had been spent in conspiracy. Without religion as the Church teaches it; without wife or child or kith or kin;* without a friend; without fear; hunter and hunted; implacable, unconquerable; alone. . . . His being was organ-

* Churchill is mistaken: Savinkov had a son, who is alive to this day.

ised upon a theme: the freedom of the Russian people. In that cause, there was nothing he would not dare or endure. . . .[1]

Sir Bruce Lockhart, British diplomatic agent in Moscow after the Revolution, was less enthusiastic:

> For some reason which I have been unable to understand [he writes], Boris Savinkov has always been regarded by Englishmen as a man of action and therefore a hero. . . . His talents cannot be denied. . . . He understood the revolutionary temperament better almost than anyone and knew how to play on it for his own ends. . . . He had mingled so much with spies and *agents-provocateurs,* he hardly knew whether he was deceiving himself or those he meant to deceive. Like most Russians too, he was a forceful speaker, who could impress his personality upon his listeners. . . . [But] there was a fatal flaw in his character. He liked luxury and although he was ambitious, he was not prepared to sacrifice his self-indulgence to his ambitions. His chief weakness [however] was a fatal capacity for short spells of frenzied work, followed by long periods of indolence. . . .[2]

Boris Savinkov had indeed been a conspirator since the age of twenty. First, he had conspired against Tsarism: as field commander of the Socialist Revolutionary party's famed "Combat Organization," he had during the first years of this century personally planned and supervised the assassination of at least nineteen high Tsarist officials, including Minister of the Interior Von Plehve and the Grand Duke Serge, uncle of the Tsar. Then, when the campaign of terror had come, temporarily, to an end, he had turned to literature and written a best-selling novel, *The Pale Horse,* in which he recounted his experiences as a terrorist. World War I had found him in France, a political exile. Unlike many of his Socialist friends, however, he had welcomed enthusiastically Russia's participation in the hostilities on the Allies' side, believing—perhaps rightly—this to be the best means of speeding up the introduction of a Western-type parliamentary democracy in his country. First, he had enrolled as a volunteer with the French Army; then, after the downfall of Tsarism in February-March, 1917, he had returned home and thrown himself heart and soul into the battle for republican Russia's continuing participation in the war.

The overthrow of Russia's first democratic government by the

Bolsheviki in October-November, 1917, which was followed in due course by their signing, first of an armistice, and then of the shameful Brest-Litovsk peace treaty, as well as their disbanding of the just elected Constituent Assembly, represented, as far as Savinkov was concerned, more than a political defeat. It constituted a personal tragedy, the end of his life's dream. For like so many of his compatriots, he regarded Russia's withdrawal from the war as an act of perfidy, a betrayal of her allies' sacred trust. As for the Bolsheviki themselves, he knew their leaders too well, he had fought far too long at their side, not to foresee that their seizure of power—whatever its long-range economic or social effects—signified in fact the establishment of a tyranny compared to which Tsarist autocracy would seem like an age of enlightenment. "Between me and Lenin," he explained to W. Somerset Maugham, who was seeing much of him at the time, "it's a war to the death. One of these days, he will put me with my back to the wall and shoot me, or I shall put him with his back to the wall and shoot him. One thing I can tell you is that I shall never run away. . . ." And Maugham adds: "I have never come across anyone who filled me with a greater sense of confidence."[3] By means which he had always regarded as morally justifiable, Savinkov had fought for freedom when it was being suppressed by the Right; unlike the majority of his Socialist friends, he was not prepared to give up the struggle merely because this freedom was at present threatened by his erstwhile allies of the Left. Without a minute's hesitation he now proceeded to place his dauntless courage, his unique conspiratorial experience, his exceptional organizing talent and his invaluable contacts in the Russian political underworld at the service of the anti-Communist cause.

Russia, throughout that winter of 1917-1918 and the following spring, offered ideal conditions of activity for a man of Boris Savinkov's particular temperament and talents.

The Bolsheviki, who had seized power in the first week of November, controlled as yet only Petrograd, Moscow and a few other industrial centers. The workers as well as the Army and Navy were largely on their side, but in the rural areas their hold was

tenuous and throughout the Cossack "Vendée"—the Don and the
Kuban—and in eastern Siberia, it was already being openly chal-
lenged. All of western and southwestern Russia as well as the
Crimea were occupied by the Germans and nobody quite knew, least
of all the Soviet government, whether they would stop right there
or resume their march eastward, with a view to putting an end to
Bolshevik rule in Russia and setting up a new government more
docile to their will.

But even in the areas nominally under Soviet control, what with
much of the country laid waste or exhausted by three years of war,
with the land unplowed, the factories idle, production virtually at
a standstill, communications in a shambles and disease and starvation
stalking the land, conditions were, to say the least, precarious.

Leningrad itself (or Petrograd, as it was then known) had become unrecognizable. Dead horses lay strewn about the streets that
had not been swept or weeded for months, their swollen bellies
coveted hungrily by the thousands of ragged people waiting patiently in the breadlines that stretched along entire house blocks. In
the daytime party agitators rushed from factory to factory rounding
up much-needed support for the new regime and elsewhere, in the
formerly sumptuous but now hopelessly run-down and mud-spat-
tered mansions of the expropriated bourgeoisie, hastily improvised
committees strove wearily but often with brutal relentlessness to
bring some semblance of order to the administrative chaos the
Revolution itself had brought about. At night the newly organized
units of the dread Cheka* played a grim and often bloody game of
hide-and-seek with heavily armed gangs of anarchists that lived off
loot and extortion. Meanwhile, in the few remaining hotels, restau-
rants and night spots, raucous reveling went on until dawn, as those
who sensed that the end of an era had come, sought to drown their
sorrow and frustration to the wailing strains of gypsy violins.

* Thus named after the Russian initials of the "Extraordinary Commission
for Combatting Counter-Revolution and Sabotage." Created on December 20,
1917, six weeks after the Bolshevik seizure of power, upon the recommendation
of the Pole Felix E. Dzierzhinski, the Cheka soon acquired under his direction
a well-deserved reputation for ruthlessness and savage cruelty, which its successor organizations, the OGPU and the NKVD did little to belie.

And yet all was not coarseness and violence in those first months of the Communist age in Russia. Cultural life, for instance, had rarely been more intense. Released from the last bonds of centuries of censorship, "symbolist," "cubist" and "futurist" poets confounded one another in the press or over glasses of tea made of apples, currants and herbs in avant-garde literary cafés. Sobinov, Chalyapin and Nezhdanova sang. Karsavina and Hessler danced. Meyerhold, Taïrov and Eisenstein dabbled in daring theatrical experiments. At the Moscow *"Chauve-Souris"* the great comic Baliyev launched daily his bitter sallies at the new regime, while at the opera houses, "the lights at the foot of the great curtain still dimmed," in George Kennan's evocative words, "to the opening strains of the indestructible 'Swan Lake' and 'Sleeping Beauty' and proletarians and *bourgeoisie* sat side by side in the gilded boxes, spellbound and subdued, reconciled—for the brief hour—in a common fascination with the choreographic re-enactment of the age-old encounter between chivalry and brutishness. . . ."[4]

Though through their unceremonious dissolution of the Constituent Assembly the Bolsheviki had put an end to political democracy in Russia, there was as yet little actual terror in the areas under their control; that would come later. True, the various so-called "bourgeois elements" were treated with scant ceremony, but anti-Bolshevik publications appeared openly, the representatives of the dissolved political parties could congregate and even conspire with impunity, and the strongly anti-Bolshevik civil servants, bank officials and railway and post-and-telegraph workers could even strike for weeks on end without fear of retaliation. Indeed, it seems safe to say that the Soviet regime survived the first winter of its rule not so much on account of its own strength as because of the weakness, profound state of demoralization and lack of unity that prevailed among its foes, and above all because, alone of all the contending groups, it had announced its readiness to give the people that which they craved for most at this point, namely, land and peace.

Against this typical background of a disintegrating society there flitted throughout those harsh winter months of 1917-1918 a continuous stream of persons of sometimes unknown nationality and

often no clearly defined occupation, whose most interesting characteristic was, surely, that they seemed to be on equally good terms
with the representatives of the new regime and with the survivors of
the old. Of these, one of the most colorful and certainly the most
versatile was a Monsieur Massino, whom his calling card described
as a "Turkish and Oriental Merchant" and who, in the spring of 1918,
could often be seen about the more elegant and expensive cafés of
Petrograd and Moscow. Well-groomed, wealthy-looking, with a high,
sloping forehead, smoldering eyes and sensuous lips, he looked every
bit the part, except that his glance was perhaps just a little too
restless, his carriage a little too erect, too military even, his face too
haggard, too tortured. . . . Only a few knew him by his real name—
Captain Sydney George Reilly, of the British Intelligence Service.

One evening, early in May, 1918, Leonid M. Karakhan, Foreign
Commissar Chicherin's deputy and a future victim of Stalin's Great
Purge, telephoned Lockhart and asked him to come to see him
urgently:

> He had [writes Lockhart] an extraordinary story to tell. That after-
> noon a British officer had walked boldly up to the Kremlin gate and had
> demanded to see Lenin. Asked for his credentials, he had declared that
> he had been sent out specially by Mr. Lloyd George to obtain first-hand
> news of the aims and ideals of the Bolsheviks. . . . He had not seen
> Lenin but he had been interviewed by Bonch-Bruevich, a Russian of
> good family and the closest personal friend of the Bolshevik leader. Kara-
> khan wished to know if the man was an impostor. The name of the
> officer, he said, was "Relli." . . . Without betraying my amazement, I
> told Karakhan that I would enquire into the matter and let him know the
> result. That same evening I sent for Boyce, the head of the Intelligence
> Service, and told him the story. He informed me that the man was a
> new agent, who had just come out from England. . . . The next day the
> officer came to me to offer his explanation. . . . He admitted that he
> had been to the Kremlin and had seen Bonch-Bruevich. . . . His sheer
> audacity took my breath away. . . . The man who had thrust himself
> so dramatically into my life was Sydney Reilly . . . known today to the
> outside world as the master spy of Britain.[5]

Few individuals in our time strove so tirelessly to turn single-
handed the tide of history and few claimed to have come so close to
success as this man, who, plotting, scheming, changing disguises

constantly, hunted, with a price on his head, betrayed but never captured, engaged for many years in what was virtually a one-man struggle against Communist rule in Russia.

As behooves one whom even his detractors still refer to as "the mystery man" of that very mysterious service, Sydney Reilly's origins are cloaked in obscurity to this day. He himself claimed to have been born in Odessa in 1874, of mixed Irish-Jewish descent. Lockhart, however, who knew him well (though he was never one of his admirers), insists that he had no drop of British blood, that his real name was Rosenblum and that nobody knew even how he had become a British subject. But the same Lockhart writes that he combined "the artistic temperament of the Jew with the devil-may-care daring of the Irishman," and he goes on to describe him as "a man of great energy and personal charm, very attractive to women and very ambitious," "a man cast in the Napoleonic mould," "who lived for danger," "who, speaking seven languages with amazing facility, spoke none of them perfectly," "who knew the extremes of poverty and wealth," "amazingly young for his years," "in short, a man who, taken all in all, deserves to be ranked with the bravest men of his time . . . an object of mystery and fascination to all those who knew him."

He had first appeared, around the turn of the century, in Port Arthur (the Russian concession on the Kuantung Peninsula in China) as partner in the firm of Grünberg and Reilly, timber merchants. Then he had worked for a time as manager of the Danish Compagnie Est-Asiatique in that city. After the Russo-Japanese War (1904-1905), he had joined the arms concern of Mandrokhovich & Chubersky, where he had amassed a fortune in commissions from various German shipbuilding firms such as Blohm & Voss of Hamburg, which were just then helping rebuild the Russian fleet. It is not officially known when exactly he began to work for the British Intelligence Service, but it can be presumed that these business contacts came in handy, once he had switched to a less prosaic type of activity. Soon after the outbreak of World War I he turned up in Japan, on behalf of the Banque Russo-Asiatique, and later in the U.S.A., in connection with Russian munitions contracts. In 1916 he gave up his

business career and enlisted as an observer with the Canadian RAF.
Shortly thereafter he was in London, where his knowledge of languages and familiarity with German maritime affairs soon brought
him to the notice of the "appropriate authorities." He spent the next
two years shuttling in and out of Germany, disguised as an officer of
Kaiser Wilhelm's Navy. Early in 1918, he was recalled to England
and dispatched, under the code number of "S.T.-1," via Murmansk
to Russia, on what was to become the mission of his life.

W. Somerset Maugham (who had been sent by the British Intelligence Service to Russia some six months earlier than Reilly) has, in
the preface to his book *Ashenden, or the British Agent,* described his
own assignment as having been essentially "to prevent the Bolshevik
revolution and to keep Russia in the war." And he adds a little
ruefully: "The reader will know that my efforts did not meet with
success."[6]
By the time Reilly arrived in Russia in the spring of 1918, it was
already too late to prevent the Bolsheviki from seizing power and
the recent signing of the Brest-Litovsk Treaty had brought to an end
Russia's onerous participation in the war. Nevertheless, there was
still some hope in the Allied camp that the Soviet government might
be induced to resume hostilities against Germany. In the first place,
the situation on the Western front was such that something had to
be done at any price in order to relieve the enemy pressure. For the
German spring offensive had just started; the newly arrived American
forces had not yet been committed in strength and the Allied lines
were in serious jeopardy. There was thus also, no doubt, an element
of wishful thinking in the hopes of certain unofficial Allied agents,
such as the Englishman Bruce Lockhart, that the Soviet authorities
could be persuaded to rejoin the Allied camp. On the other hand, it
was known that the Communist leadership had been rent with
dissension over the issue of Brest-Litovsk, that Trotsky had even
threatened Lenin with a complete break and that it was only
through sheer will power and talent of persuasion that Lenin had
been able on March 15 to obtain its ratification by the Fourth
Extraordinary All-Russian Congress of the Soviets. And then the

warehouses of Arkhangelsk, in the Far North, and of Vladivostok, in the Far East, were literally bursting with hundreds of thousands of tons of valuable supplies, sent to Russia at great trouble and expense by convoy from the West in anticipation of the 1917 offensive, which the Russian Revolution had cut short, and which had to be saved from falling into German hands. But even if all these hopes were vain, even if the Soviet government were to remain impervious to Allied persuasion or threats, there remained another card to be played, that of the numerous anti-Communist forces, which were beginning to assemble in many places throughout Russia.

Of these, the strongest and best organized at the time of Reilly's arrival in Russia and also the one that seemed most assured of broad popular support, was Savinkov's former party, the Socialist Revolutionaries, or "SR's" for short.* A minority faction, the so-called "Left SR's," had initially supported the Bolsheviki and had for a time even held a few posts in the Soviet government and especially in the Cheka. But since Brest-Litovsk and the inauguration, in the spring of 1918, of the first peasant "communes," they too had been attacking the Communists with increasing violence. Eventually they would become the new regime's most intractable foes. As for Boris Savinkov himself, he had just succeeded, with French financial help, in reviving under the flamboyant name of "Union for the Defense of Fatherland and Freedom" the famous Combat Organization of his anti-Tsarist days, with the difference that it was now made up in the main of some five thousand fanatically anti-Communist ex-Tsarist officers. Sometime after his arrival in Russia in March, Reilly con-

* Founded in 1902 as a clandestine group, the SR's had played a pre-eminent role in the first two Russian revolutions, those of 1905 and of February-March, 1917. Their program—a compound of Populist (*Narodnik*) theories with a few borrowings from Marx—advocated the socialization of the land (which was immediately to assure them the unqualified support of the peasant masses), broad administrative decentralization (which made them popular with the national minorities), and—unlike the Bolsheviki—a political regime based on liberal democracy (which won them the backing of the smaller urban bourgeoisie). Unlike the Bolsheviki also, some of them favored individual terror to achieve their aims, Boris Savinkov being long their most famous "executioner." However, after polling, in November, 1917, some 58 per cent of the popular vote to the short-lived Constituent Assembly, their influence began to decline, until in the end they could boast of having controlled only two of the many anti-Communist regimes active in Russia at the time of the Civil War.

tacted Savinkov and though they were not to meet personally until
almost a year later, the two were soon steeped in conspiracy.

For Reilly had already come to the conclusion that the original
terms of his assignment no longer corresponded to the realities of the
Russian situation. The main foe, he contended, was no longer Germany. Indeed, he wrote,

the Germans are human beings. We can afford to be even beaten by
them. [Whereas] here . . . there is growing to maturity the arch-enemy
of the human race. If civilisation does not move fast to crush this monster
while there is yet time, the monster will finally overwhelm civilisation. . . . At any price, this foul obscenity which has been born in
Russia must be crushed out of existence. . . . There is only one enemy.
Mankind must unite in a holy alliance against this midnight terror![7]

This was to be his theme song to the very last day of his life.

Early in May, 1918, Reilly showed up in Moscow, where the
Soviet government had moved soon after the signing of the Brest-
Litovsk Treaty so as to be further removed from German pressure.

He soon discovered that in Moscow, unlike Leningrad, the strongest opposition group was made up, not of Savinkov's SR's, but of the
liberal intelligentsia and of former officers who, after barely escaping
lynching at the hands of their mutinous troops, were now hiding out
by the thousand in order to avoid being drafted into the newly established Red Army. He had consequently little trouble in setting up a
fairly extensive network of agents, well supplied with funds—there
were in those days still many wealthy Russians willing to exchange
their rubles against a letter of credit on a London bank!—which soon
reached out into some of the most closely guarded offices of the new
administration. To them he was known as "Mr. Constantine, Greek
Merchant," but presently he acquired still another identity, even
more valuable.

For at the house of one of his top agents, the ballerina Dagmara K., of the Moscow Art Theater, he had made the acquaintance
of a Miss Friede, whose brother happened to be a colonel in the
famous "Lettish Rifles." Reilly contacted Colonel Friede and presently he induced him to provide the British Intelligence Service reg-
ularly with copies of all relevant Red military documents. Friede did

more: From the ex-Tsarist judge, Veneslav Orlovski, now head of the
Criminal Investigation Department of the Cheka, he obtained for
Reilly identity papers in the name of "Commissar Relinsky," of the
Petrograd Cheka. As such, Reilly had entry literally everywhere.

The Soviets' position in the spring of 1918 was becoming increasingly critical. Discouraged by their apparent reluctance to break
with the Germans or allow for the re-establishment of an Allied
Eastern front on Russian soil, the Western Powers were now inclin-
ing more and more toward open intervention in Russia, with or without Soviet consent. Since the middle of May, a corps of some 35,000
ex-Austrian prisoners-of-war of Czechoslovak origin had been in a
state of armed revolt against the Soviet authorities. Prior to Brest-
Litovsk, they had fought against their former Austro-Hungarian
masters at the side of the Russian armies, after which they had
sought to make their way in a body through southern Russia and
Siberia to Vladivostok, there to embark for France. They now held,
together with several White detachments that had hastened to profit
from the situation, most of the Trans-Siberian Railway from the
Urals to the Pacific. Indescribable chaos prevailed throughout the
country. Inflation was reaching astronomical figures. In the villages
the peasants were refusing to accept the worthless coinage for their
produce and were returning to a form of barter, while in the towns
industrial production had dropped to almost zero, trade had come to
a virtual standstill and drastic rationing had been introduced. The
authority of the government was at an all-time low. The Cossack
"Vendée" was in open revolt, with pitched battles being fought between Red troops and White. Elsewhere too, events were moving
toward a showdown. On June 23 a first detachment of British troops
disembarked in the Far Northern port of Murmansk. Three days
later British and Japanese forces landed at Vladivostok. And on
July 6 President Wilson, after much hesitation, at last committed the
U.S.A. to active intervention in Siberia too.

By now the Left SR's hostility toward their former Communist
associates had reached the pitch of hysteria. On June 20, one of their
agents assassinated Soviet press chief Volodarsky. On July 6 two of
their group gained admittance to the German Embassy in Moscow

as members of the Cheka and shot down in cold blood Ambassador Count Mirbach, who had just joined his post. Three weeks later, on July 30, Field Marshal von Eichhorn, commander-in-chief of all German forces of occupation in Russia, suffered a similar fate in Kiev. Through these two thoughtless acts of terror, the SR's seem to have hoped to provoke a renewal of Soviet-German hostilities, which they would then have exploited in order to seize power for themselves.

On the day of Mirbach's murder the Fifth All-Russian Congress of the Soviets (the Red pre-parliament) was sitting at the Moscow Opera House. Allied observers—Bruce Lockhart among them—had been invited to attend the session, which was tense and stormy. To Lockhart's surprise none of the Communist leaders was there. Then he sighted Reilly, pale and agitated, making his way toward the diplomats' box. The shot that had killed Mirbach, Reilly whispered in his ear, was meant to sound the signal for a general uprising in the capital against the Reds. But, as usual, the SR's, fooled by rumors of an imminent Allied landing in Arkhangelsk, had acted too hastily; they had seized the post office, but the Opera House was now ringed by loyal Lettish Rifles; there was firing in the streets; the government, however, seemed to have the situation under control. As he spoke, says Lockhart, Reilly kept searching his pockets for compromising papers. Presently he found one, tore it to shreds and swallowed the pieces. A French intelligence agent sitting in Lockhart's box did likewise. Then, swiftly, Reilly slipped out of the hall.

The same day, another rising, led this time by Savinkov, broke out in Yaroslavl', a textile center northeast of Moscow, where Savinkov had concentrated the bulk of his forces. It was suppressed only after two weeks of bitter fighting, which marked the beginning of all-out violence throughout the country (four hundred hostages were executed by the Reds in Yaroslavl' alone). Savinkov himself, however, escaped unscathed and succeeded eventually in making his way to White-held territory.*

Actually, although Reilly's personal sympathy and admiration for

---

* Savinkov and the SR's seem to have had advance notice of the coming Allied landings in northern Russia, which had originally been planned for the first week in July—hence the Mirbach murder and the Yaroslavl' rising. But for some reason they were not informed of its last-minute postponement.

Savinkov remained unimpaired, he was finding it increasingly difficult to work with him. For one thing, he had always distrusted the SR's as a party; their program—a sort of agrarian socialism—was far too radical for his conservative tastes. And then by now he had reached the conclusion that Russia's salvation lay in a military dictatorship and most of the White generals he knew were loath to co-operate with the former terrorist. Events now moved rapidly to a climax.

On July 16 the ex-Tsar Nicholas II and his family were brutally murdered in Ekaterinburg in the Urals, just a few days before the town's capture by the Whites. On August 2 the long-awaited British landing in Arkhangelsk took place.* Two days later British gunboats operating from the Persian coast of the Caspian Sea seized the oil center of Baku, in the Caucasus, while British and French troops disembarked in Vladivostok, followed, shortly thereafter, by the Japanese and, on August 15 and 16, by U.S. troops. The Reds seemed thus about to be seized in a vise. A lightning blow at the center could well topple their whole shaky edifice.

On August 15—the day of the first U.S. landings in Vladivostok—Lockhart was lunching in his Moscow apartment when two Lettish gentlemen called to see him.

One of them [he writes] was a short, sallow-faced youth called Smidchen. The other, Berzin, a tall, powerfully built man with clear-cut features and hard steely eyes, called himself a colonel. He was, in fact, in command of one of the Lettish regiments† . . . Smidchen brought

* Actually, these landings—which, said Lenin, "could have crushed us in a few weeks"—were carried out with such insignificant forces and such amazing incompetence that they merely exasperated the Soviets, without materially affecting the outcome of the Civil War, providing them with a choice weapon of anti-Western propaganda ("The hosts of fourteen nations out to stifle the young Revolution in its cradle!") that has remained effective to this day.

† Toward the end of World War I draftees from the Russian Baltic provinces had been grouped in separate national units, of which the Latvian or "Lettish" Rifles were the most famous. Relatively unconcerned with the evolution of the Russian internal political situation except insofar as it might benefit the resurgence of an independent Latvia, these Lettish units had, upon the Soviets' seizure of power, hired themselves out to the new regime. At the time of which we are speaking—the old Imperial Army had completely disintegrated and the new Red Army was still only in the process of formation—they constituted the Soviet government's Praetorian Guard.

a letter from Cromie.* Always on my guard against *agents-provocateurs*,
I scrutinized the letter carefully. It was unmistakably from Cromie. . . .
It closed with a recommendation of Smidchen as a man who might be
able to render us some service. . . . I asked the two men what they
wanted. Berzin did most of the talking. He explained that while the
Letts had supported the Bolshevik revolution, they could not fight the
Bolsheviks' battles indefinitely. Their one ambition was to return to their
own country. As long as Germany was powerful, this was impossible. On
the other hand, if the Allies, as now seemed likely, were to win the war,
it was clear that they and not Germany would have the final word regarding the future of Latvia. They were therefore determined not to put
themselves wrong with the Allies. . . . If they were sent to the Arkhangelsk front, they would surrender. . . . It was [Lockhart concludes]
an interesting and plausible proposal.

After consulting with his French colleagues, Lockhart decided to
issue the Letts a *laissez-passer* to Major General F. C. Poole, the
British commander in Arkhangelsk, after which he put them in touch
with Sydney Reilly who, he thought, "could keep an eye on their
movements and help to stimulate their reluctance to oppose our
troops." "Two days later," continues Lockhart, "Reilly reported that
his negotiations [with the Letts] were proceeding smoothly. . . ."
And he went on to suggest that he might even be able, with Lettish
help, to stage a counter-revolution in Moscow!

Lockhart was for a moment taken aback. For months on end now
he had been at pains to persuade the Soviet government that the
Allies, in Russia, were seeking to oppose, not Communism, but Germany; even the recent British landings in Arkhangelsk had been
undertaken, allegedly, only in order to salvage the Allied military
supplies there. And here was a top British agent conspiring openly
to overthrow that same Soviet government! "This suggestion," he
writes, "was categorically turned down . . . and Reilly was warned
specifically to have nothing to do with so dangerous and doubtful
a move. . . ."[8] Actually, the very fact that the project was regarded
as "dangerous" and "doubtful" by the professional diplomats was apt

---

* Commander F. N. A. Cromie, R.N., D.S.O. (1882-1918). An outstanding
British submarine commander in World War I and at the time of which we
are speaking British Naval Attaché in Petrograd, and one of Sydney Reilly's
closest friends and fellow conspirators.

merely to whet Reilly's appetite for it. Moreover, he had by now acquired the conviction that he had a personal stake in the Russian drama. "A Corsican lieutenant of artillery," he wrote, "trod out the embers of the French Revolution. Surely a British intelligence agent could make himself master of Moscow!"[9] He decided to disregard Lockhart's warnings and to go ahead with his plan.

A few days later a final meeting was called to that end at the apartment of French Consul General Grenard. It was attended by Colonel de Vertemont, Moscow head of the Deuxième Bureau. René Marchand, Moscow correspondent of the Paris Le Figaro, was also present. At this meeting, Reilly expounded his plan:

The proposed coup, he reported, would go off on August 28, when the Central Executive Committee of the Communist party was scheduled to convene in the Moscow Opera House. As usual the Lettish Rifles would provide the guard. This time, however, they would work for the other side. At a given signal, a picked detachment headed by Colonels Berzin and Friede and Sydney Reilly himself would rush the podium and arrest the entire party presidium with Lenin at its head. After which—a typically Reilly touch—the Red leaders would be ridiculed out of power by being promenaded about the streets of Moscow in their skin! A provisional government would then be proclaimed and the dispersed Constituent Assembly would be called back into session. The operation was to be backed in Moscow itself by the rising of some sixty thousand officers and by simultaneous outbreaks in Petrograd and other cities.

All seemed to be proceeding according to plan when there occurred a first hitch: It was learned that the Central Executive Committee had postponed the opening of its session until September 6.

Reilly, however, was not unduly perturbed. Such last-minute changes had been known to occur before. He would now take advantage of this postponement, he decided, and go with Colonel Berzin to Leningrad—where Commander Cromie was in charge—to check up on arrangements there.

Arriving with Berzin in Petrograd early in the morning of August 29, he immediately began the round of his contacts. By now, writes Kennan, "the city, famine-stricken, terrorised, deserted . . . by at

least half a million of its former inhabitants, was only the wraith of
the great teeming capital that had existed on the banks of the Neva
the year before. The cold hand of the Terror was already chilling
and laming the place, inflicting upon it that strange species of
blight—lifelessness, a furtive drabness, a sense of the sinister lurking
behind a peeling façade, and everywhere a hushed, guarded in-
scrutability—which seems to be the effect of the Communist touch
on any great urban area. . . ."[10] Presently Reilly realized that he
was being followed. This was in itself an unpleasant surprise since,
until then, his Cheka disguise had given him virtual immunity. On
the spur of the moment he decided to send Berzin back to Moscow
and to return there himself as soon as he had shaken off his "escort."
He did not know that in Moscow the game was by now already up
and that throughout Soviet-held territory the Cheka were hot on his
trail.

They had been tipped off by an unexpected source: René Marchand, the French newspaperman who had attended that fateful
last meeting in Consul General Grenard's apartment, happened to
be a secret Communist sympathizer. He had immediately reported
all he had heard to his Soviet friends.

On August 29—the day Reilly reached Petrograd—the Cheka
raided the Deuxième Bureau's Moscow headquarters. De Vertemont
himself escaped over the roofs but several of his agents were captured, as well as a stock of explosives and a large sum of money.
Later that day Miss Friede walked into a trap which the Cheka had
set in the ballerina Dagmara K.'s apartment. At the time of the outbreak of hostilities between the Czech legion and the Soviet authorities in May, the Cheka had requisitioned all private motor vehicles.
As a result, orders had been issued throughout the anti-Communist
underground never to enter or even approach a building if any vehicle was parked before it. Miss Friede ignored this warning and
upon climbing the stairs of her friend's apartment, walked straight
into the arms of the Cheka. Fortunately for Reilly, Dagmara herself
was not arrested, no doubt in order to serve as a bait for her ever
elusive chief; moreover, she was able to conceal on her person some
two million rubles, which were to come in very handy a couple of

weeks later, when Reilly found himself with the whole Cheka at his heels. Nevertheless Miss Friede's capture dealt the plotters a blow from which they were never to recover, for in her music satchel she carried compromising documents, including a list of members of Reilly's proposed provisional government. That same night the Cheka arrested the two Lettish colonels, Berzin and Friede. Put to the torture, they confessed all.

Meanwhile Captain George Hill, a British intelligence agent who worked independently of Reilly, had been able to dispatch an agent to Petrograd to warn him. But by now the chase was on—the messenger was arrested on the train.

The following morning, August 30, Uritzky, the dread chief of the Leningrad Cheka, was shot and killed as he was entering his office. That same evening Lenin addressed a workers' meeting in Moscow. His speech was both violent and demagogic. "There is only one of two ways out for us," he thundered, "either victory or death!" As he was leaving the plant, he was approached by a young woman, a Left SR by the name of Fanya Kaplan, who fired two shots with poisoned bullets and gravely wounded him. The Soviet authorities were now seized with panic. For all they knew, Sydney Reilly's plot was perhaps just one facet of a much broader conspiracy, timed to coincide with the Allied landings and aimed at beheading the party by picking off its leaders one by one. The Cheka all over the land was called upon to strike without mercy.

It required little encouragement. One of Lenin's top lieutenants, Grigori E. Zinovyev (who was later to become famous as the leader of the so-called "Left Opposition" and as one of the first victims of Stalin's Great Purge), who in those days held the position of head of the Leningrad Soviet, promptly ordered five hundred hostages to be seized at random in the city prisons and shot without trial, while many others suffered a like fate in Moscow at the hands of his friend and future companion in misfortune, Lev B. Kamenev. After which it was announced that 750 further hostages would perish in reply to each subsequent outrage.[11] On September 1, Lockhart, Grenard and two hundred French and British nationals were thrown into prison and it was officially announced in the Soviet press that were Lenin

to die of his wounds, Lockhart too would be shot. The Terror—in
Engels' apt words "the domination of men, who are themselves terrorised"[12]—had begun in earnest. Though varying in intensity over the
years, it was never quite to cease until the day of Stalin's death,
some thirty-five years later.

A day earlier, on August 31, suspecting that Reilly might be hiding
out with his friend Cromie at the British Embassy in Petrograd, the
Cheka had raided the building.

Reilly was indeed on his way there. Having successfully shed his
"shadows," he had vainly awaited Cromie at their usual secret
rendezvous and when Cromie had failed to appear, he decided to
risk a visit to the Embassy. Now, as he approached the street in
which the latter was situated—at present semideserted and already
overgrown with weeds—he heard the sound of shots. Presently he
saw men and women running and then diving into doorways and
side streets. A truck roared past him, crammed with armed men;
then another. He broke into a run. As he rounded a corner, he came
to an abrupt halt. For the street was cordoned off with troops. Several trucks had halted opposite the battered doors of the Embassy,
in front of which a couple of bodies lay, sprawled out in grotesque
poses. First cautiously, then quickening his pace, Reilly slipped
away, out of sight.

Later he learned that Cromie had sought to bar the way to the
Cheka. Warned that if he persisted, he would be "shot like a dog,"
he had nevertheless opened fire, killing two of his opponents, and
had then himself been cut down on the Embassy staircase.

Next morning Reilly took the first train back to Moscow. By now
the newspapers carried a detailed account of what they persisted in
calling "the Lockhart conspiracy," based on Marchand's story and
the Lettish colonels' confession. Shortly thereafter Reilly himself was
proclaimed an outlaw and a reward was offered for his capture.

Reilly's first move was to contact Captain Hill, who, not having
been a party to the plot, was living in disguise but in relative security. "Reilly's bearing, when I met him," writes Hill, "was splendid.
He was a hunted man; his photograph with a full description and a
reward for his capture was placarded throughout the town; he had

been through a terrible time in getting away from Petrograd and yet he was absolutely cool, calm and collected, not in the least down-hearted and only concerned in gathering together the broken threads and starting afresh."[13] At one point he even considered giving himself up to the Cheka in order to exonerate Lockhart. But in the end even he had to concede defeat; there was clearly nothing more he could do for the anti-Communist cause in Russia at the present.[14]

For close to two weeks more he hid out in Moscow under the very nose of the Cheka in the apartment of a prostitute in the last stages of a professional disease (who happened to be one of Hill's secret couriers), changing disguises almost daily, going out only at night, until Hill was able to provide him with forged papers with which he then made his way back to Leningrad. There he was able to find a Finnish fisherman who, for a substantial sum of money— Dagmara K.'s two million rubles were coming in handy!—on September 11 smuggled him out of Russia and over the Gulf of Finland to the German naval base at Revel, from where he eventually made his way back to England via Helsinki and Stockholm, his pockets characteristically crammed with secret information on the disposition of German naval forces in the Baltic.

Yet, as far as Reilly was concerned, the great adventure had only just begun.

In London Reilly found himself at first—as is so often the case with intelligence agents who have played a losing hand—without a job. Eventually—thanks largely to his friendship with Winston Churchill, who had masterminded the Allied intervention in Russia—he was sent back to Russia together with his friend and fellow conspirator, George Hill (who had just himself escaped from Moscow), disguised as merchants on a lightning tour of the Black Sea coast. Then he was transferrred, late in March, 1919, as semiofficial contact man with the White Russian "Council of Ambassadors," which was seeking at the time, with little success, to uphold Russia's interests before the Versailles peace conferees.

It is in Paris that he at last met Boris Savinkov. They took an

immediate liking to each other. Savinkov was now the Whites'
official representative in the Western capitals, "in which quality,"
says Churchill, "he displayed every capacity, whether for command
or for intrigue."[15]

The defeat of the White armies had not put an end to Savinkov's
activities. Indeed, if anything it acted as a release, since he was now
able to give up the game of diplomacy, for which, for all Churchill's
glowing words of praise, he had never really felt much affinity, and
to revert to the career to which he was most suited, that of a
terrorist.

Though an armistice had been recently signed between the two
countries, Poland was still formally in a state of war with the
Soviet Union. In the fall of 1920, therefore, Savinkov proceeded to
Warsaw, where with Marshal Pilsudski's material support he had
soon organized a force of thirty thousand guerrillas, which was for
a time active in the forest of Byelorussia. He had never been too
chary about the means he used to achieve his ends and many of
these so-called guerrillas revealed themselves as out-and-out bandits,
who could hardly be dignified with the term of counter-revolutionaries. The initial idealism of the White movement was beginning to
become corrupted by despair.

The Riga peace treaty having put an end to the Soviet-Polish War
in March, 1921, Savinkov was soon a less welcome guest in Poland
than a few months earlier. In the summer of 1921, therefore, he
moved to Prague, where he and General Rudolf Gayda (one of the
leaders of the Czech legions in Russia in 1918) organized yet another group of anti-Communist terrorists, the so-called "Green
Guards,' who were for a while active in the western Ukraine.*

In the spring of 1922, Savinkov turned up with a group of accomplices in Berlin, where he and Sydney Reilly planned to assassinate Soviet Foreign Commissar Chicherin and several other top Red
officials, who were scheduled to pass through that city on their way

---

* Late in 1926, it was discovered that Gayda (who had, by then, risen to the
position of Chief of the Czech General Staff) had for some time already been
working for the Soviet Military Intelligence.

back from the Hague Conference. The attempt misfired at the last minute, however, the Soviet delegation having been held up at a state banquet.

In due course Savinkov also succeeded in re-establishing contact with the scattered remnants of his underground organization inside the U.S.S.R. Thereafter, subsidized in turn by virtually every government, group or individual that wished to cause the Moscow government embarrassment, he and his agents were to engage in a hit-and-run campaign of terror and sabotage against the Red authorities that was to continue until the fall of 1923.

Mrs. Reilly—Sydney Reilly's wife—met him shortly thereafter. He was, she writes, a great disappointment to her.

A portly little man strutted in with the most amusing air of self-assurance and self-esteem—a little man with a high brow, a beetling forehead, little eyes and an undershot chin [who] posed in front of the mantelpiece. Now he gave us a view of one side of his profile, now of the other. Now he thrust his hand into his breast in the approved Napoleonic manner, now he flourished it in the air with a theatrical gesture. Every pose was carefully studied and had been studied so long that he had passed beyond the stage of taking even a glance at his audience to gauge the measure of its appreciation. . . . His little court fully shared Savinkov's estimate of his own importance. When he frowned, a cloud settled on the assembly. When he smiled, answering smiles appeared on every face. When he condescended to joke, which was but seldom, it was greeted with discreet and respectful merriment.[16]

In 1922 Reilly had introduced him to Winston Churchill. Though both in temperament and in politics the two men differed widely, they saw eye to eye on the subject of Communism and on the means of combating it. Indeed, unlike Mrs. Reilly, Churchill was, according to Lockhart, "entirely captivated."[17]

For Churchill had come to the conclusion that in Russia the time was ripe for an Eighteenth of Brumaire and in Savinkov, he decided, Russia had her Buonaparte. The outcome of the Civil War had indeed shown that, for all their temporary successes, the White generals had been unable to find a language that could arouse the enthusiastic support of the Russian masses. Moreover, even in the

Western capitals there had always been a lurking fear that their victory might lead to a restoration of Tsarism in Russia—a highly un-
desirable development in the eyes of Western liberal public opinion.
Boris Savinkov was another matter. When he attacked Lenin and
Trotsky as usurpers and tyrants, his accusations had behind them all
the weight and impact of a lifetime spent in fighting for democracy,
however undemocratic his methods. His was not the unrepentant
monarchist's poorly suppressed craving for a return to the old regime,
or even the wishful thinking of a well-meaning if unrealistic Westernized parliamentarian, but the instinctive, soil-bound reaction of
the born rebel to any form of tyranny. Until 1917, in fact, he had
been a hardly less important, and certainly a much more spectacular,
figure in the Russian revolutionary movement than either Lenin or
Trotsky. His continuing hostility to Soviet rule was, hence, not only
materially damaging, but also highly embarrassing morally to the
Kremlin.

Churchill decided to take him to see Prime Minister Lloyd George
at Chequers. The time, however, was ill-chosen for such an interview. For at this point, Great Britain wished only for one thing:
peace, peace at all cost, "so that the boys could come home." Gone
was the crusading fervor that had induced her, in the spring of 1918,
to champion and spearhead anti-Communist intervention in Russia.
After all, the main if not the sole reason for such an intervention,
Germany, lay now defeated, crushed at the Allies' feet. Besides, the
feeling was spreading in Europe that for all the White Russians
could do or say, Bolshevism had come to stay. So long as it was
kept out of Eastern Europe, Russia herself could be left to stew in
her own juice.

Lloyd George was thus understandably skeptical about Churchill's
and Savinkov's plans for a resumption of the armed struggle against
Soviet rule. And then he had just spent a pleasant afternoon singing
hymns with a group of Welsh divines and was therefore in an un-
belligerent mood generally. The worst in Russia, he said confidently,
was over. The Red leaders, having failed in their utopian dreams of
an early world revolution, would no doubt presently start fighting

one another and their power would disintegrate. Russia could just as well be written off the world map as a major power for at least one generation. Meanwhile one could trade "even with cannibals!"* As for the "World Communist Menace," about which both Churchill and Savinkov seemed so concerned, it simply did not exist!

Boris Savinkov, who, with his formal black frock coat, his stiff wing-tipped collar, patent-leather boots and frigidly polite manner, resembled more an undertaker than a terrorist, listened to Lloyd George impassively until he had finished. Then, in French, in his quiet, indifferent voice, he remarked: "Mr. President, you will permit me the honor of observing that after the fall of the Roman Empire, there ensued the dark ages!"[18]

He emerged profoundly discouraged from this interview. Gradually the conviction grew within him that the White Russians had been duped by the Allies, that they had simply been used as pawns in a sordid game of power politics in which there had never been any room for Russia's real interests—indeed, that her trials and tribulations were in a way welcomed by the West.† And parallelly there grew within him the belief that Russia's salvation could be brought about only by Russian hands and specifically by the Russian peasant masses and the Red Army, in which these were so strongly represented. And then also by now he had become disgusted with Russian émigré politics generally. Going or gone, he felt, was the spirit of dedication that had animated the White cause in its beginnings. Those who claimed, at present, to speak for a "National Russia," as opposed to the "Third International," were often the very same discredited politicians who, whether they belonged to the former Right or to the former Left, had had little or no part in the White movement or had even actively opposed it.

On this point both Savinkov and Reilly saw eye to eye. Of the

* To which Lenin is reported to have shot back with contempt: "Those people would trade even in the very cords that are destined to hang them!"
† Thus, for instance, in the agreements by virtue of which she had recognized and subsidized the Wrangel, Petlyura and Transcaucasian anti-Communist governments, France had secured for herself, by way of collateral, a fifty-year railway-building and operating contract, as well as a five-year control over these governments' financial, commercial, industrial and even military policies.

White Russians as a whole, Reilly had no very high opinion either. He regarded them with few exceptions, such as Kutyepov and Savinkov himself, as vain, talkative and ineffective. They were full of words and schemes, but seemed incapable of translating their ideas into action. Many were undisguisedly apathetic, of many others their loyalty was more than doubtful. Were Russia to be saved from Communism, such salvation would have to come from within.

Where Reilly differed with Savinkov, however, was in his continuing belief that even now individuals, groups and interests could be found to back such a venture—if not in Europe, then in the U.S.A., and if not among the politicians, then among the financiers, such as Sir Henri Deterding or Henry Ford. Meanwhile every effort should be made to keep up the economic blockade of the U.S.S.R., thereby slowing down the country's economic recovery, exacerbating the social strains and finally strangling the regime into capitulation. Reilly's personal business took him often to New York in those years and he was thus able to put his knowledge of Russian affairs, his charm and talents of persuasion to good use there.

It was in New York that he learned, early in the spring of 1924, that Savinkov was about to take a fateful step: that he had decided to go back to Russia.

Some time early in 1924, Savinkov had received a highly confidential message from inside Russia from a Colonel Serghei Pavlovsky, one of his most trusted lieutenants and his top agent there. The latter informed him that a full-scale uprising was being planned against the Soviet government, which, strife-ridden since Lenin's death in January, was not expected to put up much of a fight; that the first blow would be struck in Georgia, Stalin's motherland, which had only recently come under Soviet rule and where anti-Bolshevik feelings were still strong; that the plotters had at their disposal large sums of money, obtained in a raid on a branch office of the Soviet State Bank; and that the signal to start would be given as soon as he, Savinkov, appeared on the scene to assume over-all command.

In June, 1924, Savinkov received yet another invitation to return

to Russia, this time from some of the Soviet leaders themselves.*
They appealed to his patriotism, but also to his vanity, and promised
him, were he to agree to return to Russia and to stand a mock trial,
that he would be immediately amnestied and given a good position
with the Soviet administration.

Another month went by. In July Savinkov received a second, still
more pressing message from Colonel Pavlovsky. Time, said the latter,
was running out. The plotters could not afford to delay action any
longer, and he enclosed a detailed itinerary and twenty thousand
rubles for expenses.

It is still not clear to this day whether Savinkov sensed the trap.
He himself was to claim that he had known all along what would
befall him were he to accept Pavlovsky's invitation, but that by now
his mind was made up and this was as good a way as any of going
back into Russia without delays and formalities. Life abroad, far
from his beloved homeland, had always been unbearable to him.
Distrusted, or at best just tolerated, by the more conservative White
Russians (who could never completely forgive him his terrorist past);
himself distrustful of them; shunned or denounced by his erstwhile
friends of the non-Communist Left as an opportunist who had "sold
himself out to the militarists and the reactionaries";† beset by constant financial worries (Reilly's funds were now virtually exhausted
and his own recent attempts to obtain a subsidy from Mussolini had

* In his *Great Contemporaries* Churchill writes that this invitation stemmed
from Trotsky and Kamenev (both of whom were in those days still members
of the Politbureau).[19] By this time, however, Trotsky was already engaged in
a life-and-death struggle against the so-called "Triumvirate" of Stalin, Zinovyev
and Kamenev for Lenin's succession. The invitation could thus well have
originated with one of them, but hardly with both. Neither is it likely that
Trotsky would in those early days have chosen to ally himself with such a
well-known anti-Communist as Savinkov, however difficult his own position.
† It was one of the tragedies of the non-Bolshevik Russian intelligentsia that,
unlike the German Social Democrats, few of them were willing to accept the
fact that there are times when freedom has to depend on the use of force to
prevent its own extinction. Loath to fight for freedom themselves now that it
was threatened by the Left, they were equally unwilling to help the Right do
so. For in their view, a leftist policy could only be exercised by leftists and
since the only "leftists" in power on Russian soil were the Bolsheviki, whom
many of them regarded now as tyrants, they found themselves reduced to verbal
attacks directed at both the Bolsheviki and their armed opponents.

ended in failure); no longer even convinced of the justice of his cause, Savinkov had reached literally the end of the road. Lockhart met him for the last time in 1923 in a night haunt in Prague. "He was a pathetic figure," he writes. "For whom one couldn't help feeling the deepest sympathy. He had exhausted all his friends and when later he returned to Moscow . . . I was not surprised. Doubtless, behind that tortured brain there was some grandiose scheme of striking a last blow for Russia and carrying out a spectacular *coup d'état*. It was a gambler's throw, but then Savinkov had always played a lone hand. . . ."[20]

Be this as it may, his friends' warnings—including those of Reilly, who traveled purposely to Paris in the hope of talking him out of his project—fell on deaf ears and on August 10, 1924, he set out, in great secrecy, on his return trip to Russia. He traveled with a forged Italian passport in the name of "Stepanov," via Berlin and Warsaw. He was accompanied by his secretary, Dickhoff-Daehrenthal and the latter's wife, with whom Savinkov had long been on very close terms.*

For a little while nothing more was heard of him.

On August 28 the ill-fated rising of the so-called "Paritary Committee" broke out in Soviet Georgia. At dawn a troop of armed Mensheviks seized the town of Chiaturi and killed off the local Communist officials. Simultaneously other outbreaks occurred elsewhere in the Caucasus and an attempt was made to seize the oil fields. But the rebels were poorly armed and few in numbers and their actions were ill co-ordinated, so that the rising was fast suppressed. To this day it is not certain whether the whole business was

* The exact role played by this couple in the Savinkov affair has never been elucidated. Although they had been associated with virtually every one of his anti-Soviet ventures, after being arrested together with Savinkov, the Daehrenthals were released, supposedly at his request, and allowed to reside thereafter in Russia unmolested. In a moment of candor, Deputy OGPU Chief Yagoda was later to admit to an American newspaper correspondent that Savinkov had been lured back to the Soviet Union by a "beautiful OGPU operator" and he went on to complain that the OGPU was having trouble now with the lady, for she had fallen in love with Savinkov and insisted on being allowed to spend nights in his cell. Since Mrs. Daehrenthal is the only woman known to have enjoyed this privilege, it would seem that she was the "beautiful OGPU operator" in question.[21]

not a Soviet police provocation, timed to coincide with Savinkov's capture.

For next day, August 29, the Soviet press came out with an announcement that created an immediate sensation:

> On or about the 20th. of this month, our security services arrested in Soviet territory Citizen B. V. Savinkov, the most irreconcilable and persistent foe of Russia's Workers' and Peasants' Government.

The papers went on to report that at his trial, which had just come to an end, Savinkov had made a complete confession and had proclaimed his unqualified recognition of the Soviet regime.

The exact circumstances of Savinkov's capture have been described by a former high Soviet official, Grigori Z. Bessedovsky, ex-Chargé d'Affaires in Paris, who was to "choose freedom" late in 1929 by jumping over the Embassy wall.

The Politbureau, says Bessedovsky, had been seriously alarmed by Savinkov's reported activities. "The factional fight in the party," he writes, "had begun to assume threatening proportions and it was felt that in view of these circumstances, a new campaign of terrorism by Savinkov might have created a situation extremely dangerous to the very existence of the Communist dictatorship."[22] Instructions were therefore given to the OGPU to liquidate Savinkov and his organization at whatever cost and without delay.

Early in 1924 the OGPU scored a first success: it captured Colonel Pavlovsky. The latter was tortured, threatened with death and finally broken: He agreed to betray his chief and help lure him back to Russia.

Upon crossing the Soviet border, Savinkov and the Daehrenthals were met by several of Pavlovsky's emissaries, who drove them to a secluded house in Minsk where they were told to await further instructions.

"They did not have to wait long," says Bessedovsky. "Almost immediately after their arrival a young man, of medium height, shortsighted, entered the room and announced in a quiet voice: 'I am Pilar, head of the Byelorussian OGPU. The house is surrounded by my men. You are under arrest!' "

This was the well-known ex-Baltic Baron R. A. Pilar von Pilhau, one of OGPU Boss Dzierzhinski's most feared lieutenants, who was later to perish in Stalin's Great Purge.

"Savinkov remained perfectly calm," continues Bessedovsky. "He was silent for a moment or two and then said: 'I congratulate you. . . . You have done a good job. . . . As a matter of fact, I suspected Pavlovsky's letter from the first. . . . But I decided to come anyway. I'll tell you why. . . . I have decided to give up my struggle against you.' "

Pilar smiled but said nothing. The same day Savinkov was taken by special train to Moscow where he was brought before Dzierzhinski. Though they belonged to rival revolutionary parties, the two men had known each other for many years. To Dzierzhinski Savinkov now repeated all that he had said to Pilar in Minsk.

Dzierzhinski assured Savinkov that he personally believed him, but that he could not vouch for his life as the Politbureau was thirsting for his blood. However, if Savinkov agreed to make a full confession, he would undertake to intercede with them on his behalf and obtain his release. Whereupon Savinkov promised that he would say all. More, he insisted that he be given a job in the Soviet administration so that he might "atone for his sins" by working for the new regime.

At first the Politbureau was adamant. Stalin, in particular, kept insisting that Savinkov be shot forthwith. As the then still influential Karl Radek put it to a foreign journalist: "As melodrama it is perfect. Cesare Borgia in the role of Hamlet. . . . Myself, I would shoot him out of hand. He is so utterly the plotter, so wholly devoted to murder and destruction as to be incapable of anything else. . . ."[23] Little did Radek suspect that before very long he too would be made to act as one of the protagonists in a drama of like quality, but that he, unlike Savinkov, would grovel despicably at his judges' feet! Finally, says Bessedovsky, a compromise was reached: Savinkov would be condemned to death, after which his penalty would be commuted to life imprisonment. On no account, however, would he be set free.

His trial could now begin. Lasting two days (August 27-28), it was one of the first of those show trials for which the Kremlin was soon to become so grimly famous, and one of the few, perhaps, at which the Hamlet-like quality (to quote Radek's apt simile) was relatively genuine. Only some two hundred hand-picked guests were permitted to attend the proceedings, but these included some of the top dignitaries of the regime. The foreign press was excluded, with the exception of the last session, when three foreign correspondents were whisked off after dark in great secrecy to hear the last plea of the defendant, whose identity had not at first been revealed to them, as well as the court's verdict. Walter Duranty of the *New York Times* was fortunate to be one of the three. He has described the scene:

No keener first-night audience could be found in Moscow. Every man and woman was athrill with interest, intensely conscious of the treat before them and ready to enjoy its piquancy to the uttermost.

They were not disappointed.

The court entered; three youngish men in uniform, with the Supreme Judge of the Military Tribunal, Ulrich, in the center. Then came the guards and soldiers and surprisingly, two sailors; and the prisoner, Boris Savinkov.

A small man, quite bald, about forty-five, who walked with rather weak and faltering steps, he wore a cheap, double-breasted gray sack suit, with a starched white collar and shirt and a narrow black tie. His face suggested the pictures of young Napoleon, but was drawn and white, with deep shadows under the eyes. He was quite unafraid, and glanced around with curiosity like a man taking his last look at human beings and their petty lies. . . .

Judge Ulrich ordered the prisoner to make his last statement.

Slowly [Duranty continues] he rose from the wooden bench and ran his eyes over the spectators. . . . Just as the tension became almost unbearable, he began to speak in a low, weak voice but one which was quite audible throughout the small courtroom.

"I am not afraid to die," he began, "I know your sentence already, but I do not care. I am Savinkov, who always played on death's doorstep; Boris Savinkov, Revolutionary and Friend of Revolutionaries, now to be judged by your Revolutionary court. . . ."

And he went on to recount the story of his revolutionary career.

He told it [writes Duranty] either with supreme skill or with utter sincerity. In words which every person in the audience could understand, for he spoke to the audience rather than to his judges, he reviewed his terrorist adventures, the death of Plehve, of Sergius and the rest; told how he lived always cut off from human life, cut off from the workers and peasants, always under the shadow of shameful death, always apart from men and women who lived and loved in the sunlight.

Often Savinkov paused so long that the whole room quavered with emotion. Was it sincerity? Was it weakness? . . . Was it art?

"And then," he exclaimed, "came the triumph of the idea to which I have devoted my life, the triumph of Revolution."

His voice deepened as he turned toward the audience with a pathetic gesture of both hands.

"Then you, who now represent Revolutionary Russia, seized the reins. I turned against you for four reasons. First, my life's dream had been the Constituent Assembly. You smashed it. . . . Second, I believed the Brest-Litovsk treaty was a shameful betrayal of my country. . . . Third, I believed that Bolshevism could not endure, that it was too extreme, that it would be replaced by the other extreme of monarchism and that the only alternative was the middle course. . . . Fourth and most important reason, I believed that you did not represent the Russian masses. . . . I thought they were against you and so I, who have given my life to their service, set myself against you also. . . ."

Then he went on to describe the beginnings of his doubts: Russia had shown that she was not ready for such organs of self-government as the Constituent Assembly. . . . Brest-Litovsk had turned out to be merely the lesser of two evils, a respite which Lenin had later fully exploited for Russia's benefit. . . . The Soviet regime had proven its durability through years of stress and hardship. . . . As for the genuine feelings of the Russian "masses" toward the new regime, what did he know about them? Hadn't he been handicapped in correctly assessing them by the fact that he himself had always lived in the watertight compartment of the conspirator? And all of a sudden, he had felt that he needed to see things for himself, and so he had returned—of his own free will, without bombs or revolvers, without plots or supporters. . . .

"Now," he exclaimed, "I know. . . . Here, before your Court whose sentence I know already, surrounded by your soldiers of whom I have no fear, I say that I recognize without condition your right to govern Russia. I do not ask your mercy. I ask only to let your

revolutionary conscience judge a man who has never sought anything for himself, who has devoted his whole life to the cause of
the Russian people. But I add this: Before coming here to say that I
recognize you, I have gone through worse suffering than the utmost
you can do to me!"

"The last words," writes Duranty, "were spoken in the same low
voice as the rest. Savinkov sat down, opened a box of cigarettes,
asked for a light from a guard and began to smoke."

Judge Ulrich announced a recess.

Long after midnight, [says Duranty] the court re-entered the hall and
Ulrich read the verdict. The prisoner was sentenced to death on four
counts: espionage, incitement to assassination, incitement to brigandage
and partisan warfare and counter-revolution. There was, however, a
recommendation of mercy.

The audience received the verdict in silence. Savinkov, standing, heard
it with unmoved face. But at Ulrich's final phrases, his dark eyes blazed
for a moment. He knew that he had won the biggest and most daring
stake of all his desperate life.

Actually, whether his repentance was sincere or whether he had
all along been acting a part in the hope that, once free, he would be
able, in Lockhart's words, to carry out his "spectacular *coup d'état,*"
the final sentence which condemned him to ten years' imprisonment
was a terrible blow to Savinkov. As he himself candidly admitted, he
had been all along convinced that his trial could have but two
possible outcomes: either he would be shot—the most likely solution!
—or his change of heart would be taken at face value and he would
be allowed to go free. A third solution had never entered his mind.
After all, the crimes he had committed could not possibly be atoned
for by mere imprisonment; it was no longer necessary to "reform"
him—life had seen to that!

He kept pleading with Dzierzhinski and reminding the latter of
his earlier promises and at first Dzierzhinski sought to bolster his
spirits by assuring him that his jail sentence was just a temporary
measure, to lull public opinion, that it would be reduced. He was
given a comfortably appointed two-room apartment in the Butyrki,
the dread "Inner Prison" of the OGPU, and allowed to write books,

to correspond with his friends abroad (including Reilly), to receive
guests, to go for drives—escorted, of course—in and around Moscow,
and even to be interviewed by foreign journalists. But further the
Kremlin would not go.

An AP correspondent, William Reswick, was among the news-
papermen allowed to visit the jail in which Savinkov was being held
at the time. He has described the scene:

The first prisoner shown us was a tall, handsome man in his thirties.
His sparsely bearded face was as white as the whitewashed wall behind
him. His eyes were feverishly aflame in a sudden paroxysm of fear, his
bluish lips mumbled some incoherent words. As if in a last effort to snatch
a few more minutes of life, he backed up against the wall, stretched out
his arms, and, trembling from head to foot, stood before us like a cruci-
fixion, with knees sagging and weeping head bent in a last unspoken plea
for mercy. . . . There was a moment of breathless suspense, pierced
suddenly by a stifled cry: *"Tovarishchi!"* (Comrades!) In the gathering
dusk of the oncoming night the man at the wall seemed to me an eternal
symbol of mankind's pain and undying hope. Like Christ on the cross he
smiled as we turned to go. Our sudden departure must have brought him
heavenly relief, almost a sense of resurrection. . . . Savinkov's cell—the
last one we visited—was the biggest surprise of the day. It was a beautifully
furnished room with thick carpets on the floor, a large mahogany desk, a
blue-silk-upholstered divan, and pictures on the walls. . . . The great
conspirator was clean-shaven and smelled of perfume as though a barber
had just left him. Most astonishing of all was his state of mind. He be-
haved like a wealthy and gracious host receiving visitors. Is this mere
bravado, I wondered, or absolute courage? . . . We plied Savinkov
with questions, to each of which he had a quick, tactful, brilliant answer.
He spoke Russian and French with equal ease. Asked why he had returned to Russia, he stepped to the window. Pointing to the Kremlin, he
said: "I would rather see those towers from a prison cell, than walk
freely in the streets of Paris!" . . . In our admiration and pity, for to most
of us he was not only a valiant leader, but a brilliant writer, we avoided
asking any questions that might embarrass him in the presence of his
jailers. But there was one exception. Much to our chagrin, a French correspondent asked a question that instantly put Savinkov on the defensive,
compelling a choice between evasion and danger: "Are the OGPU horror
stories true or false?" . . . The prisoner replied: "Speaking for myself
they are obviously untrue." I looked at Trilisser [a senior official of the
OGPU about whom more will be heard later, who was accompanying

the correspondents on their tour]. His black eyes flashed with anger. The prisoner, like everybody else in the room, could not help noticing the poor impression "speaking for myself" had made on the *Chekist*. Yet Savinkov went on talking like a free man until Trilisser put an end to the interview with one word: *"Pora!"* (Time is up!) The effect of that word was instantaneous. Savinkov turned pale and stopped talking. He still smiled as he saw us to the door, but it was a forced smile."[24]

For he had served his purpose, he had been brought to his knees and made to abjure the cause for which he himself and many likewise dedicated men had sacrificed so much. As an opponent, he was no longer dangerous; as a friend, the Reds had no use for him.

Finally, on May 7, 1925—i.e., some eight months after his capture—shortly after breakfast, he sat down to write Dzierzhinski a last letter (which was later reproduced in the Soviet press). Once again he reminded his jailer of the latter's promise to obtain his release in exchange for a complete confession. He ended it with the words: "Either shoot me or give me the opportunity to work. . . . I cannot endure this half-and-half existence of being neither with you, nor against you, of merely lingering in jail and becoming one of its denizens. . . ."[25]

He does not seem to have hoped for an answer, for presently he called for his car and ordered the chauffeur to drive to Yaroslavl'—the scene of his 1918 luckless uprising against the young Soviet regime. There he lunched at a roadside tavern, after which he drove back to Moscow, at breakneck speed, to jail. As he climbed the stairs to his fourth-floor apartment, he caught sight of an open window that gave out onto the flagstoned courtyard. A minute later he had crashed to his death.

No foreigner was allowed to see his body. Indeed even this, the official version of his death, was published only a week later, on May 12. "The *Butyrki*," says Duranty, "guards its secrets well."

Yet this may not be the true story of Boris Savinkov's end. For sometime in 1928 Walter Duranty met in Paris the daughter of the famous Prince Piotr Kropotkin, "the noblest of the old-school Russian revolutionaries," as he calls him. She related to him that she had met Savinkov in Moscow *after* 1924 and that although he was disguised,

she had recognized him—having known him well before the Revolution—by his trick of drooping his eyelids "like an owl." She actually
spoke to him, she said, and in the end he had admitted his identity.

> I know the Bolsheviks [writes Duranty]. Either he thought he could
> bluff them, and get an independent post—he would never on any account
> be a subordinate—and when these hopes failed, committed suicide; or
> they thought they could bend him to their will, and when they found
> they could not, had him thrown from the window.*
> Those are the likeliest alternatives, with the odds in favor of the
> former. . . . Yet it is fascinating to imagine that somewhere along the
> vast frontier, where the Soviet-Union marches with China, Afghanistan
> and Persia, there is posted a small comrade called Ivanov, or Smirnov,
> or some such common Russian name. . . . In Mongolia, it may be,
> where they brew strife between Russia and Japan for the mastery of
> North China; or among the Afghan hills, where the Lion and the Bear
> are waiting, Boris Savinkov perhaps stares southward, drooping his heavy
> eyelids.†[26]

At first Savinkov's friends abroad were so stunned by the news of
his capture and behavior in court that they refused to believe it. In a
letter to the editor of the London *Morning Post* Reilly claimed that it
was all a farce, that Savinkov had in reality been killed while crossing the frontier. As "one of his most intimate friends and devoted
followers," he said, a sacred duty devolved upon him to vindicate
his honor. But presently even Reilly was obliged to bow to the facts.
In a second letter to the *Morning Post* he now admitted bitterly that
"by his act, Savinkov has erased forever his name from the scroll of
honor of the anti-Communist movement." However, he added, "the
moral suicide of their former leader" would serve, as far as his
friends and followers were concerned, merely as "an added incentive
to close their ranks and 'carry on'!"[27]

---

* Several years later an ex-Left SR by the name of Brunovsky shared a death
cell with one Zapol'sky, a former high official of the OGPU. Shortly before
being taken away to be shot, the latter admitted to him that Savinkov did not
commit suicide, as the Soviets claimed, but that he had indeed been slain in
jail soon after writing his last letter to Dzierzhinski, after which his body had
been thrown out of the window.

† There are indications that Savinkov's mother continued to receive a Soviet
state pension until her death, several years later.

Winston Churchill, to whom Reilly had confided his dismay and indignation, was inclined to be more understanding. "I do not think," he replied, "that you should judge Savinkov too harshly. He was placed in a terrible position; and only those who have sustained successfully such an ordeal have a full right to pronounce censure. . . ."[28] And in his *Great Contemporaries*, he has dedicated to him a magnificent epitaph:

Whether he was quietly shot in prison or committed suicide in despair [he writes] is uncertain and unimportant. They had destroyed him body and soul. They had reduced his life's effort to a meaningless grimace, had made him insult his cause and had fouled his memory forever. Yet when all is said and done, and with all the stains and tarnishes there be, few men tried more, gave more, dared more and suffered more for the Russian people.[29]

The most unexpected discovery, however, that emerged from the investigation of the circumstances of Savinkov's last trip was that Yakushev and the Trust generally had been closely involved in it: the route chosen was one often favored by Trust couriers; Yakushev himself had accompanied Savinkov's party as far as Warsaw and after the Soviet border had been crossed, it was again the Trust that had arranged for them to be met and taken as far as Minsk where they had also been arrested!

Savinkov's tragic end found Sydney Reilly again in New York, where he had returned from Paris in order to sabotage, through public lectures and personal pressure, the efforts which Soviet agents were just then making to obtain a loan on the Wall Street market. He was still in New York when, some time early in 1925, he received a letter in code from an ex-colleague in the British Intelligence Service, one Commander E., who was at present attached to one of the British consulates in the Baltic. The letter, which was dated January 24, read:

Dear Sydney,
    There may call to see you in Paris from me two persons named Krasnoshtanov, a man and wife. They will say they have a communication from California and hand you a note consisting of a verse from Omar

Khayyam which you will remember. If the business is of no interest to you, you will say: "Thank you very much. Good day."

Now as to their business. They are representatives of a concern which in all probability will have a big influence in the future on the European and American markets. They do not anticipate that their business will fully develop for two years, but circumstances may arise which will give them the desired impetus in the near future. It is very big business and one which it does not do to talk about. . . . They refuse at present to disclose to anyone the name of the man at the back of the enterprise. I can tell you this much—that some of the chief persons are members of the opposition groups. You can therefore fully understand the necessity for secrecy. . . . I am introducing this scheme to you thinking it might perhaps replace the other big scheme you were working on but which fell through in such a disastrous manner. . . .[30]

And Commander E. went on to say that certain other foreign groups—German, French and British—were much interested in what he described as "this deal."

For all his readily awakened love of intrigue and adventure, Reilly was by now too experienced and wary a conspirator to fall an easy prey to provocation. He had already eluded several attempts to lure him back to Russia and Savinkov's fate was bound if anything to make him even more cautious. On the other hand, Commander E. himself was clearly above suspicion; moreover, he too was a highly experienced agent. If, therefore, he had decided that this project was worth Reilly's while, there surely must be something to it. And then, like Savinkov, Reilly was a man born to action and intrigue who could not endure prolonged idleness. Lockhart suggests yet another reason: By now, he says, Reilly had expended most of his considerable fortune on various anti-Communist ventures, including some of Savinkov's operations; he may thus have been forced by circumstances to take another, supreme chance.

Be this as it may, when he and his wife returned from New York to Paris early in September, 1925, Reilly was distinctly interested and this interest deepened following his talks with General Kutyepov, who seemed *au courant* of the new situation. Between them it was decided that Reilly would go to Finland—whose Chief of the General Staff, General Wallenius, was a personal friend of Kutyepov's and

an active sympathizer with all anti-Communist ventures—and interview the two emissaries, but that on no account would he allow himself to be talked into going back into Russia.

He traveled to Helsinki without mishap, though he was obviously
being followed. But then he was used to that! In Helsinki he learned
that the woman who called herself "Mrs. Krasnoshtanova" was none
other than the celebrated Maria Vladislavovna Zakharchenko-
Schultz, one of General Kutyepov's most trusted couriers, about
whom he had already heard much. He knew that the laughing gray
eyes and gay, lively, outwardly carefree manner of this slight, deli-
cately built, but rather plain-looking young woman—she was about
thirty-five years old at the time—concealed a will of iron, a dauntless
courage and a seemingly fanatical dedication to the anti-Communist
cause. Twice a war widow, she had herself served throughout World
War I as a private in a Tsarist cavalry regiment and had been among
the first to offer her services to General Kutyepov when the latter
began recruiting volunteers for his Combat Organization. By now
she was regarded as one of the most experienced and resourceful
White agents in Russia.

To Sydney Reilly, Maria Schultz (as she will hereinafter be known)
related that the survivors of his own network and those of Savinkov's
organization had joined forces, that important contacts had been
made in high Soviet opposition circles and that, as Reilly himself
was presently to put it, "something really entirely new, powerful
and worthwhile"[31] was going on in Russia.

Coming as it did in the wake of continuing unrest throughout the
U.S.S.R. and of a known sharpening of the conflict between Stalinists
and Trotskyites over Lenin's succession, this information sounded
entirely plausible. In order to explore the situation further, Reilly
now agreed to proceed with the two agents to Vyborg, close to
the Soviet border, where several of the leaders of the new Russian
underground were waiting. One of them turned out to be Yakushev.

Reilly emerged from the meeting deeply impressed and on September 25 he wrote his wife a letter, in which he informed her that
it was absolutely necessary that he go to Leningrad and Moscow
for three days. "I am leaving tonight," he said. "And will be back

here on Tuesday morning. . . . There is absolutely no risk to it. . . . If by any chance I should be arrested in Russia, it could only be on some minor insignificant charge and my new friends are powerful enough to obtain my liberation. . . ."[32]

In the night of the twenty-eighth to the twenty-ninth of September, Reilly, escorted by Maria Schultz and an especially assigned Finnish border patrol, crossed over into Russia near the hamlet of Alekul. He traveled with a passport in the name of one "Nikolai N. Sternberg, merchant," which Yakushev had provided. Maria Schultz later described the scene:

> For a long while [she said] we waited while the Finns listened anxiously for the Red patrol, but everything was quiet. At last one of the Finns lowered himself cautiously into the water and half-swam, half-waded across. Sydney Reilly followed. Then went one of the men out of Russia, until all were across. . . . Peering over the water we could distinctly see them filing obliquely across the field on the further bank. Then they vanished in the gloom. By-and-by we saw their figures faintly outlined one by one against the sky as they crossed the crest. . . . All was silent as the grave. . . . Georghi [Maria Schultz's husband, Georghi Radkovich] returned the following day with the news that they had boarded the train to Petrograd without incident. All had gone well. . . .[33]

Shortly thereafter there appeared in the Soviet press the following brief announcement:

> In the night from the 28th. to the 29th. of September four smugglers attempted to cross the Finnish border into the U.S.S.R. . . . They were intercepted by our frontier troops. In the ensuing skirmish two of them were killed, a third—a Finnish soldier—was captured and the fourth mortally wounded.

For nearly two years this ambiguous statement constituted all that the Soviet authorities seemed willing to disclose about the circumstances of Sydney Reilly's death. Thus his end—like his beginnings—seemed fated to be cloaked in mystery. And yet despite this news blackout the rumor persisted that Reilly had not died that September night in 1925 at Alekul. And in the end the Soviet government admitted as much.

On June 8, 1927, the Soviet press came out with an official communiqué that listed the most recent instances of violations of Soviet territory by White saboteurs or terrorists. Among others the communiqué mentioned specifically the case of one Sternberg, who had been wounded and captured some time late in the summer of 1925 while attempting to cross into Russia from Finland with a forged Soviet passport and who, upon being questioned had admitted that he was Captain Sydney George Reilly, "the notorious British spy." The papers followed this up next day with a detailed confession of guilt, which Reilly was purported to have made to his captors. What his subsequent fate had been, however, they did not say.[34]

3

OPPERPUT

The circumstances of Boris Savinkov's last trip pointed to the possibility of a "sensitive spot" within the Trust. Sydney Reilly's tragic end made this a certainty. Even General Kutyepov was now heard to voice surprise at the Trust's continuing survival, considering its agents' lack of caution. For her part, Maria Schultz, who regarded herself rightly as responsible for Reilly's fateful voyage, was now determined, in defiance of Kutyepov's orders, to go back to Russia to find out the truth.

Just as all these misgivings, doubts and dawning suspicions were about to crystallize, there occurred an episode which for a little while longer helped to some extent to still the skeptics. This episode has come to be known as the "Shulghin Affair."

A former right-wing member of the Tsarist *Duma* or Parliament, Vassili Vitalyevich Shulghin had been active in the Russian anti-Communist movement both during the Civil War and after. One day, late in 1923, he learned that a favorite son, of whom he had been without news since his own escape from Russia, had been finally located in a Soviet mental institution near Vinnitsa, in the Ukraine. With Baron Wrangel's consent he contacted Yakushev (whom he had met earlier that summer in Berlin, together with General Klimovich) and, reminding him of his offer to organize the safe passage of a White emissary to Russia and back, informed him that he was willing to undertake the trip. Almost two years went by in hesitations—on Shulghin's part—and preparations—on the part of the Trust. Finally in September, 1925, Shulghin set out.

He traveled by one of the Trust's favorite routes: by rail to Warsaw and then by horse-drawn cart to Rovno, a small town close to the Soviet border, where he stayed some six weeks in hiding, growing a beard and acquiring generally a more "proletarian" appearance. It is here that sometime early in December he learned from his Trust contacts in Poland, that a "misfortune" had recently (!) befallen an Englishman while the latter was trying to cross over into Russia—Reilly's alleged death had taken place at the end of September!—that the Englishman had been killed and that his own trip was being delayed while new arrangements were made.

A less dedicated man might now well have turned back. After all, if the OGPU had gone to so much trouble to get Savinkov and Reilly into their clutches, they could be expected to go to no less trouble in order to seize hold of one of the more active and prominent émigré politicians. However, Shulghin, though a naïve man, was no coward; he decided to go ahead with his plans.

He crossed over into Russia without mishap. At the border he was met by emissaries of the Trust, who thereafter rarely left his side. First, he was taken to Kiev, then to Moscow and lastly to Leningrad. He remained in the Soviet Union until the following spring, residing under various false identities in secret lodgings especially prepared for the occasion. Wherever he went—all in all, he made the acquaintance of nineteen members of the Trust during his stay—he found what seemed to him like convincing evidence of the existence of a widespread, well-organized and highly disciplined anti-Communist underground.

He had a number of talks with Yakushev and other leaders of the Trust. One of them took place in a country villa outside of Moscow. He little suspected that this was precisely where Reilly had been arrested only a few months earlier. It was here that he was introduced to yet another of the organization's leaders—a quite young man, tall, red-haired, with cold shifty eyes, a catlike, insinuating manner and a small pointed goatee with which he constantly toyed

—whom Yakushev presented to him as "Edward Ottovich, our Minister of Finance." Shulghin took an instant dislike to him. But later he learned from Maria Schultz (who had herself just slipped back into Russia) that this "Edward Ottovich" was her immediate superior. A man of great energy and considerable business acumen, he was, she informed Shulghin, in charge of the Trust's business enterprises, which provided the organization with most of its income. However, she added, though he ranked immediately after Yakushev in the Trust's hierarchy, there was at this juncture a serious conflict between the two men. For if Yakushev acknowledged the potential advantages of terror he insisted that any premature use of it would merely provoke police reprisals; that the overthrow of the regime should strike the Communists "as a bolt out of the blue." Opperput (as he will hereinafter be known) and most of the rank-and-file were growing increasingly impatient over this wait-and-see attitude and were threatening Yakushev with an open break were he to persist with his tactics. This "conflict" was to acquire particular significance in the light of subsequent events.

Curiously enough, though Shulghin's whole trip had been undertaken, allegedly, for the purpose of arranging a meeting with his son, he was not allowed near Vinnitsa, a Trust man going there instead. Presently the latter returned with the news that the boy was no longer there, that he had recently been moved to an unknown destination! Profoundly disappointed, Shulghin now began to prepare himself for the return trip. On several occasions during their talks Yakushev had hinted that "if and when he got home safely," he might wish to publish his impressions of the voyage. Though this had been said casually, *en passant*, as it were, Shulghin had been quite taken aback. Surely, he protested, any disclosures of the Trust's existence would be fatal to that organization! But Yakushev had shrugged away his objections. The Trust, he boasted airily, was so powerful that it was virtually immune from reprisals, as Shulghin could judge for himself from the smoothness with which his trip had proceeded. For their part, the White Russian *émigrés* would be heartened to know that Russia had not succumbed under Communism, that she still "lived" and that the anti-Communist underground there was a reality. Indeed—and Shulghin began to suspect that this was, perhaps, the crux of the whole matter—even General Wrangel (about whom Yakushev spoke invariably with the greatest respect) might as a result be persuaded at last to co-operate with the Trust.

And so in the end Shulghin agreed. His return trip was uneventful. By April, 1926, he was back in Belgrade, where the story of his stay in Russia was soon the talk of the town. For a little while longer it seemed as if the skeptics had been wrong after all.*

On May 12, 1926, a military coup in Warsaw returned to power Marshal Josip Pilsudski and his "Cabinet of Colonels." Pilsudski had long been critical of the Polish Military Intelligence; in particular he had repeatedly warned against exclusive reliance being placed in the Trust's reports. He now ordered a thoroughgoing investigation.

For that purpose the Polish military attaché in Paris was instructed to contact the local Trust resident and to procure from him a copy of the latest Soviet mobilization plan in the event of a Polish-Soviet conflict. The resident notified Yakushev, who happened to be on one of his periodic trips to Western Europe at the time. But Yakushev (who had only recently, at a private ceremony in Warsaw, been awarded a silver-initialed revolver in recognition of his services to the Polish Intelligence) reacted unexpectedly: The Trust, he protested angrily, did not have any reliable contact in the competent department of the Red General Staff "at that particular moment" and it would cost at the very least ten thousand U.S. dollars to obtain the information from another source. The Poles, however, were adamant; the price was irrelevant, they said. Thus Yakushev had perforce to comply. Even then, several months were to pass before the document was handed over. It was carefully studied and the findings confirmed Pilsudski's worst suspicions: it was clearly a

---

* Shulghin's book appeared in Berlin in January, 1927, under the title of *Three Cities* after the manuscript had been sent back to Moscow, to Yakushev, for clearance. An odd mixture of cloak-and-dagger intrigue and mystical soul searching, it caused an immediate sensation. At the end of World War II, Shulghin, who had been residing in Yugoslavia, was handed over to the Soviets by the Titoist authorities. He was, reportedly, until recently in a Soviet slave-labor camp. His present fate is unknown.

"plant." As is often the case in such matters, it was now suddenly remembered that in 1925 the Polish military attaché in Tallinn had already on his own initiative undertaken to check those of the Trust's dispatches which passed through his hands against information received from other, absolutely unimpeachable sources. He too had discovered a number of unaccountable discrepancies.

Pilsudski immediately ordered that all contacts with the Trust and its agents be severed.

Throughout the summer of 1926 distrust of Yakushev and the Trust grew in all quarters. Those Western intelligence services which had until then been working most closely with them began gradually to slacken their contacts; certain British agents who had been involved in Reilly's operations were assigned to other posts. Even General Kutyepov found it increasingly difficult to restrain those of his followers who kept denouncing Yakushev for his "immobilism" and pressing for a campaign of active White terror inside the U.S.S.R.

One day, early in November, General Von Monkewitz, Kutyepov's evil genius and the Trust's most zealous promoter in White military circles, vanished from his Paris apartment. He left a suicide note in which he explained that he had chosen this particular way of putting an end to his life "in order to spare his family the funeral expenses." But presently the rumor spread that he had simply defected to the Reds, that he had in fact for a long time already been an agent of the OGPU.

A couple of weeks after Von Monkewitz's disappearance Maria Schultz reappeared unexpectedly in Paris. She confided to Kutyepov that she had slipped out of Russia without the Trust's approval or even knowledge, that she had had to do so because her investigation of the circumstances of Reilly's end had progressed to the point where she was convinced that the OGPU had succeeded in infiltrating the Trust, though to what extent she was as yet unable to tell. She counseled Kutyepov in any event to make as little use as possible of Trust-sponsored channels of communication, but instead to send back into Russia with her three reliable couriers (for whom she had already obtained clearance from Yakushev, without of course

disclosing her real intentions) to whom she would confide her defini-
tive findings.

Another winter went by. Spring came. The spring of 1927.

On the night of the thirteenth of April two unknown persons, a
man and a woman, presented themselves at a Finnish command post
close to the Soviet border, announced that they had just fled from
the U.S.S.R. and asked to be taken to Captain Rozenström, Chief
Intelligence Officer of the Second Finnish Division, which was stationed in that area. The woman's name was apparently familiar to
that officer, for a few hours later she and her companion were being
driven in a swift car to Finnish Army headquarters in Helsinki. To
the senior officers there, Maria Schultz (for it was she) now introduced her companion. His name, she said, was Edward Opperput
(although he was known also by many other aliases). Until recently
a top official of the OGPU's Counter-Intelligence Department, he
had in the latter capacity worked closely with a group which in
Russia went by the name of the "Moscow Municipal Credit Association," but which abroad was better known as the Trust.

The effect of this announcement can easily be gauged. General
Wallenius, the Finnish Chief of Staff, for one, must have immediately
realized that if what she said was true—and he had no reason to
doubt her word—Opperput's defection could have the most incal-
culable consequences. The two fugitives were held incommunicado
and the whole matter was kept secret until the Finnish Intelligence
had completed their questioning.

Exactly one week later, on April 21, the Soviet Tass agency came
out with the announcement that a "monarchist group operating
under the leadership of the ex-White General Kutyepov" had been
recently uncovered in Moscow and liquidated. In the days that
followed there were rumors of mass shootings in Leningrad and
other Soviet cities.

On April 24, General Kutyepov (who had himself visited Finland
briefly in March, when he had met with Yakushev and other leaders
of the Trust) received a letter by special courier from Moscow.
Dated April 16 (i.e., three days after Opperput's flight to Finland)
and signed by Yakushev's second deputy, General Potapov, it in-

formed Kutyepov in almost panicky terms that the OGPU had just carried out a vast mopping-up operation against the Trust; that many of its members were under arrest; that the organization was virtually smashed; but that Potapov himself, as well as Yakushev and, in general, "all those who had had little or no connection with Staunitz and Zakharchenko-Schultz" (!) had survived and were now regrouping their forces. And Potapov ended by imploring Kutyepov not to lose heart and to maintain close contact. The letter was followed by a stream of cables, signed alternately by Potapov and Yakushev, in which Kutyepov was again reminded in veiled terms to beware of Staunitz and Schultz and to stay, at all cost, in touch.

By now, the Finnish press had got wind of the whole affair and were hinting that "in the words of a prominent recent Soviet defector," the so-called "monarchist organization" which had been liquidated lately in the U.S.S.R. was nothing but an OGPU front.[1]

And then the story broke. On May 17 the Riga Russian language daily *Sevodnya* came out with a letter to the editor which started with the words:

In the night of April 13th., I, Edward Opperput, a resident of Moscow under the name of Staunitz since March 1922 and a secret collaborator of the OGPU's Counter-Intelligence Department since that date, escaped from Russia with the purpose of disclosing all the OGPU's secret operations and of thus furthering, to the best of my ability, the Russian national cause.

It is to be presumed that General Kutyepov was informed at an early date by his Finnish friends of the arrival of the two fugitives. At General Wallenius' invitation he traveled in great secrecy with two of his officers to Finland, early in May, to interview them. In any event, by the time Opperput's open letter appeared in the press and the whole affair thus became public property, he was certainly aware of Maria Schultz's side of the story.

At first, she said, everything had gone smoothly. The three White couriers—Colonel Sussalin, Karinsky and Shorin—had reached Moscow safely and taken up their stations. But presently Sussalin had become careless. Ignoring her explicit warnings, he had begun to

hint darkly that abroad people were getting suspicious of the Trust
and that he had come to Russia to find out the truth. And one fine
morning what she had feared all along had happened: Sussalin went
out for a walk and was never seen again and when she inquired of
the Trust as to his whereabouts, she was informed that a Bulgarian
Communist, who happened to have known him abroad, had recognized him in the street and denounced him to the OGPU, which had
shot him before the Trust could intervene.*

Throughout that winter of 1926-1927, Maria Schultz continued,
relations between Opperput (or rather Edward Ottovich Staunitz, as
he was then still known to her) and Yakushev grew increasingly
strained. Staunitz kept insisting that the Trust should pass to positive
action against the Soviet regime. Yakushev kept hedging. And then,
one fine day in April, just when this conflict was about to reach a
head, Staunitz had come to her with a shattering confession.

He was, he had told her, an old-time agent of the OGPU. Moreover he was not alone: Yakushev, Potapov and many others, the
entire leadership of the Trust, in fact, had also from the first sold out
to the Communists. Personally, however, he had always hated this
role of a double agent (which he had agreed to assume only under
torture in the first place) and he was now resolved to quit. At first he
had hoped to stay on in Russia and even to outwit the OGPU by
building up within the Trust a hard core of sincere anti-Communists
of proven loyalty, immune from police infiltration, since they would
assume that he had the situation under control. It was because of this
that he, for one, had backed her request to bring in the three
couriers. But Colonel Sussalin's indiscretion had wrecked all this,
and now he had been informed by a friend well versed in the innermost secrets of the OGPU that his role in the Reilly affair (about
which more will be told later) and his recent controversy with
Yakushev had made him a marked man. Besides, the OGPU was a
self-consuming machine that lived off the bones of its own personnel.
The reaction abroad to the Savinkov and Reilly incidents proved

* Actually, Colonel Sussalin does not seem to have been executed until
several months later, for his name figures, together with nineteen others, on
the list of persons shot by way of reprisals for the Larionov bombing attempt
and the murder of Ambassador Voykov (see p. 84).

clearly that the Trust had overplayed its hand and that its days were
therefore numbered. Sooner or later it would have to wind up its
activities as a Communist front and when the time came to do so,
the OGPU—of that he was sure—would use the usual trick. Thus,
while those of its members who had not been compromised were
saved for future use elsewhere, the rest, together with the Trust's
rank-and-file, having served their purpose and being by definition
expendable, would be liquidated, their end being then blamed on a
"traitor" who had allegedly penetrated their ranks. After which this
"traitor" himself would be sacrificed. And Opperput claimed to have
good reason to suspect that he had been earmarked for this role.
One way or another, therefore, he had no choice but to flee abroad
right away, while the Trust's "passers" at the border still obeyed his
orders. And he urged her to do likewise.

This was far worse than anything she had suspected. As she now
realized that all she had worked and fought for these past years, that
her entire world, in fact, had suddenly crumbled about her ears,
Maria Schultz seems to have lost her head. She had now only one
urge—to get out and away and to rejoin her friends abroad so as to
collect her thoughts and plan her future anew. And so she agreed.

Staunitz had suggested that they postpone their flight only so long
as was necessary to enable three White couriers—the two surviving
"trainees," Karinsky and Shorin, and Maria Schultz's husband,
Georghi N. Radkovich (with whom she had been traveling, as "Mr.
and Mrs. Krasnoshtanov," when she first met Reilly about two years
earlier)—to make good their escape. On April 10 the three men
crossed safely back into Poland via the "bushes," i.e., on their own,
as Staunitz had recommended, and three days later, on April 13, they
themselves escaped to Finland.

And presently Opperput gave his story, which opened up at last
the whole incredible background of the Trust.

It had all started with Yakushev's first visit to Captain X in
Tallinn, that late summer of 1921. For shortly after his return to
Moscow from the Oslo lumber conference, Yakushev was arrested
and confronted by Commissar Kiakowski, of the Counter-Intelligence

Department of the OGPU* with a copy or a summary of Captain X's letter to his Berlin friend. Presently, despite all his protestations of innocence, he was tried by the OGPU's dread "Secret Collegium" and condemned to death.

His account of his meetings with Captain X, however, had suggested to Kiakowski an ingenious plan: Under the name of "Kolesnikov," Kiakowski himself now proceeded to Revel, where he contacted Captain X, allegedly on behalf of "his good friend, Aleksander Aleksandrovich Yakushev," with the results that we know. Then, returning to Moscow, he summoned Yakushev from his death cell and put to him the following proposition.

Whether one liked it or not, the old order was gone, gone forever; as a result of almost eight years of never-ceasing war, revolution, civil strife and foreign intervention, Russia was now bled to the point of collapse. Such a collapse could benefit neither those who believed in Communism nor those who opposed it; it could benefit only those Western powers who, aided and abetted by disgruntled White Russian émigrés whose patriotism had become dulled by their thirst for revenge, were now preparing to deal her the death blow in order, under the cover of friendship with a non-Communist Russia, then to divide up among themselves the once mighty empire of the Tsars. In the face of such a threat, continued Kiakowski, it was the sacred duty of all Russian patriots, whatever their political beliefs—and he assumed that Yakushev was one—to forget their petty resentments and to rally around the Soviet government, which, for all its possible shortcomings, was nonetheless the sole present custodian of Russian historical continuity.

What the country needed most, Kiakowski went on, was peace, a

* Kiakowski, whose real name was Victor Stetskevich, was himself an interesting character. Having started his career during the Soviet-Polish War of 1920-1921 as one of Poland's most daring agents behind the Red lines, he had eventually been captured. Hauled before Polish-born Dzierzhinski, the founder of the Cheka, he had soon been persuaded by the latter (who liked to surround himself with compatriots) to join the Soviet secret police, in whose ranks he rose rapidly to a position of prominence. He first served, under the alias of "Kossinsky," with the Soviet legations in Riga and Helsinki, after which in 1926 he participated, under the name of "Petrovsky," in yet another *cause célèbre* of the twenties—the kidnaping in full daylight in Moscow of the Estonian Minister to the U.S.S.R., Ado Birk.

respite, during which it could heal its wounds and get back onto its
feet. At home the Communist authorities had inaugurated such a
period of respite with the introduction of the NEP. A similar NEP—
the expression "peaceful coexistence" had not yet been coined—was
needed in the field of foreign policy. To this end, the Western Powers
had somehow to be dissuaded from renewing their intervention in
Russia or from encouraging the Whites to start another civil war.
One way to achieve this was to convince them that such an intervention was no longer needed, that "something was happening in
Russia," that Communism was being gradually undermined from
within, and that under these circumstances any outside shock was
bound to vitiate the natural process of evolution toward "normalcy."
And this, Kiakowski concluded, was where Yakushev came in. Why
shouldn't *he* undertake a trip abroad in order to contact White
circles there and, posing as a dedicated anti-Communist, make this
theory sound plausible? The framework for his mission could be
provided by an underground anti-Communist organization, which
called itself the MUCR and which had recently come to the Cheka's
notice.

As Yakushev sat pondering Kiakowski's proposition, he was given a
cellmate. Tall, red-haired, in his thirties, the latter introduced himself
as Edward Opperput. He had many a grim tale to tell.

Of Latvian origin, the son of wealthy farmers, he had served in
World War I as a subaltern in Tsar Nicholas II's Army until the
Bolshevik Revolution. Then (like so many of his fellow officers) he
had been arrested, only to be released shortly thereafter and posted
to the so-called VOKHR or Internal Security Troops of the Revolutionary Military Council, an ill-famed outfit which performed in the
early days of Soviet rule roughly the same functions as those later
taken over by the Cheka-OGPU. As such, he had been assigned to
fight Boris Savinkov's guerrillas in Byelorussia, but being at heart a
sincere anti-Communist, instead of fighting them, he had contacted
Savinkov and even organized on his behalf a secret network behind
the Red lines. In the spring of 1921, however, he had been sold out
to the Cheka, where he had been tortured until he was broken and
had agreed to write propaganda pamphlets denouncing Savinkov

and his activities. It was on account of this affair, he assured Yaku-shev, that he was now still in jail. What his ultimate fate would be, he knew not, though he feared the worst. In any event, he was at the end of his tether.

The two men remained together in the same death cell for approxi-mately three months, until January, 1922, during which time they were subjected to some of the Cheka's more effective methods of persuasion. Thus, they were made to witness a few mass executions and, in Opperput's words, this spectacle—what with the lamentations and cries for mercy of the victims and the drunken oaths of the executioners—was in itself something which none of those exposed to it were ever able to survive without breaking. After that they were themselves several times taken out to be shot, only to be dragged back to their cells at the last minute, supposedly under a temporary reprieve.* Although Yakushev was supposedly sincere when he first visited Captain X in Revel in the summer of 1921—or at least so Opperput claims—this ordeal, coupled with Opperput's constant harpings on the OGPU's omniscience and ruthlessness and his own understandable disgust with the carelessness or treachery of Captain X's Berlin correspondents, was bound in the end to make him pretty well amenable to anything Commissar Kiakowski sug-gested.[3]

Be this as it may, some time in January, 1922, the Cheka appointed a special task force, which in its turn set up a front organization or "legend" (as these were known in Russian secret police jargon) to "cap" the MUCR. Headed by the notorious Artuzov, Chief of the Counter-Intelligence Department (KRO) of the Cheka,† the latter included, in addition to Kiakowski, Yakushev and Opperput himself

---

* Not everyone got off so easily. Thus Kalamatiano, the head of the U.S. In-telligence Service in Moscow at the time of the Bolshevik Revolution, who had been arrested on the occasion of the "Lockhart Conspiracy," was also made to witness a few mass executions, until one fine day he himself was pushed into the line of fire and shot.[2]

† Short, gray-haired, with a small goatee, Artuzov was a native of Genoa, who had come to Russia in 1917 under his real name of Renucci and had started off by teaching French in a girls' school. A lover of music and a model family man—something in itself exceptional among senior Soviet police officials in those days—he was to rise eventually to top positions, first in the Cheka and OGPU and later in the NKVD, only to perish in Stalin's Great Purge.

(who now became "Edward Ottovich Staunitz"), some fifty other men and women agents of widely varied background and qualifications. Thus "capped," the Trust served a dual purpose:

On the one hand, *inside* Russia—where it operated officially as the "Moscow Municipal Credit Association" and where it was led by such supposedly bona fide anti-Communists as the ex-Tsarist Generals Zayonchkovsky and Potapov—it helped identify and channel into the ranks of an OGPU-run organization such dedicated foes of the regime as Maria Schultz, who otherwise might have remained long undetected. These now became all the easier to observe and control, inasmuch as they willingly accepted what they regarded as elementary rules of conspiracy, i.e., iron discipline and blind obedience to the "initiated few" (all of whom were, of course, trusted agents of the OGPU). Occasionally, even, the zeal and idealism of the rank-and-file would be fanned and then promptly neutralized by what seemed to them like useful "clandestine action." Thus, for instance, anti-Communist leaflets would be run off on OGPU presses, then distributed to bona fide Trust couriers, only to be immediately impounded again and stored, pending further use, in OGPU strong rooms. Occasionally, too, when the rank-and-file showed signs of restlessness, the leaders would rig yet another comedy: One group would urge a "tougher" policy vis-à-vis the Soviet regime, while the other insisted on greater caution. As a result of the ensuing debate, the more fanatically minded or less gullible elements would be duly identified and, if need be, quietly liquidated.

Furthermore, since the existence of the Trust was a carefully kept secret even within the OGPU itself, by checking the latter's watchfulness against the Trust's internal security measures, it became possible to ascertain to what extent the secret police was able to prevent the establishment or survival of a genuine anti-Communist underground in the Soviet Union.

Outside the U.S.S.R., masquerading as the Trust, the organization served to keep an eye on the activities of Kutyepov and his group and thus effectively to neutralize them, while at the same time acting as a sort of clearinghouse, both for the Western and White Russian agents and propaganda coming *into* the country and for the information (or, more often as not, "misinformation") going *out* of it, most of which, for greater speed and security, traveled by Soviet diplomatic pouch!

The results surpassed the OGPU's wildest expectations. Even Dzierzhinski, who had at first viewed the project with considerable skepticism, was amazed. At one time the sums of money received from Western intelligence sources in payment for the "information" supplied through the Trust were large enough to cover, not only the operational expenses of the entire Counter-Intelligence Department of the OGPU, but even some of the Foreign Department's own espionage activities abroad! One thankful Western intelligence bureau donated to the Trust eight solid gold watches, which were promptly distributed to Artuzov, Kiakowski and other deserving OGPU pundits! Indeed, so successful was the Trust in infiltrating the White para-military groups, that this formula became thereafter the standard pattern for the countless "legends" or "lines" (as they were also known in OGPU jargon) with which the Soviets sought to blanket their foes and which, according to Opperput, numbered some forty to fifty at the time of his defection.

Opperput also provided an exhaustive account of Sydney Reilly's capture and death, with which he himself had been closely associated.

Thus, he said—though we again have only his own word for it—it had not been the Trust's original intention to kill Reilly. Indeed, to kill anyone would have defeated the organization's very *raison d'être*, which was to infiltrate, delude and thus disarm the White groups against which it operated.

And at first all had gone well with Reilly too. He reached Leningrad safely, being met there by Yakushev, Opperput, Styrne (Artuzov's right-hand man in the Counter-Intelligence Department of the OGPU) and an ex-Tsarist police colonel by the name of Shatkovsky. After spending the night in a luxuriously appointed apartment in the very center of the city, he was driven next morning by Shatkovsky to an OGPU-owned villa in the hamlet of Malakhovka, outside of Moscow. In the beginning he was quite unsuspecting. True, the OGPU patrols that kept stopping their car on the road were possibly just a little too perfunctory in checking Shatkovsky's papers and this seemed to worry him. At one point, however, their car broke down and they had to proceed to the nearest railway station on foot. There his escort flagged down to a stop the first passing express train to Moscow, with which they continued on to their destination without further mishap. Reilly's openly voiced misgivings were laughed off with the explanation that this merely proved the "pull" from which the Trust benefited in all quarters. But this time he did not appear entirely convinced.

Meanwhile the rest of the Trust's "welcoming committee" had driven straight to Moscow, to Opperput's lodgings, where they waited while Styrne went to the OGPU to report to his chief Artuzov the successful completion of the first part of their mission. He was gone for quite some time and as the hours dragged on, Opperput began to suspect that the OGPU might be up to one of its usual "tricks." But Yakushev brushed his misgivings aside. Prior to leaving for Leningrad to meet Reilly, he said, all three top OGPU officials in charge of the operation—Artuzov, Styrne and Savinkov's captor, the ex-Baltic Baron Pilar von Pilhau—had emphatically assured him that the Englishman would be allowed safely out of the country. And presently, as if in confirmation of his words, Styrne reappeared and said that they must now rejoin their guest.

As they sped along the Ryazan highway toward Malakhovka, they sighted Shatkovsky's car approaching from the opposite direction. All, he said, was well; Reilly was waiting for them. Whereupon Styrne pulled out his wallet, handed Shatkovsky a wad of money and instructed him to purchase two first-class return tickets to Leningrad for himself and Reilly. They would be leaving that very night, he added, so that Reilly could be back in Finland within forty-eight hours, as he had originally planned.

Opperput breathed a sigh of relief. But on reaching Malakhovka, his suspicions were instantly revived. For the villa was literally surrounded by suspicious-looking characters in varied disguises, who looked pointedly away as their car drove up. Yet Styrne had an explanation even for this: the plain-clothes men were there, he said, to keep the local police, the militia, from being unduly inquisitive.

Entering the house, they now sat down to talk with Reilly about those matters for which, allegedly, he had come to Russia in the first place. But somehow the conversation never got off to a real start. Reilly seemed uneasy; he kept looking apprehensively at the door and his nervousness communicated itself to Styrne, who kept jumping up and walking over to the window or out into the hall. The hours dragged on. Darkness fell. Styrne began to complain that the cars were late, that they should have been back long ago, that Reilly would miss his train connection. Opperput, however, suspected that this was all just make-believe, that Styrne was playing for time. Presently he could control himself no longer. Getting up, he walked out onto the porch. He had been right; the cordon of plain-clothes men had drawn closer. White with anger, he turned back into the house. Styrne met him in the hall. "Pull yourself together!" he hissed, and added hurriedly: "Very well, I may as well admit it! You were right: we are about to arrest him. The cars are due any minute now. Pusinsky [Artuzov's second deputy] is coming over in person! That way the Trust will be kept out of it!"

Opperput began to plead with him and they were presently joined by Yakushev. Were Reilly to be arrested, they warned, it would be the end of the Trust, of all their painstaking and so successful efforts. First Savinkov and now this—why, the Whites were bound to smell a rat! Was it worth it? Wasn't it better to let Reilly go and have him confirm far and wide the existence of the Trust as a bona fide anti-Communist organization? But Styrne would not be moved. He himself was powerless, he said. Indeed, he agreed with them, as did all those of the OGPU who were connected with the Trust. After all, wasn't the latter their common "baby"? But the matter was now beyond the control even of Artuzov, even of Pilar von Pilhau. The Politbureau itself had ruled that Reilly could not be allowed out of the country alive. It was said that Stalin had asked to be informed every half-hour about the progress of the operation.

They had been arguing for some time, when two cars ground to a stop outside the house and Pusinsky jumped out, followed by several other Chekists. Again Opperput pleaded with him and Styrne that

the OGPU should stick to its original bargain with the Trust, and
in the end Styrne agreed to talk the matter over with Artuzov and
Pilar von Pilhau, but on one condition: Pusinsky and his party would
have to remain with Opperput's group. Whereupon everybody, including Reilly, piled into the cars and drove back to Moscow, to
Opperput's apartment, while Styrne proceeded to OGPU headquarters in Lubyanka (now Dzierzhinski) Square.

In Moscow they were met by Shatkovsky with the tickets. Handing one of them to Reilly, the latter told him that they had better
go to the station separately and meet on the train. After which he too
left them. He hadn't been gone more than a quarter of an hour, when
the telephone rang. Opperput picked up the receiver. It was Pilar
von Pilhau. Pusinsky, he said dryly, was to act according to his
orders! This settled it.

Reilly was told that he would now be driven to the station. He,
Opperput, Pusinsky and two other Chekists thereupon climbed into
one of the waiting cars and drove off. As they were passing through
the Zlatoustovsky Pereulok, Pusinsky suddenly whipped out a pair of
handcuffs and swiftly clicked them shut about Reilly's wrists. "Not
a word!" he barked. "You're under arrest!" Five minutes later the
great steel gates of the Lubyanka had swung closed behind them.

A little later Opperput was driven home, where he was presently
joined by the top leaders of the Trust—Artuzov and Styrne, plus
Pilar von Pilhau. They seemed a little embarrassed. All would be
done, nevertheless, to preserve the Trust, they said. To fool the outside world, a shooting fray with "contrabandists" would be staged on
the Finnish border at about the time Reilly could be expected to
have crossed back into Finland. There would be a couple of victims,
and Reilly would be listed as one of them. In fact, Pusinsky had
already left with a few men for Leningrad on the very same train
Reilly was to take.

At first, Opperput related further, Reilly was treated very correctly. He was given Savinkov's former apartment in the "Inner
Prison" of the Butyrki, was—like Savinkov—allowed to go for drives
in the country and was even treated to his favorite brand of
whiskey. But presently, as he kept denying any knowledge of the

British Intelligence Service and of his own activities in that organization, assuring his listeners that he had come to Russia solely with a view to convincing himself of the failure of the Soviet system and writing a book about it, entitled *The Great Bluff*, the OGPU got tough. For a while he continued to hold out, claiming that a British officer did not betray. But in the end, after he had been made to witness several particularly gruesome executions and been subjected to other types of pressure, he too was broken.

The OGPU had now no further use for him and for fear that rumor of his survival might cause diplomatic complications, it was decided to finish him off. As an exceptional favor to a nevertheless respected enemy, however, he was not killed—like the rest of the OGPU's victims—in the porcelain-tiled cellars of the Lubyanka. One brisk November morning, as he was taking his daily walk in the Vorobyovy Hills—now Lenin Hills—he was quietly shot in the back by the OGPU's top marksman, the notorious Ibrahim.*

* And yet even this may not be the true story of Sydney Reilly's end. As late as June, 1927, for instance, Mrs. Reilly claimed to have positive knowledge that her husband was still alive in April of that year.[4]

Many years later, a former inmate of the Butyrki related that sometime in 1926, i.e., several months after Reilly's assumed death, he had been in "water-pipe correspondence"—a favorite practice among inmates of Soviet jails, which consists in rapping out messages in Morse on communicating pipes—with a fellow prisoner, who would not give his name, claiming that he was better known as "S.T.-1" (which had been Reilly's cover number on his first assignment to Russia in 1918!).

Shortly thereafter, the man who called himself "S.T.-1" had gone silent. Throughout that spring, however, there were persistent rumors among the inmates of the prison that an important captive, a British spy, was being held incommunicado under an assumed name in one of the so-called "cells of special designation," that had been installed in the loft of the Butyrki's "Inner Prison," and whose inmates were known only by numbers. The man had gone mad; occasionally he would be taken out for walks, escorted by two Chekists.[5]

4

THE END OF THE "TRUST"

General Kutyepov now faced a dilemma.

For it was obvious that, for close to four years, all those who had in one way or another worked with Yakushev and his group—and this was especially true of his own Combat Organization—had in effect been unwitting tools of the OGPU. For all one knew, Opperput, despite his alleged pangs of conscience, despite even his disclosures, might *still* be working for the OGPU. Somehow his story sounded just a little too glib, and the Soviet-inspired press reports about his past just a little too easy to disprove. Moreover, with the exception of his disclosures about Sydney Reilly's end and his denunciation of Yakushev and the Trust—who were by now suspect anyway—he had not named *a single* other Soviet agent abroad, had not identified *a single one* of the forty to fifty "lines" which, in his own words, blanketed the White Russian emigration at the time of his defection.

What would he, Kutyepov, have done in the OGPU's place?

Assuming that the OGPU had come to the conclusion that the game was up, its next concern, surely, would be to save as much of Yakushev's laboriously built apparatus as possible. For this it was essential that it wind up operations on its own initiative, *prior to* any action on the part of the Whites. In this way the latter would be lulled into a sense of false security, whereas in reality only those whom the OGPU had chosen to unmask, only those who were "scalded" and could not be protected any longer anyway, would be out of action. Better still, one of the Trust's most trusted and experienced agents, say, Opperput, would be sent out of the country, to Finland, for instance, as a self-professed defector; he would proceed to make elaborate, well-publicized disclosures about matters which either were of secondary importance or were already largely known, and his credibility would be still further enhanced by the simultaneous unleashing of a campaign of defamation, which would be promptly traced back to Moscow. Thus, if Kutyepov believed him and agreed to recruit him into his organization, the OGPU would have someone in the General's immediate entourage despite the Trust's liquidation. But this was not all. As a sort of "counterinsurance," Opperput would also be denounced by Yakushev and Potapov, so that if Kutyepov, contrary to all expectations, continued to believe their word against Opperput's, their position in his eyes would be further strengthened and a new "legend" would be promptly built up to succeed the Trust.

All in all, it seemed wiser to have nothing to do with the fellow.

And yet Maria Schultz and the many other members of the Trust's rank-and-file, to whose sincerity she could testify, were a living proof of the fact not only that there existed real discontent in Russia with the Communist regime—in the view of a man of Kutyepov's character and beliefs, such discontent could not *not* exist—but that there were also people willing to do something about it, even at the risk of their own lives. And with the international situation heading, as he saw it, for a crisis, this was hardly the time to break off all contacts with a potential anti-Communist underground in Russia.

Maria Schultz herself was, needless to say, not the person to offer him counsels of wisdom. In the first place, she personally believed that this time Opperput was sincere. Hadn't he risked his life by staying on in Russia until her husband and the two White couriers had made safe their escape? And then, now that Kutyepov had decided to step up his clandestine activities in Russia, he could surely not afford to waste the talents of a man of Opperput's intelligence, energy and experience. Besides the latter's loyalty could be put to a test. A first team of White terrorists was just then about to

cross over into Russia from Finland. She would join it. Why not have
Opperput accompany them, on a mission of self-redemption, as it
were? She herself would watch his every step and at the first sign of
betrayal, she would shoot him like a dog!

For Kutyepov had indeed made up his mind. The period of
immobilism—Yakushev's greatest achievement—was over. The time
had come for White terror to start in earnest. In Finland he had
now a group of nine volunteers, all of them dedicated anti-Communists, equipped—partly through his own efforts, partly with the
help of his Finnish friends—with a fairly substantial, if heterogene-
ous, arsenal of firearms and explosives and burning with the desire
to re-enact the revolutionary prowesses of the nineteenth century
Nihilists. This represented the largest team that had ever been
committed at one time for underground work in the U.S.S.R. since
the days of Savinkov's "Green Guards."

But if the men and the spirit were there, the organization, experience and training were pitifully inadequate. In a memorable
conversation with Captain Hill (Sydney Reilly's companion in the
days of the "Lockhart Conspiracy"), Savinkov had once commented
on the difficulties he had encountered every time he had sought to
make a bomb-throwing terrorist out of a former Tsarist officer. Not
that they lacked courage, he said, or dedication or even fanaticism;
but from childhood they had been brought up in the Christian concept that "Thou shalt not kill!" And although many of them were by
now hardened by years of war and revolutionary violence, when it
came to murdering someone in cold blood, something within them
rebelled. And Savinkov had gone on to evoke nostalgically the companions of his young days, all of them simple people, whose Christian ethics either were blunted by ignorance or else had been
dulled by years of godless and materialistic propaganda. What
terrorists *they* had made![1] Kutyepov was about to come up against
the same problem.

Maria Schultz seems always to have exercised a strange fascination over all those who happened to meet her. On the other hand,
Kutyepov had been greatly angered by her return to Russia against
his explicit orders, the preceding autumn, following General Von

Monkewitz's mysterious disappearance. Now, with two of his officers, he proceeded to Helsinki to interview the fugitives and study
the situation on the spot. He found his worst suspicions confirmed.
The shock had been too much for her. Maria Schultz was clearly a
sick person, who needed above all a long rest.* Ordering his two
men to stay on in Finland to watch over her, he then returned to
Paris, only to learn to his horror, a short while thereafter, that she
had again given the watchers the slip and gone back to Russia.

For on May 31, i.e., barely six weeks after their escape from
Russia, Maria Schultz and Opperput had recrossed the Finnish
border, this time as members of a six-man team of White terrorists
who had been ordered into the U.S.S.R. to carry out bombing attempts in Moscow and in Leningrad.

According to the plan of operations (which had been drawn up in
all its details by Maria Schultz), as soon as they reached Soviet
territory, the terrorists were to split up into two teams of three, one
of which, headed by young Captain Victor A. Larionov, would proceed straight to Leningrad, while the other, under Maria Schultz's
personal leadership, pushed on to Moscow. Opperput accompanied
her. On no account was Larionov to go into action until he heard
that the Moscow coup—the main operation—had already taken place.

This plan had one major flaw: If Opperput happened still to be a
Soviet agent and if he succeeded in giving his two companions the
slip, chances were that he would promptly betray their presence to
the OGPU before they reached their target and then lead it back to
Larionov's hiding place, where the latter would still be waiting for
news of the Moscow group. Whether this was indeed Opperput's
intention, we will doubtless never know. In any event, it would have
misfired. For Larionov had taken an instant dislike to Opperput and
being a man of strong character and independent judgment, he now

* Some time after her husband's disappearance, Mrs. Reilly had herself
been recruited by Maria Schultz into the Trust. Late in 1926 she had
received a letter from Yakushev and Opperput inviting her to come to
Russia to "join in the search," but had been dissuaded from doing so by
Kutyepov. Now, curiously enough, from Finland and despite all that had
happened, Maria Schultz again urged her to go back into Russia with her!
Her own departure was so precipitate, however, that Mrs. Reilly did not
have time to do anything about it.

decided to ignore his instructions and to act as circumstances demanded.

The border was crossed without mishap. "They left us," Larionov writes, "and followed a footpath into the forest. . . . For a while we could see them as they moved fitfully through the fir underbrush. Presently they vanished from sight forever. . . ."[2]

For a week Larionov himself and his two companions, Vladimir Monomakhov and Serghei Solovyov, hid out in a small forest clearing near Levashovo, some twenty kilometers north of Leningrad, one man guarding the camp with the weapons and supplies, while the others went into town daily to study the lay of the land. Their targets—the choice and order of priority of which represented Opperput's sole contribution to the planning of the venture—were first the Leningrad District Soviet, then the Central Party Club and lastly the headquarters of the Association of Militant Atheists or the School for National Minorities. Finally Larionov decided to wait no longer. By now his nerves were pretty much on edge. Besides, they couldn't hide out in Levashovo forever! After lunch, on July 6, therefore, he and his friends made their way to the Leningrad District Soviet. They found it so heavily guarded, however, and their bombs were relatively so small that chances of success seemed slim and so Larionov decided to try the Party Club instead.

As they entered the club building, at No. 59 Moyka, a clock struck 8:45 P.M. A woman receptionist was seated in the lobby, checking the passes of all visitors. This was a nasty surprise since it had been agreed among them that Monomakhov would immediately open fire at anyone who happened to stop them, after which they would throw their bombs and make a break for it. But a woman? They had not reckoned with *that!*

"What do you want, comrades?" she asked tersely. She looked suspicious.

"Where is the meeting of village agitators?" Larionov asked casually (having read about it in the morning paper).

"But who are you?" the woman insisted.

"Why, Communists, of course!" he replied, acting surprised.

"Oh, I see! Very well then, second floor up. First door to the right. But first sign in here: your name and your party card number. You can leave your coats over there."

Larionov signed in. "Fedotov, No. 34," and then he could have kicked himself, for the number was obviously far too low. Solovyov did worse: He pulled out his party card, a rather crude forgery, the cover of which was, moreover, of the wrong color. The woman was quick to notice it.

"Have we such cards?" she asked with growing hostility.

"Sure," Solovyov muttered hurriedly. "We're from Moscow. . . ."

They had been told to leave their coats in the lobby, which meant that they would have to transfer the guns and the bombs from their coat pockets to their jacket pockets before the woman's very eyes. Just then, as luck would have it, a bunch of Young Communists came clattering down the stairs; for a split second the woman's attention was distracted. And that split second was all they needed. Bounding up the stairs, they opened the first door to the right and looked in. There were only six or seven people in the room, including several women; surely they hadn't come all the way from Finland for *that!* Larionov shook his head, beckoned to his companions to follow him and walked down the stairs and out into the street. As they passed the woman in the lobby, she turned to them, visibly surprised.

"So soon?"

"We must have come to the wrong address," Larionov replied. "You see, we're strangers here, we're country chaps. . . ."

But as they boarded the tram back to the railway station, he whispered: "Tomorrow . . . Same time . . . Same place . . . And this time without fail!"

The following evening, toward 8:45 P.M., they were back inside the building of the Central Party Club. This time the woman at the desk was busy talking to some other visitors and they were able to sign in without her seeing them. Hurrying up the stairs, they opened a door and peeped in. This looked like better pickings. The Rector of the Leningrad Communist University Pozern was presiding over

a fairly large meeting, at which a Comrade Schirwindt was speaking
on the subject of "American Imperialism." At the sound of the opening door, a few faces turned in their direction.

"Now!" Larionov commanded.

Two bombs whipped past his head. The first one bounced off
along the floor without exploding, but the second burst with a roar,
filling the room with acrid yellowish smoke. Someone lunged at
Monomakhov. Firing at his assailant point-blank, the latter slammed
the door shut and ran down the stairs after his fleeing companions.
He could hear the sound of wailing behind him.

As they rushed past, the woman jumped up from her desk.

"What's happened?" she cried out.

"Someone threw a bomb! Call the militia! Hurry!" Larionov
shouted back and ran out into the street, where a crowd was
already gathering.

Two days later they were safely back in Finland. *

The fate of Maria Schultz and her two companions remains a
mystery to this day.

According to the original plan of operations, the first target of the
Moscow team was to be the Community Home for OPGU officials,
at Nos. 2 to 6, Malaya Lubyanka, just around the corner from the
OGPU's main headquarters in Lubyanka Square. The actual job of
planting the bomb had been assigned to Opperput, who was to enter
the building, kill the sentry and set the explosives in the stair well,
while the others stood guard outside. In the first place, he knew his
way around, having often met there with his colleagues of the
OGPU. And then this was to be something in the nature of a trial by
fire, by means of which he would cement, once and for all, his new-
found loyalty to the anti-Communist cause. The escape route lay by
way of the Polish border.

* The youngest of the three, Monomakhov, barely made it. He lost sight
of his accomplices during their flight and now, as he boarded the train for
Levashovo, he noticed that he had spent all his money and that he hadn't
even got fifty kopecks for his fare. He decided to try and slip through
without a ticket. As ill luck would have it, he was stopped by the controller
who was about to report him to the Railway Militia, when an old Jewish lady
volunteered to pay for him.

Nowadays, the choice of this particular target may seem somewhat surprising. For if Opperput knew the building as well as he claimed —and it is he who is said to have made the choice—he must also have known that it was inhabited primarily by the "small fry" of the secret police. The "brass"—OGPU Boss Metcheslav Menzhinski (Dzierzhinski had died the year before), his First Deputy Genrikh Yagoda, Counter-Intelligence Chief Artuzov, in other words, all Kutyepov's opposite numbers in his long-standing struggle against the Communist police state—worked and lived elsewhere.

For over a week following their parting with Larionov and his two companions, there was no further news of them. Then, on June 10, the Tass agency came out with the unexpected announcement that an attempt had recently been made to blow up the headquarters of the Moscow OGPU. The authors of this attempt had succeeded in laying a bomb containing four kilograms of melinite, but the fuse had gone out and the device had been discovered before it could cause any damage. A similar attempt—more successful this time, since many persons had been injured, some severely—had been made in Leningrad.

Three more weeks went by. On July 5, Tass issued another statement, according to which all three members of the group responsible for the Moscow bombing attempt had been caught and liquidated: Opperput on June 19, and Maria Schultz and Georghi N. Peters, alias "Vosnessensky," a couple of days later. Next day Deputy OGPU Boss Yagoda called a special press conference in which he reported that a diary had been found on Opperput, which proved conclusively that both the Moscow and Leningrad attempts had been engineered by "the White General Kutyepov" and a Captain Ross of the British Legation in Tallinn.

For two years nothing else was heard of this episode. Late in the fall of 1929, however, a top official of the OGPU's Foreign Department, the INU's "resident" in Turkey, G. A. Agabekov, defected to the West and shortly thereafter published a volume of memoirs.* Agabekov claims to have been in Moscow at the time of the attempt

---

* After a man hunt which lasted nearly ten years, the NKVD finally caught up with Agabekov in Belgium, where he was assassinated early in 1938.

in the Malaya Lubyanka, which, he says, took the OGPU completely
by surprise. As one of his colleagues from the Counter-Intelligence
Department put it to him: "Three agents arrived from abroad to
contact an alleged counter-revolutionary organization over here. One
of them, of course, was our man [*sic!*]. Everything had been prepared: phony counter-revolutionary leaders with whom they were
supposed to meet, phony conspiratorial meeting places, etc. And
then—Bang! All three vanished into thin air, including our man! We
had been combing Moscow for them for days when, suddenly, yesterday evening, we found a bomb in our people's Community Home
in the Malaya Lubyanka: the floor was soaked with kerosene and
two jerry cans and a case of melinite stood in a corner. Fortunately
the fuse had gone out. . . ."

"Who do you suppose did it?" Agabekov asked.

"No doubt our man and his companions. He alone knew his way
around the place, for we used often to meet there. One of the two—
either he bungled his assignment or else he betrayed us!"

"What was his name?"

"His name was Opperput, but he had a pile of documents in other
names which he used in order to lure the Whites over here."[3]

Some time before, in 1928, the Moscow government had published
an official account of White underground activities in the U.S.S.R.[4]
Curiously enough, this account differs considerably in its description
of the bombing attempt in the Malaya Lubyanka, not only from
Agabekov's version (which is understandable) but also from Tass's
official statements at the time as well as from Yagoda's comments to
the press. Thus Opperput's name is not mentioned at all; the Moscow
team of terrorists is said to have consisted of only two persons and
the famous diary implicating Kutyepov and the British Captain Ross
is said to have been found on Vosnessensky's body! And it goes on
to give further particulars of the two agents' end.

Thus, June 16, at about 5 P.M., a stranger was sighted walking
through the grounds of the Yanovsky Liquor Distillery, near Smolensk. A factory guard hailed him, whereupon the man pulled out a
revolver, wounded the guard and then took to his heels. The whole

area was cordoned off by the local OGPU and the man was finally ambushed and killed later in the day. A diary was found on him, which gave his name as Peters.

Two days later, on June 18, an Army vehicle was held up at pistol point in the same area by a lone woman, who demanded a lift. When the driver refused, she opened fire, wounding two soldiers gravely, and then vanished into the forest of Dretun'. There she was presently ambushed by a unit of the Red Army. She died in the ensuing skirmish. Her name was Maria Zakharchenko-Schultz.*

Thus, either Tass and Yagoda himself spoke the truth at the time—and in that case it is difficult to understand why a year later the official Soviet account should choose to cover up Opperput's role in the affair—or else this latter account is correct, and then the question arises: what became of Opperput? Did he place a dud bomb and then give Maria Schultz the slip? In September, 1927, the London *Morning Post* reported that Opperput had on July 27, i.e., fully a month after his alleged "liquidation" by the OGPU, been awarded the order of the Red Banner "for exceptionally meritorious services" and that he was now working for the OGPU in China! Or did he simply bungle his assignment? Or did he indeed escape to Finland on the OGPU's instructions and then undergo a genuine change of

---

* Not only is the official Soviet version as stated in the above-mentioned Blue Book in contradiction with Yagoda's first account; it conflicts also with some of the evidence that has become available since World War II.

Thus, for instance, during the Nazi occupation of Smolensk, Captain Larionov (the surviving leader of the Leningrad bombing coup) had the occasion to interview the German-appointed mayor of that city, a former Soviet lawyer by the name of Menshaghin. The latter related that some time late in 1927 he had been appointed to defend in court a railway switchman, who was accused of having given shelter to a "White Guardist." Shortly thereafter, the latter had been shot down in a neighboring factory by an OGPU patrol. The switchman, who had described the man as tall, powerfully built and red-haired, was condemned to ten years at hard labor.

A former Soviet DP by the name of Ivan Repin (at present in this country) happened to be doing his military service in a Red Army summer camp near the railway station of Dretun' at the time. He and his comrades were engaged in rifle practice in a forest clearing, he relates, when all of a sudden, two strangers—a man and a woman—stumbled out of the underbrush, torn and disheveled, straight into the line of fire. They may have suspected an ambush, for they opened fire out of their revolvers. They were immediately cut down. Their bodies were never identified.

heart and return to Russia with the intent of striking a blow at his former masters, as Agabekov's informer suggested?

We will probably never know.

Actually, whatever Opperput's real motives in fleeing to Finland, there is some evidence that the Soviets had already decided to wind up the Trust by the spring of 1926, at the time of the Pilsudski coup. For barely a month later, in June, the Soviet branch of the so-called "Eurasian" movement, which had until then functioned as a supposedly clandestine group within the framework of the Trust, broke away from the latter and set up its own "Managing Center," as it was called, which was to retain its contacts with the *émigré* "Eurasians" long after the Trust was no more. Clearly the OGPU was looking to the future.[5]

There exist in the game of police provocation three golden rules, which the OGPU had partly inherited from the Tsarist Okhrana, partly perfected itself: The first rule is that the same formula of provocation should not be used under two different sets of circumstances or for two different purposes. The second (which has already been mentioned in connection with Opperput's defection) is that when the time comes to wind up a given "legend"—whether because one's opponent has begun to suspect the truth, or because circumstances have changed—the initiative for such a suspension should always be taken by those responsible for this "legend's" operation and *prior to* its denunciation by the other side, even if this means denying oneself a few additional successes. And the third rule is that in winding up operations, one should invariably seek to provoke the maximum of disarray in the enemy camp by sowing confusion among the rank-and-file and suspicion and distrust in the leadership, while at the same time covering up those agents who happen to have still escaped suspicion.

It should be remembered that the Trust was essentially an adjunct of the NEP. And for almost four years, while the NEP helped put Russia's economy back on its feet, the Trust had successfully contributed to lull the more extremist White *émigrés* and their Western friends into a state of complacent optimism. But 1926 and 1927 were again years of crisis for the U.S.S.R. Due, on the one hand, to the Kremlin's persistent refusal to honor Tsarist Russia's debts and, on the other, to the stepped-up activities of the Comintern, a new wave of anti-Sovietism was beginning to sweep the world.

The mid-twenties were to see a veritable tidal wave of spy trials which showed only too clearly that the Soviet government had hastened to take advantage of the diplomatic immunity granted it by those countries that had reluctantly recognized it, in order to tighten its hold over the local Communist organizations and build up its intelligence network. This wave of scandals culminated, on May 12, 1927, in Scotland Yard's raid on the premises of Arcos Ltd. and of the Soviet Trade Mission in London, both of which yielded much compromising material. Three days later, on May 15, 1927, Great Britain broke off diplomatic relations with the Soviet Union. By the late spring of 1927, Soviet sources were proclaiming far and wide the imminence of a break between the Western Powers and the U.S.S.R. and the threat of another joint crusade against the young Communist state, in which even Germany, this time, would participate.*

It will be recalled that some time in March, 1927, General Kutyepov had met with Yakushev and other leaders of the Trust in the Finnish border town of Terijoki, where in answer to a specific question by Yakushev, he had asserted that the chances of a war against the U.S.S.R. "had never been so good" and that "decisive events" could be expected within the next three to six months. Coming, as it did, in the wake of wild rumors of an alleged remobilization of the Wrangel Army in the Balkans, and of secret talks between certain White leaders and prominent Western statesmen—Churchill,

---

* Germany had, in the spring of 1925, been the scene of a widely publicized trial, that of General Gorev-Skoblevsky, top Soviet military adviser to the German Communists, before the Leipzig High Court of Justice. In the fall of 1927, another sensational trial was to open in Frankfurt against a group of Georgian émigrés, charged with counterfeiting Soviet currency.

In the vastly different outcome of the two cases—while Gorev-Skoblevsky was condemned to death (he was later exchanged for three German citizens, whom the Kremlin had hastened to seize as hostages), the Georgians were acquitted—the Moscow government chose to see an indication of Germany's abandon of the so-called "Rapallo policy."

Lord Birkenhead, Poincaré and Briand—this announcement, even
though it stemmed from a highly subjective analysis of the situation
on Kutyepov's part, was bound to cause alarm in Soviet circles.

Actually, even in the Trust's days of glory (1923-1926), it had not
been possible to put a complete stop to White terror. For if Kutyepov's Combat Organization had been for a while successfully neutralized, there existed several other militant groups, which were for
years active inside Russia and which—due, perhaps, to better security
—were long immune to OGPU infiltration. And finally there were
those fanatical individuals who, governed by no laws or discipline
other than their consciences, were the most dangerous of all, since
they acted in most cases on the spur of the moment, without much
preparation and without consulting those groups which the OGPU
had already infiltrated. And their list of successes added up already
to a tidy balance sheet that was to culminate, on June 7, 1927, in
the assassination in broad daylight in Warsaw of Soviet Ambassador
Pavel I. Voykov—one of the murderers of Tsar Nicholas II and his
family—by the sixteen-year-old Boris Koverda. That same evening
Captain Larionov's bombs exploded in the Leningrad Central Party
Club and two days later, Iosif K. Opansky, an old-time Chekist and
Deputy Head of the Byelorussian OGPU, was shot down in the
neighborhood of Minsk.

As in August, 1918, following Uritzky's assassination and Fanya
Kaplan's attempt on Lenin's life, the Kremlin may well have believed again that open aggression on the part of the Western Powers
was being preceded by a softening-up period, designed to sow terror
in the ranks of the Soviet leadership. The OGPU (which, as usual,
needed little encouragement) was ordered to strike without pity.

Actually, taken in the light of contemporary Soviet accounts, the
outcome of the whole 1927 crisis seems nowadays so anticlimactic
that one cannot escape the feeling that the so-called "Right Opposition" within the Soviet Communist party was not exaggerating when
it charged that the Kremlin's reactions were based not so much on a
genuine fear of war—however ominous the symptoms—as on Stalin's
desire to find a convenient pretext for settling his long-standing accounts with his various foes within the party.

For these had seized upon the growing food crisis in the U.S.S.R. and the repeated failures of his foreign policy to step up their concerted onslaught against the ever growing concentration of power in his hands. On June 1, War Commissar Voroshilov had admitted, in a memorable speech before the Soviet Trade Unions, that the Red Army was not fit for war. Assuming that the worst happened and that the U.S.S.R. found itself involved in a conflict, Stalin had every reason to think that he would be confronted with a united front composed of all those he had so persistently sought to divide, from Zinovyev and Kamenev to Trotsky. Indeed Trotsky, in his famous "Clemenceau Statement" (about which more will be said later) had hinted as much.

In any event, this was clearly not the time to allow the continuing existence on Soviet soil of an organization which, capped and controlled though it might be by the OGPU, included nevertheless a fairly large number of genuine counter-revolutionaries and whose business consisted, among other things, in facilitating contacts between the latter and their White Russian sympathizers abroad. No police system is ever completely infallible and in a police state this is more true than elsewhere. Even the omniscient OGPU could, alongside many spectacular successes, boast a few major slips as well. Another such oversight, one well-placed bomb and the Soviet government might literally go up in flames. The Trust had simply no longer any *raison d'être*. Indeed, its liquidation imposed itself as an elementary prophylactic measure against a threat it was by definition unsuited to handle.

Besides, the OGPU had recently succeeded in placing in General Kutyepov's immediate entourage yet another agent, one who had never been directly connected with either the Trust or his Combat Organization and who was, thus, presumably, above suspicion. It is this man who, in the years to come, was destined to deal the decisive blows to the Russian anti-Communist movement, both within the U.S.S.R. and abroad.

Not much is known about the subsequent fate of the main actors in the Trust.

Artuzov and Kiakowski both attained high rank in the NKVD. At one point, in the mid-thirties, the former headed the famous INU, the NKVD's Foreign Department, and was in this capacity responsible for the appointment of many of those who will play a primary role in the later stages of this narrative. All of which did not save him from sharing, together wth Kiakowski and Styrne—the organizer of Sydney Reilly's capture—the fate of the many high secret police officials, who were to perish in Stalin's Great Purge.

General Zayonchkovsky, the alleged founder of the MUCR and the Trust's ranking "front" with the White para-military groups, died in 1934. His deputy, General Potapov, was reportedly still teaching military history at the Frunze Military Academy in Moscow in 1938. General Von Monkewitz's defection to the Reds has never been actually established, though the interest shown at the time by Soviet agents in its investigation would seem to imply that they had a personal stake in the affair.

As for the outstanding "hero" of them all—the "Gentleman from Revel," Aleksander Aleksandrovich Yakushev, alias "Mr. Feodorov," his ultimate fate is unknown.

General Baron P. N. Wrangel.   Captain Sydney Reilly.   Maria Schultz.

B. L. Savinkov before the Soviet Tribunal. (X) Savinkov, (XX) Judge Ulrich.

Keystone

The Headquarters of the OGPU in Moscow's Lubyanka (now Dzierzhinski) Square, as it was in Sydney Reilly's day.

General A. P. Kutyepov.

Facsimile of a letter bearing the signatures of "Klein" (Yakushev) and "Levine" (Opperput), in which the "Trust" urged Mrs. Reilly to come to Moscow, allegedly to participate in the search for Sydney Reilly.

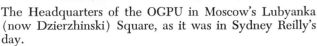

avec vous dans le même but final.
Que Dieu vous vienne en aide
dans votre douleur et vous donne
une consolation dans le travail,
que vous désirez partager avec
nous.

Vos amis lointains

Klein   Levine
           = Padunokun
              Ring

The scene of General Kutyepov's kidnaping today. Right: the entrance pavilion of the Clinique St. Jean-de-Dieu. Left: the Rue Rousselet. (X) Kutyepov's house. (XX) Window from which Steimetz observed the kidnaping.

L'Illustration

A contemporary artist's reconstruction of General Kutyepov's kidnaping in Paris.

The OGPU's top leaders at Dzierzhinski's tomb. (1) Trilisser, (2) Yagoda, (3) Artuzov, (4) Menzhinski.

S. M. Kirov.   K. Radek.

J. E. Rudzutak and F. E. Dzierzhinski.

The lull before the storm: J. Stalin, A. I. Rykov, L. B. Kamenev, and G. Y. Zinovyev in 1927.

N. I. Bukharin (center) with J. Stalin (left) and G. K. Ordzhonikidze on the eve of Stalin's rise to absolute power.

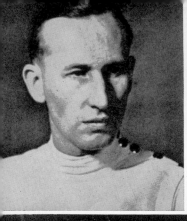

Left, Gestapo chief R Heydrich.

Right, Marshal M. N Tukhachevsky.

Chief Political Commissar J. B. Gamarnik wit Marshals A. I. Yegorov and V. K. Blücher.

Operation "Kama" in action: President von Hindenburg greets Marshal Tukhache sky (third from left), General Y. E. Yakir (with whom he is shaking hands) and oth Red Army observers at the 1932 summer maneuvers of the Reichswehr.

Oscar Tellgmar

Left, General I. P. Ubore-
ich.

Right, General R. P. Eidemann.

Left, General V. K. Putna.
Wide World

Right, General A. I. Kork.
International News

Left, G. G. Yagoda.

Right, N. I. Yezhov. *Wide
World*

General N. V. Skoblin.

N. V. Plevitzkaya.

General E. K. Miller.

Where General Miller met his doom: the corn
of the Rue Jasmin and Rue Raffet.

Wide World

INTERLUDE

5

THE KIDNAPING OF
GENERAL KUTYEPOV

"There are two or three people," Sydney Reilly had once remarked
prophetically, "during whose lifetime the Bolsheviki will never sleep
in peace. General Kutyepov is one of them. Then there is Boris
Savinkov. There are two or three others. The Bolsheviki will get
them back to Russia if they can. And then . . ."[1] And Reilly had
passed his hand significantly across his throat. Though he had not
mentioned his own name, it probably headed the list.

By 1926 both Savinkov and Reilly himself had been successfully
disposed of. There remained Kutyepov.

Lieutenant General Pavel Aleksandrovich Kutyepov represented,
in a way, the Tsarist combat officer at his best. Powerfully built, with
a head shaped like a cannon ball, slightly Oriental eyes, and a boom-
ing voice, he had emerged from World War I with the reputation of
a man of personal integrity and great physical courage and as a stern
disciplinarian to boot—all in all one of the most outstanding younger
regimental commanders (he was thirty-six years old at the time) in
the Imperial Guards. By the end of the Civil War he had risen to the
position of Wrangel's second-in-command. Thanks, largely, to his
selfless and sometimes ruthless energy and his vibrant personality,
the White troops retained their morale and soldierly appearance
throughout the harsh months of internment on Gallipoli and Lemnos,

and later, after they had been resettled in Bulgaria and Yugoslavia, it was again Kutyepov who presided over their fate. And as a result, the feeling of dread which his severity in battle had hitherto inspired among his men (and which had earned him the rather unflattering nickname of "Kutyep Pasha") gradually gave way to one of admiration and then of devotion, that has survived among them to this day.

His appointment, in March, 1924, to the Grand Duke Nicholas' staff in France, where he was put in charge of all White undercover activities inside Russia, had been viewed by at least one person, however—namely, General Wrangel himself—with considerable misgivings. For Kutyepov was above all a first-rate combat officer in the strictest meaning of the word, with little or no experience in staff or intelligence work and with a somewhat limited horizon. Moreover, his fiery temper and generally passionate disposition were apt to make him dangerously prone to following the dictates of his heart rather than those of reason. And future events were to prove Wrangel right.

Besides, there was also another major point of difference between the two men. For even if this does not appear in his official statements at the time and though his personal papers are still unavailable to the general public, there are indications that Wrangel differed with Kutyepov and the other White generals on the fundamental issue of the future of the Russian anti-Communist movement as such. The only real soldier-statesman among them, Wrangel had been an early critic of a strictly military approach to the struggle against Bolshevism. Partly because a different approach would have meant the condemnation of certain features of the old regime, a condemnation which few of them were willing to pass, this strictly military approach had prevailed, until it was too late, even for Wrangel, to reverse the tide of political fortunes in Russia. This lack of vision on the part of most of the White leaders, the neutrality or actual betrayal of all but a handful of ex-Tsarist officers and government officials (though these stood, seemingly, to lose all from the triumph of Communism in Russia)* and the ambiguous attitude, bordering on

* In 1919, for instance—the crucial year of the Civil War—four-fifths of the Red officers' corps and most of the senior Red commanders in the field were officers of the old regime.

bad faith, of the Allies, had all combined, in Wrangel's judgment, to deprive Russia of the one opportunity that had been given her of nipping Communism in the bud. Now that the Civil War had been lost, now that the disease had been allowed to gain a foothold in what was potentially one of the richest and most dynamic countries in the world, it would have to take its course until the Russian people, at doubtless immense cost, succeeded in building up the necessary antibodies. This would take, in all probability, one or two generations or more. And here Wrangel showed once again a breadth of vision and a sense of realities that contrasted sharply with the shortsighted, purely revanchist dreams of so many of his associates. *

Needless to say, this reasoning was bound to subject to considerable strain Wrangel's personal relations with Kutyepov and the Grand Duke—a strain which Yakushev, for one, had consistently exploited for his own ends.

But on April 26, 1928, General Wrangel had died in Brussels of a long illness,† and less than a year later, in January, 1929, the Grand Duke had passed away in his turn and Kutyepov found himself the undisputed leader of all the White para-military organizations.

If Wrangel had emerged from three years of Civil War profoundly skeptical about the future of the White movement, Kutyepov, for his part, seems to have regarded the latter's disastrous outcome as something in the nature of an ordeal by fire, the lessons of which, if properly analyzed and exploited, could point the way to salvation. And then Kutyepov was profoundly conscious of the danger for any *émigré* movement of losing touch with the homeland. To him any contact, even a flimsy underground one, was preferable to complete isolation. It is to his credit that his motives were not tinged with any revanchist spirit; he drew a clear distinction, for instance, between

---

* Curiously enough, Russia's top Marxist theoretician, Georghi Plekhanov, had already in the fall of 1917 come to very similar conclusions. "The strength of Bolshevism," he wrote, "lies in the weariness and ignorance of our people and also in our backward economic conditions. Bolshevism will last many years and our people will only attain consciousness after this hard lesson. Then there will be an end of Bolshevism. But that day is far off."[2]

† It was rumored at the time that he had been poisoned by means of a continuous administration of tuberculosis bacillae.

92 THE CONSPIRATORS

the Red Army as representative of the Russian people and the Communist leadership.*

Actually, the end of the Trust must have come as an embarrassing, but nonetheless welcome release, as far as Kutyepov was concerned. For although he had been among the first to succumb to Yakushev's talents of persuasion, his was far too dynamic and restless a nature not to chafe under the policy of enforced idleness which the Trust demanded of its friends abroad. Now, at least, he could go ahead with no holds barred.

We have seen that by the summer of 1927 Kutyepov had in the Baltic a force of close to a dozen volunteers who, far from being deterred or discouraged by their comrades' fate, seemed burning with eagerness to go back into Russia to avenge them.

Early in July, Georghi Radkovich, the late Maria Schultz's widower, whom Sydney Reilly had once described as "a very brave young nincompoop," arrived in Helsinki from Poland (where he had fled from Moscow at the time of Opperput's defection in April) to take charge of the next operation. This time the two teams consisted of two men each. The first—Aleksander B. Balmassov and Aleksander A. Sol'sky—was to head for Kiev, while the second— Aleksander A. Shorin and Serghei V. Solovyov (who had accompanied Captain Larionov on the Leningrad raid a month earlier)—was to operate in Leningrad or Moscow, depending on Soviet security arrangements in these two cities.

For several weeks the men assigned to the operation had been training in the use of small arms and dummy grenades in an abandoned gravel pit outside Helsinki. On August 14 they set out. They traveled first by rail as far as the station of Leppe-Suriya, near the

---

* His successor, General Miller, was later to disclose that at one point Kutyepov had been in contact also with the future Red Marshal Tukhachevsky.

Tukhachevsky was at the time, it appears, also in touch with the German generals Von Seeckt and Gröner, and this at Stalin's personal initiative. It is therefore not excluded that Tukhachevsky's contacts with Kutyepov (if they indeed existed) were established for the same purpose. And this is all the more likely if they dated back to the years 1927-1928, when, what with the Trust's liquidation and despite the fact that another *agent provocateur* was beginning to establish himself in White circles, the OGPU had, at least temporarily, less insight into Kutyepov's activities than in the past.

town of Suoyaervi, and then by car to a rendezvous close to Gheb-Ozero, where they had arranged to meet the Finnish "passers," who were to take them into Russia.

Despite the stepped-up precautions of the OGPU in all frontier zones since Larionov's successful escape eight weeks earlier, they crossed the border successfully and presently the Finns turned back, leaving them to proceed inland on their own.

Shorin and Solovyov started out first, on August 20. For a while all went well. The following morning, however, they chanced upon a game warden who asked to see their papers. Two shots cut him down. The whole episode had taken but a couple of minutes. Nevertheless, the firing had been heard by the inhabitants of a neighboring village who, following it up, came eventually upon the game warden's bullet-ridden body. The local OGPU was alerted and before long the whole area had been cordoned off and was being combed by patrols equipped with police dogs.

By now Balmassov and Sol'sky, unaware of the mishap that had befallen their comrades, were groping their way through the Karelian forest in their turn. It was they whom the OGPU picked up first. They seem to have been taken by surprise, for they made no use of their arsenal of weapons or of the poison capsules with which they had been equipped precisely in the event of such a contingency. Solovyov and Shorin were sighted again only four days later, on August 26. By then they were already deep in Soviet territory and approaching the regional capital of Petrozavodsk. They, however, opened fire, perishing in the ensuing skirmish.

Balmassov and Sol'sky were tried in Leningrad early in October, together with three other of Kutyepov's agents, Stroyevoi, Samoylov and Aderkass, who, entering the U.S.S.R. from Latvia shortly thereafter, had been captured near the town of Ostrov. With the exception of Aderkass, all four of them were condemned to death and shot. The OGPU had clearly shed its kid gloves.

On September 29, the Finnish authorities—acting, presumably, under strong Soviet diplomatic pressure—decided at last to put an end to Kutyepov's embarrassing activities. Radkovich, Larionov and Monomakhov were expelled from Finnish territory and Kutyepov himself was discreetly advised to transfer the scene of his anti-Soviet intrigues elsewhere.

And yet, even though the circumstances were growing increasingly unfavorable to the sort of action which, according to Kutyepov, could alone have any impact on Soviet policies; even though his agents—despite the end of his contacts with the Trust and his generally increased security precautions—were now being captured with a monotonous regularity that indicated only too clearly that there were still traitors in the ranks of his organization, and even though in one respect, i.e., the degree of co-operation to be expected from the Soviet population, Kutyepov had been clearly overoptimistic, the flow of volunteers for underground work in Russia did not cease, and attacks, by groups or individuals, upon Soviet institutions and officials continued.

On July 10, 1928, i.e., almost one year to a day after Maria Schultz's unsuccessful venture, the Moscow *Izvestya* came out with the sensational announcement that a bomb had exploded inside the Kommandantura of the OGPU in Lubyanka Square. One terrorist had perished on the spot; the two others had succeeded in escaping in a stolen car. Some eight hundred OGPU officials were immediately sent out on a man hunt that brought them eventually to a blood-spattered car, stalled in the forest of Lossino-Ostrovskaya, just outside of Moscow. While a Red Army battalion cordoned off the area, the Chekists went into the forest with police dogs. They presently came upon another of the terrorists, who thereupon opened fire and was immediately cut down. The two men were eventually identified: they were Georghi Radkovich, Maria Schultz's widower and Vladimir Monomakhov, one of Captain Larionov's accomplices in the Leningrad coup of the year before. The third man was never caught.

Radkovich's coup was, aside from Larionov's spectacular but useless venture, the only sortie by Kutyepov's Combat Organization that came anywhere close to achieving its purpose. For the offices of most of the top leaders of the OGPU were situated in the same wing as the Kommandantura, a couple of floors up.

Actually, if one matches the over-all results of Kutyepov's cam-

paign of White terror against the efforts invested in it, one cannot
fail to wonder at his agents' continuing dedication. In the first place,
as Savinkov had already noted, not many of them were really made
of the stuff that goes to produce a first-rate terrorist à la Savinkov
to whom killing was, in his own words, "something one gets accustomed to, as one does to any other business."[3] And then, compared
to the conspiratorial techniques and resources of those whose example he and his men sought to emulate, i.e., the Nihilists and
Socialist Revolutionaries of Tsarist days, Kutyepov's methods were
amateurish in the extreme and the material means at his disposal
ludicrously inadequate, so inadequate that some of his agents would
insist on performing odd menial jobs at their point of assembly—
Helsinki or Riga or Warsaw—merely in order to economize on their
subsistence allowances and thus save their organization unnecessary
expenses. Moreover, they suffered from another handicap. For years,
now, it had been drummed into them, and they had, naturally,
gladly believed, that the Russian people were literally groaning under the Communist yoke, that they dreamed of only one thing,
namely liberation, that returning White agents would therefore be
treated as heroes and allies and that just as the SR terrorists of yore
had gradually undermined the Tsarist administrative machine, so
they with their hand grenades and pistols would gradually sap the
Communist administrative apparatus until another major upheaval,
such as World War I had done in the case of Tsarism, sent it
tumbling altogether. But the few who went back into Russia and
came out again safely had soon to admit that, however unpopular
the regime might be with many sections of the population, especially
the peasants, this discontent did not as yet measure up to a state of
open revolt—this would come later, with Stalin's drive for collectivization—and that the most White agents could expect was indifferent
neutrality. And in many cases they could not even count on that!
Moreover, most White leaders chose to forget or to ignore the fact
that, besides giving the Russian people that which they desired
most at the time—namely, land and peace—the Bolsheviki, and not
the SR's and other Socialist groups, had triumphed in the long run
in Russia precisely because, instead of concentrating on hit-and-run

terror they had, for years, steadily and patiently built their following from the roots up. Thus, those who perished—the Balmassovs, the Sol'skys and others—were victims as much of Kutyepov's cloud castles and wishful thinking as of a Yakushev's duplicity or the watchfulness of the OGPU.

In any event, Radkovich's bomb, following as it did upon the Chekist Opansky's assassination and Maria Schultz's attempt on the Malaya Lubyanka, must have made it clear to the OGPU that it had also a personal stake in the matter when, some time in the fall of 1928, orders were given to wipe out "Kutyepov's wasp's nest" once and for all.

From the very first, intelligence and subversive work among the White Russian *émigrés* had been the responsibility of the OGPU's so-called "Foreign Administration" (*Inostrànnoye Upravlèniye*) or INU. Brought to a high peak of efficiency by its long-time head, a taciturn, harsh-voiced Chekist of outstanding intelligence and ability by the name of Mikhail A. Trilisser,* the INU had by now evolved into an intricate but at the same time smoothly running apparatus. It had secret branches headed by so-called "residents" in virtually every country, with a whole army of informers—more or less benevolent—that included prominent journalists and politicians, the Chief of the Rumanian *Siguranza* and princes—both royal and of the Church—and was geared to work autonomously, though in close cooperation with local Soviet diplomatic and trade missions, thus safeguarding the latter against unnecessary unpleasantness, were any of

---

* Trilisser had long been known as one of the more independent top Chekists. When Stalin ordered the OGPU to execute Count Mirbach's assassin, Blumkin, on the charge of contacting Trotsky abroad, Trilisser was reportedly the only member of the specially appointed secret tribunal to abstain from signing the verdict. Shortly before, he had joined with OGPU Boss Menzhinski and the latter's deputy, Yagoda, in warning Stalin that the OGPU could not guarantee internal security in the country unless the speed of collectivization was slowed down. Earlier still, he had on his own initiative inquired into the fairly questionable moral and political background of that same Yagoda and the findings had proven so interesting that he had seen fit to report them personally to Stalin. The latter feigned to take objection to such a procedure (though much of Trilisser's material was eventually used against Yagoda at his trial in 1938). In the fall of 1929 Trilisser was removed from the OGPU and appointed to the Comintern, where he remained until his arrest and death in the Great Purge.

its highly questionable operations ever to come to light.

These "residents" disposed of vast discretionary powers and considerable funds—the Berlin "residency," for instance, had in 1929 a monthly budget of 25,000 U.S. dollars!—and were in effect the "long arm" of the OGPU outside the Soviet Union. This at times led to embarrassing situations. Thus Victor Prassolov-Kepp, a former high official of the OGPU in China, who had been appointed to the Paris residency in 1927, took such a liking to some of the less reputable amenities of capitalist life that he promptly went and gambled away ten million francs in INU secret funds at Deauville and then added insult to injury by trying to blackmail Moscow into paying off his debt with the threat that he would otherwise make disclosures to the French police. Needless to say, he failed. Nevertheless, the INU had to go to the risk and trouble of luring him out of the Deauville Casino, kidnaping him and then driving him all the way to Antwerp and shipping him home from there aboard a Soviet steamer. Luckily for Kepp, his sister was married to a high Soviet official, and he therefore got off with ten years at hard labor in an Arctic concentration camp.

His successor at the Paris residency at the time of which we are speaking was a tall, personable and suave Chekist of good standing by the name of Lev B. Helfand, who officially held the title of second secretary at the Paris Embassy. Actually he was seen there but rarely, for within the Embassy itself there existed another, separate outpost of the OGPU headed by the Embassy archivist, Vladimir B. Volovich, alias "Yanovich." The latter, a thick-set, powerfully built, old-time Chekist with cruel little eyes, a snub, turned-up nose and a shock of unruly fair hair, besides keeping an eye on the personnel of the Embassy from Ambassador Dovgalevsky downward, acted as a sort of clearinghouse for the transmittal of funds, information and instructions (all of which traveled, of course, by Soviet diplomatic pouch) between Trilisser's office in Moscow's Lubyanka Square and "resident" Helfand.

Contact between Yanovich and Helfand was assured, characteristically, not at the Embassy itself (although they were both officially employed there) but by a third person, in this particular case Yanovich's wife Aleksandra, a good-looking and exceptionally intelligent young woman with a rare gift for languages, who seems to have been an even more important figure in the INU's Paris apparatus than her husband. The Yanovich couple rented a villa in Normandy, near the small seaside town of Villers-sur-Mer, which was often used by the Embassy personnel and which was to figure prominently in the Kutyepov drama.

For all their influence and power, the INU's foreign "residents" and "undercover groups" were rarely entrusted with the actual carrying out of such admittedly hazardous operations as, say, an assassination or a kidnaping. Though they might help to procure the information required to insure the latter's success, these, for reasons of greater security, were the responsibility of a special mobile "task force" of some fifteen hand-picked operatives recruited, as an additional precaution, more often as not from among non-Russian nationals (Latvians, Austrians, Hungarians, etc.), all of whom carried forged or otherwise doctored foreign passports. At the time of which we are speaking, this unit was headed by a former Latvian convict, a good-looking, ruthless and resourceful young daredevil by the name of Michel Avatin, alias "Kuzmich," and was stationed, much to Ambassador Krestinsky's displeasure, in Berlin, where it thus came under the authority of the INU's "resident" there.

Shortly after his arrival in Paris, Helfand had stepped up the infiltration of the White organizations and soon he and Mrs. Yanovich (who seems to have been in charge of this aspect of the INU's operations in France) could register substantial results.

A former White officer by the name of Petrov, who served for many years as an OGPU informer in *émigré* circles before defecting in 1928, has described some of his assignments, which were directed primarily against the entourage of the Grand Duke Nicholas and General Kutyepov.[4]

Thus, having contacted Z (an officer on the Grand Duke's staff) Petrov was to arrange for the photo reproduction of all documents coming to and going from Kutyepov. He was, furthermore, to procure a sample of the passes used by members of the Grand Duke's bodyguard, as well as the photographs and the personalia of its members. Then he was to organize the shadowing of two officers of Kutyepov's personal staff. He was also to note down the addresses of all those connected with the Grand Duke's headquarters, whatever their capacity, and to ascertain their material circumstances and their political convictions. Finally Petrov was to inquire into the results of the investigation of the circumstances of General Von Monkewitz's recent disappearance [sic!]. For this particular assignment (which was expected to last from one to three months) he was paid a bonus of twenty thousand francs, plus expenses.*

Shortly before Soviet Chargé d'Affaires Bessedovsky fled the Paris Embassy by jumping over the garden wall (October, 1929), Yanovich was able to boast to him that the OGPU had "a little fellow" (as he put it), a White general, married to a singer, in General Kutyepov's immediate entourage so that the latter's activities were "as clearly visible to us as if we were watching them under a glass bell."5

By the end of 1929, it had become apparent that the net around General Kutyepov himself was indeed closing in and that the manhunt was now on.

On October 29, a meeting of senior ROVS leaders was called at the organization's headquarters in the Rue des Carmes. A few minutes before it was scheduled to begin, a telephone message came through to Kutyepov's private secretary. The General had been unexpectedly detained, it said; the meeting was therefore canceled. Just then, Kutyepov himself walked into the room. Needless to say, he knew nothing of the message.

From the second to the sixth of January, 1930, Kutyepov was in Nice to unveil a memorial plaque to the late Grand Duke Nicholas. From there he returned to Paris, though not for long, for on January 17 he was off again, this time on a highly secret trip to Berlin, to meet with two emissaries of an anti-Communist underground organization who had just arrived there from Russia.

Another week went by.

---

* Kutyepov himself was living off a monthly salary of fifteen hundred francs at the time!

On Saturday, January 25, the Grenadiers' Regimental Association gathered for their annual celebration. As everybody was leaving, a taxicab driver was seen to approach the General, salute him, and offer his services. Kutyepov stared hard at the man and, failing to recognize him, turned away and climbed into the cab of a Lieutenant Fortunato (one of thirty hand-picked White officers—all of them Gallipoli veterans—who had organized a special "Taxicab Brigade" to provide their chief with safe round-the-clock transportation). As they parted outside his home, he informed Fortunato that he would not require the latter's services on the morrow, Sunday. Fortunato was never to see him again.

As a general rule, Kutyepov attended Sunday mass at the Church of the Association of Former Gallipoli Veterans, 81 Rue Mademoiselle, in the Fifteenth Arrondissement. Sometimes, he would drive there in a cab of his "Special Brigade," which in such cases, so as to attract less attention, awaited him at the corner of the Rue de Sèvres and the Boulevard des Invalides. Sometimes, in fine weather, he would proceed there on foot, the Rue Mademoiselle being only some fifteen to twenty minutes' distance from his home in the Rue Rousselet.

On Sunday, January 26, 1930, a requiem for a recently deceased comrade had been scheduled to be held immediately after the mass. General Repyev, the Association's President, who usually made a point of greeting his chief at the church entrance, arrived this time, for once, late. The latter, however, was not yet there. A quarter of an hour went by . . . half an hour . . . three-quarters. . . . Assuming that Kutyepov had been unexpectedly detained, Repyev ordered the chaplain to proceed with the service without him.

Meanwhile, Mrs. Lydia Kutyepova too was becoming increasingly impatient. On leaving the house that morning at ten-thirty "to go to church," her husband had promised to be back for lunch around 1 P.M. and he was a very punctual man. It was now 2 P.M. and there still was no sign of him. As three o'clock struck, she decided to send Fedot, the General's batman, to the Gallipoli Association to hurry him. Fedot returned at about 4 P.M. with the news that the General had been neither seen nor heard of there. Now seriously alarmed, Mrs. Kutyepova summoned the head of her husband's Military Secretariat, who suggested that they alert the French police. That night, at 10 P.M., General Miller, Kutyepov's first deputy, was notified of the latter's disappearance.

The police's initial reaction had been that the General had had an accident or that he had been taken suddenly ill or that he had gone away on a sudden trip—something he had occasionally done in the past—or even that he had departed on a secret mission to the U.S.S.R. By 8 A.M., Monday, the hypothesis of an accident had been definitively discarded. So had that of a secret trip to the U.S.S.R. or elsewhere. A last hypothesis, that of suicide, was not even seriously considered. The General had never been in better spirits; indeed, he was not the despondent type; his family life could hardly have been happier; besides, he was deeply religious. There remained but one last possibility, one which as yet only his family and friends had dared evoke, that of a kidnaping. As a first step, Kutyepov's photograph, together with his detailed personalia, were now circulated to all frontier, harbor and airport authorities, to the provincial police and to French military attachés abroad. Shortly thereafter, Mrs. Kutyepova filed through her attorneys an information "against person or persons unknown" (as French legal terminology requires in such cases) for the "involuntary abduction and sequestration" of her husband, and from London (where he was attending a Naval Disarmament Conference) French Premier André Tardieu ordered that a full inquiry be initiated with all possible speed. A force of some four hundred agents of the Paris Préfecture and of the Sureté Nationale was put to work under the orders of Commissioner Fauxpas-Bidet, the Sureté's acknowledged top expert in Russian affairs.

It was obvious immediately that General Kutyepov's mysterious disappearance in broad daylight in the middle of Paris contained all the ingredients of a *cause célèbre* and that, irrespective of the moral and ethical issues involved, the episode could and indeed would be exploited to the hilt by the various political factions then, as now, grappling for power in France.

Premier André Tardieu had been elected to office on a strongly anti-Communist and generally conservative platform. Moreover, although the so-called "forces of the Left," i.e., the Socialists and Communists (who were in those days loosely allied against the bourgeoisie), were making strong inroads among the industrial workers, they did not as yet have in the trade unions the predominant position they were to achieve a few years later and still hold today. For their part, those middle-of-the-road and rightist circles which, only three years earlier, had, both out of financial and ideological considerations, insisted that France follow Great Britain's example and break off diplomatic relations with the Soviet Union, now saw in this dramatic episode a heaven-sent opportunity to revive their campaign. Before long the growing world economic crisis and the events in Central Europe and the Far East would compel even them to swallow their grievances against the Moscow government and focus their attention on other, more immediate problems, but for the time being the issue was simple. As the well-known journalist Gustave Hervé put it succinctly in the weekly *Victoire:*

> If it were ever to be proven that the Red rulers or the OGPU were so bold as to do such a thing, no French government, however craven, could tolerate more than 24 hours the presence of the ambassador of these barbarians and bandits in French territory!

The Moscow government could hardly have been unaware of the explosive potentialities of such a situation. In fact, it seems to have been so well aware of them that it did not hesitate to expose itself to complete ridicule by virtually jumping the gun in its eagerness to disclaim all responsibility in the affair.

For five days the Soviet press remained silent. For all the Russian readers were given to know, General Kutyepov could just as well have never existed. Then on Friday, January 31, the Moscow papers came out with a communiqué which, they claimed, had been circulated by the French Agence Havas on behalf of the French police and according to which "the White General Kutyepov had left Paris for an unknown destination," which was as good a manner of putting things as any, were it not for the fact that the Agence Havas had never circulated such a communiqué and the French police had

never issued it! And First Secretary Ahrens, acting as spokesman for
the Soviet Embassy in Paris, made matters no better when he presently suggested in an interview with the press that Kutyepov had
been kidnaped by . . . the French police! Finally, on February 3,
i.e., a full week after the event, the Moscow *Izvestya* came out with
the official Soviet version of the mystery, which was of course immediately echoed by the Communist and fellow-traveling press
everywhere: General Kutyepov had decamped to South America
with all the funds of his organization!

And yet, irrespective of the visible confusion in the Soviet camp,
the very fact that the Kutyepov Affair had such obvious and far-
reaching political implications made the task of the investigators if
anything still more difficult. M. Jean Chiappe, the able Paris Préfet
de Police, who was in over-all charge of the case, was known as an
ardent anti-Communist, who had made life virtually as hard for the
agents of the Comintern as he had for the procurers and prostitutes
of the city's red-light districts. And most of his subordinates at the
Préfecture were known to share this attitude. The Sureté Nationale,
however, was subordinated to the Minister of the Interior and was
not averse, on occasion, to dabble in politics, and at this point it had
the reputation of being under strong leftist influence. Then, quite
aside from these political considerations, there was also between the
two institutions a lot of that interservice rivalry that is found in all
administrations everywhere, but which in this particular case served
often merely to slow down or neutralize their respective efforts.

Since his arrival in France from Yugoslavia, early in 1924, General Kutyepov had been living in a modest four-room apartment on
the second floor of a rather run-down building at No. 26 Rue Rousselet, in the Seventh Arrondissement.

Though nowadays the sidewalks are apt to be cluttered up with
parked cars and some of the houses seem to have recently received
a fresh coat or two of paint, the street—short, narrow and rather
dark—has survived to this day much as it was at the time of Kutyepov's disappearance: a double row of fairly decrepit houses, with
dank back yards; dark, steep and creaky stairways; the traditional

dusty geraniums in the lodge windows of the concierges; an inexpensive grocery store or two, a coal-and-firewood merchant who doubles as an *estaminet* and the equally traditional *marchand de couleurs*—all in all, a typical vestige of late eighteenth-century Paris, with an air of quiet, remoteness, even boredom about it which somehow precludes the very idea of crime. On the right-hand corner, looking down the Rue Rousselet from the sleepy, distinguished Rue Oudinot toward the populous, bustling Rue de Sèvres there stands a low, sprawling Louis XVI pavilion. This is the entrance to the Clinique St. Jean-de-Dieu, a tall, three-storied, unprepossessing building that towers above the street and was destined to play a decisive role at a later stage of the affair. Facing the clinic are the only modern houses in the street, a couple of elaborately façaded apartment buildings in the typical *art nouveau* style of the early part of the century, that look slightly incongruous in this particular environment. Further on to the right, beyond the pavilion, stretches a span of high, blank wall, inscribed with the traditional "Défense d'Afficher, loi du 10 Avril 1929" in fading, weather-beaten letters, which forms the eastern boundary of the clinic's fine garden. No. 26 is situated on the right-hand side of the street, beyond this wall.

As the police proceeded with their inquiry, it became clear that Kutyepov could hardly have found a worse location for his residence. For he had been from the first under virtually constant observation by suspicious-looking individuals, whose business could only too well be guessed.

The windows of his apartment, for instance, looked out onto a small garden—an unexpectedly pleasant, restful sight for this otherwise fairly dismal neighborhood. The building opposite his, however, on the other side of this garden, served as a boardinghouse for Soviet students in Paris! In addition, habitués of the two cafés at the end of the street, "Le Rousselet" at the corner of the Rue Rousselet and the Rue de Sèvres and "Le Petit Beaumarchais" in the Rue de Sèvres itself just opposite the Rue Rousselet, reported that for some time strangers had been spending hours there over their *jus*. Relayed at regular intervals, they would sit in pairs at the window, watching the street and scribbling notes. They seemed to take their orders from a small man in a black beret, who walked with a limp. Occasionally the latter would join them in their vigil, but as a rule he merely showed up two or three times a day for a few minutes, to check up on them. Presently it was discovered that another observation post had operated in a small laundry establishment, two houses away from the General's home, while a third, which served apparently as the co-ordinating center of the whole system, had been set up in the *estaminet* of the coal-and-firewood merchant, almost directly opposite the entrance of No. 26. The *estaminet* had remained mysteriously shuttered up since the morning of the General's disappearance. Moreover, Kutyepov was followed wherever he went and as he was a great walker and insisted in doing his own marketing, he must have led his watchers quite a dance. More often as not, this was the privilege of a privately owned yellow Citroën taxicab, driven by a young man, pink-cheeked and sturdy-looking, who seemed never to bother to pick up a fare and who was a frequent visitor to the above-mentioned laundry establishment.

Yet despite these ominous signs, of which he himself was only too well aware ("They are protecting me!" he would joke), the General had refused to accept the services of a personal bodyguard. He himself could not afford it, he said; as for the funds of his Combat Organization, they were for combat purposes and not to pay for his personal safety. It had not even been easy to prevail upon him to make use of his special "Taxicab Brigade." In fact, the only precaution he took was that of never accepting a lift from an unknown person and of never entering an unfamiliar building unaccompanied.

A first routine questioning of sundry concierges and lodgers of the neighborhood and of the many cab and other drivers who had passed there during the day yielded nothing. On Monday evening, the news blackout, upon which the police had insisted during the first twenty-four hours that followed Kutyepov's disappearance, was at last lifted and soon the press was appealing for voluntary information and the first reports were beginning to come in.

Thus a Mr. P. told the following story: On January 18, toward 2 P.M., he had boarded in Cannes the Paris Express No. 24. In Marseille three men had entered his compartment and had stayed up,

talking, all night until they reached Paris, at 9:30 A.M. the following
morning. At first they had chatted casually on a variety of subjects;
then they had turned to him with a couple of questions in French.
He had answered in English and shortly thereafter had feigned to
fall asleep. In due course, they had switched to another language,
one which he happened to know well, namely Latvian, and from
their conversation he had gathered that they had recently been involved in Nice in an attempt against a "top-ranking White," which,
however, had been called off at the last minute. They were now on
their way to Paris, to repeat the operation. They would apparently
be staying in the suburbs, at Fontenay-aux-Roses.

The Sureté searched Fontenay-aux-Roses. The search yielded
nothing.

The police thereupon concentrated their attention on the question
of the itinerary which Kutyepov could be presumed to have followed upon leaving home at ten-thirty that Sunday morning. By
Wednesday, January 29, this itinerary—at least in its first stages—had
been fairly well established, thanks to the testimony of three witnesses who knew the General well by sight. Thus the owner of the
hardware store in the Rue Rousselet had noticed him as he went by
that Sunday morning, between ten-thirty and eleven; then the White
Russian owner of the "Sèvres-Pathé" movie theater in the Rue de
Sèvres remembered greeting him as he passed, going in the direction
of the Boulevard des Invalides, at about 10:45 A.M. Shortly before
11:00 A.M., he was sighted by an officer of his acquaintance at the
corner of the Rue de Sèvres and the Boulevard des Invalides. He was
standing close to the stop of tram No. 89 at the time and seemed to
be waiting for someone, for several trams went by without his paying
any attention. He looked preoccupied, for the officer had greeted
him and was a little surprised when Kutyepov, usually so courteous,
failed to return his salute. A little later, a White Russian taxicab
driver saw him walking away; he was going, strangely enough, not
in the direction of the Rue Mademoiselle, but along the Boulevard
des Invalides toward the Rue Oudinot. From that point on, his
movements remained a complete mystery.

Several questions now arose: In the first place, *had* he been waiting for someone at the stop of tram No. 89 and if so, for whom? And why hadn't he mentioned the appointment to his closest assistants? Or was he merely hesitating whether to continue on to church (as he had originally intended) or to go elsewhere? And if this was the case, where was this "elsewhere"? Was it somewhere in the neighborhood of the Rue Oudinot? And did the mysterious appointment, if any, have anything to do with his sudden change of plans? Or was he simply going home? And if so, why? And why hadn't he ever reached home? And why had he taken the longer route, by way of the Rue Oudinot, instead of retracing his steps via the Rue de Sèvres? Was it in order to elude the watchers in the two corner cafés? And if so, why this sudden shyness? Was that too in connection with his mysterious appointment?

The police leafed through his appointment book. He rarely went out without it. On that fateful Sunday, however, he had forgotten it on his writing table and for a while it was even thought that he might have been on his way home to pick it up when he vanished. But it mentioned nothing of an appointment around 11 A.M.

And then, suddenly, the mystery began to clear, for several witnesses spoke up, who had seen all.

The Paris daily L'Echo de Paris had from the very first taken a keen interest in what had now become known as "L'Affaire Koutiepoff," and its correspondent Jean Delage had even done some private sleuthing on his own. On Thursday, January 30, a Brother Denis, of the Asile des Jeunes Garçons Infirmes et Pauvres (a charitable institution to which Delage had had the occasion of rendering some service), called to see him. He had a strange tale to tell. For he had just talked with Father Robert, the Superior of the Clinique St. Jean-de-Dieu, at the corner of the Rue Rousselet and the Rue Oudinot, and the latter had confided to him that he suspected that General Kutyepov had been kidnaped just outside the clinic.

At about 11 A.M. on that fateful Sunday, he related, a ward attendant by the name of Auguste Steimetz was shaking out a carpet from a third-floor window, when he chanced to glance down at the street below. At that hour, Steimetz told him, the street was deserted but for two cars and a solitary policeman. One of the cars, a

large, powerful-looking, grayish-green Alfa-Romeo sedan, was parked
in the Rue Rousselet alongside the entrance pavilion of the clinic.
Its nose pointed, oddly enough, toward the Rue Oudinot, and Steimetz remembered wondering why it had parked on the wrong side
of the street and why the policeman was not doing anything about
it. But then he decided that it had come to pick up a patient, for
one of its doors was wide-open and two men stood nearby, waiting.
One of them, a tall, slim but powerfully built young man, wearing
dark clothes and a soft fedora hat, stood calm, nonchalant even. His
companion, hatless, in a light-colored coat, was on the contrary visibly impatient. He kept hurrying over to the corner of the Rue
Oudinot and glancing down that street in the direction of the Boulevard des Invalides, as if he were expecting someone. The policeman,
a young fellow, tall, clean-shaven and pink-cheeked, lounged close to
that same corner and seemed, again to Steimetz's surprise, equally
unconcerned over the fact that the second car, a conventional red
Renault taxicab, had stopped plumb in the middle of the Rue
Oudinot at the foot of the Rue Rousselet, so effectively blocking the
entrance into that street that another passing taxicab had to slow
down and weave around it to get by. The red Renault's nose also
pointed toward the Boulevard des Invalides.

Leaning over the window sill, Steimetz had been taking in this
peaceful scene when all of a sudden the two cars started up their
engines. Just then an elderly gentleman in a dark coat and a soft
black hat—whom Steimetz later easily recognized by the photographs in the papers, because of his striking-looking black spade-
shaped beard, as being General Kutyepov—rounded the corner of
the Rue Oudinot and turned into the Rue Rousselet. As he came
level with the gray-green sedan, the two waiting men quickly
walked up to him, said something and then, seizing him, one by the
left arm and the other by the right, pushed him, struggling fran-
tically, into the back of the car, climbed in beside him and slammed
the door shut. The young policeman, who had sauntered up casually,
now jumped into the front seat beside the driver. The car sprang
forward and, rounding the corner with screeching tires, vanished
down the Rue Oudinot in the direction of the Boulevard des In-

valides, followed closely by the red Renault. Steimetz recalled motioning to a colleague "to come and see the police make an arrest," but when the latter rushed up, it was all over: the two cars had disappeared from sight.

Shortly after 11:05 A.M., Police Officer Chauveau, on duty outside the Italian Consulate in the Avenue de Villars, noticed a grayish-green sedan approaching at great speed from the direction of the Rue Oudinot. It was followed by a red Renault taxicab and as it passed him, he could see people struggling inside. But a policeman was seated next to the driver and so he thought no more about it until he read about Steimetz's testimony in the newspapers.

Then the kidnapers' luck nearly changed. For a little later, a Madame Flottes was picking her way through a traffic jam at the Left Bank end of the Pont de l'Alma when, edging past a grayish-green sedan, she observed in the back seat a man holding a handkerchief to the face of his neighbor. A young policeman sat next to the driver. In answer to her question, the latter explained that "le malheureux" had had his legs crushed in an accident and that they were administering ether to him to relieve the pain. Later she recalled noting that the young man did not have the usual numbers on his cap and collar tabs and that his French was surprisingly pure for a simple policeman. Presently he got out of the car and sauntered over to have a couple of words with the driver of a red Renault taxicab that had come to a halt close behind them. Then he went on to organize the traffic in a most professional manner until the way was clear. After which, climbing back into his seat, he directed the driver to turn left, down the Quai Branly. Soon both cars had vanished in the direction of the Pont d'Iéna.

Around 11:20 A.M. they were again sighted, this time at the Porte de St. Cloud. They were proceeding at such speed that, so as to avoid a traffic island, they had at one point to swerve sharply and thereby come close to crashing into the cab of one of Kutyepov's subordinates, of all people, who happened to be coasting along leisurely in the opposite direction. From then on, the coast was clear.

Around noon both cars were seen speeding through the town of Evreux. At 12:30 P.M. they were sighted passing through La Rivière-

Thiberville. At 1:30 P.M. they were seen as they slowed down at a
railway crossing between Pont-Levèque and Trouville and shortly
thereafter they were observed by Maître Grandcollot, the mayor of
the village of Bonneville-sur-Touques, and by his brother as they
turned off road No. 27 toward Cabourg.

The seashore between Trouville and Cabourg is fairly straight and
consists of steep chalk cliffs, somewhat like the famous Cliffs of
Dover, which drop suddenly, cut like a knife, some two hundred
feet to a broad expanse of fine sand beach below. About halfway
between the small towns of Villers-sur-Mer (where the Yanovichs
had their villa) and Houlgate, however, there is a curious rock con-
figuration where the cliff, under the impact of erosion, has crumbled
in a huge, disorderly mass onto the beach. This is known as the
Falaises des Vaches Noires. The countryside here is barren, but for a
few hedgerows, and rarely frequented. It bears the significant name
of *Le Désert.* A dirt road, rutted and impassable in bad weather,
branches off from the neighboring hamlet of Auberville and ventures tentatively into this wasteland, only to lose itself, presently,
in the moor. This forlorn spot had been chosen by General Kutyepov's kidnapers for his transfer aboard the vessel that was to take
him to his ultimate destination.

Shortly after being seen by the Grandcollot brothers in Bonneville-
sur-Touques, the two cars vanished from sight. At first it was suspected that they might have stopped off at the Yanovich villa at
Villers-sur-Mer. But presently witnesses came forward who had
seen them parked in an orchard at the crossroads of routes Nos. 27
and 163, at a spot known as *La Croix d'Heuland.* The passengers—
among them a young policeman and a blond woman in a beige
coat—were peacefully picnicking on the grass. An idyllic scene.

Sometime around 4 P.M., a couple of young lovers were strolling
across *Le Désert,* when they were startled to hear the muffled purr
of automobile engines. Presently two cars hove into sight and came
to a stop at the end of the dirt road. Peering through a hedgerow,
they saw a policeman descend from the first car and pull out a
longish package rolled up in sacking, which he and several of his
companions then hoisted onto their shoulders and proceeded to carry

down a tiny path, which at this point winds its way down the cliff face to the beach. Intrigued, the two watchers waited until they had vanished from sight and then crept up to the edge of the cliff and looked down. A motor launch was riding the waves close to shore, while a cargo vessel lay at anchor further out to sea. As the group waded their way toward the launch, one of them—a blonde young woman in a beige coat—uttered a little scream as she was splashed by a wave. The package was hoisted over the gunwale and dumped into the bottom of the launch. Two of the men climbed in after it, the engine sputtered into a roar and presently they were off in the direction of the waiting ship, while the others turned back up the path to the parked cars. By now the two watchers had regained their hiding place behind the hedgerow, from where they could see and hear all without themselves being seen. "Mind you clean up everything," one of the men remarked to his companions as they went by. "The car must be spick-and-span!" Then the engines started up and they were off.

A litle later, around 4:30 P.M., Maître Grandcollot sighted them for the second time as they passed through his village. They had to slow down in turning the corner near which he was standing and he was now able to take a good look at one of the passengers: a hefty-looking fellow, with a shock of fair hair and a snub, turned-up nose. Afterward, from the photographs in the press, Grandcollot had no difficulty recognizing him: it was the Chekist Yanovich.*

Half an hour later, the two cars were again observed speeding through Pont-l'Evêque toward Paris. They were never to be seen again.

The fact of General Kutyepov's kidnaping and the exact circumstances thereof had now been definitely established. What remained to be determined was the identity of his kidnapers and, even

---

* Yanovich was generously rewarded for his role in the Kutyepov affair. First he was for years Stalin's favorite chauffeur. Then he was elevated to the coveted position of deputy commander (under the notorious K. V. Pauker) and later commander of Stalin's personal bodyguard. As deputy head (under the same Pauker) of the NKVD's Operations Department, he was to play an important part in the investigation of the Kirov affair, which was probably the reason why he too was eventually purged.

more important, the identity of the person or persons who had lured
him back to the corner of the Rue Rousselet and the Rue Oudinot on
that particular day and at that particular hour, to his doom. For it
was obvious that the organizers, whoever they were, had known or
seen to it beforehand: (a) that the General would *not* go straight to
church, as he had originally planned, but would return home instead; and (b) that in so doing, he would take not the usual route,
via the Rue de Sèvres and the Rue Rousselet, but the longer one,
via the Boulevard des Invalides and the Rue Oudinot.

That the authors of the outrage were agents of the OGPU was, of
course, at present denied only by the Soviets themselves and their
friends. Again and again demands were voiced that the Soviet Embassy in the Rue de Grenelle be searched. But apart from the fact
that the evidence connecting the Soviet government with Kutyepov's
disappearance was, however convincing, largely circumstantial and
thus insufficient to allow for a formal violation of the extraterritorial-
ity of the Embassy, it seemed most unlikely that the authors would
be so naïve as to leave any loose clues lying around there. For
several days following the General's disappearance, dense clouds of
smoke could be seen billowing forth from the Embassy chimneys
and the lawns of the neighboring *hôtels particuliers* were speckled
with paper ash. And what could not or dared not be burned was
packed up in a large trunk and taken on Saturday, February 1, by
First Secretary Ahrens to Brussels. Neither would the police have
been able to lay hands on Yanovich even if they had wanted to, for
both he and the INU's "resident" Helfand had left Paris shortly after
the fateful event, while Mrs. Yanovich was whisked away in Ambassador Dovgalevsky's personal car to Belgium a few days later.
The Kremlin was clearly taking no chances.

Besides, the Soviets' responsibility was in a way merely incidental. What it was important to know was what, or rather who,
had lured the General into the trap. Was it the person he had allegedly been waiting for near the stop of tram No. 89, at the corner
of the Rue de Sèvres and the Boulevard des Invalides? And if so,
who was it? Was he—or she—still around? Was it a friend? An as-
sociate? A confidant?

The police's task was not made any easier by the fact that some-one was very obviously doing his best to cover up the tracks. Within ten days of the event eighty clues had been reported and followed up. Some of them proved valid and helped establish the General's itinerary. Many others, however, stemmed either from eager but ir-responsible well-wishers or else from more sinister sources.

Thus a mysterious plane was mentioned that had, allegedly, taken off from Le Bourget on the evening of Kutyepov's disappearance, the crew's behavior arousing the suspicions of the customs authori-ties. But a quick check showed that only three planes had left the airport that day: two regular line planes for London and one for Moscow. All their papers were in order, no mysterious package had been taken aboard and nothing suspicious had been observed.

Then it was reported that a Russian anarchist worker employed near the Bastille had boasted drunkenly that: "In a few days we will do away with Kutyepov!" On the day after the General's disappear-ance, he had repeated this boast, adding that for a consideration he would be willing to talk. The police located him and questioned him. He had nothing to tell. He was booked anyway, having entered France without a permit.

Kutyepov himself was reported to have been seen on that fateful Sunday in various parts of Paris, but the description made of him never accorded with his appearance that day. Sometimes he wore a Homburg hat, sometimes a derby; sometimes he carried a stick, sometimes he didn't.

The two cars—the grayish-green sedan and the red Renault taxi-cab—turned out to be even more ubiquitous. Their presence was re-ported variously at virtually every point of the compass within a radius of some two hundred miles from Paris, long after the Nor-mandy trail had been definitely established.

Several days were spent by the police digging in the woods of Meudon following reports that a mysterious-looking, oblong package had been buried there.

Neither did the inquiry into the young policeman's identity yield any results. The Préfecture had soon ascertained that none of its own men had been on duty at the corner of the Rues Rousselet and

Oudinot that day. The man's role was obvious: he had been posted there in order to allay to the very last any suspicion Kutyepov himself or a chance witness might have had at the sight of the two parked cars and to give the operation the appearance of a routine arrest. He had first been seen at that particular spot three or four weeks earlier. He would appear there only on Sundays, remaining at his post the greater part of the day and chain-smoking—which for a policeman on duty was in itself rather unusual. Every now and then a blonde woman in a beige coat would walk up, exchange a few words with him and then depart, only to reappear a little later. The last time she had been seen was on that fateful Sunday, just a few minutes before the General rounded the corner of the Rue Rousselet to his doom. By her description, she was probably the same woman who was seen later that day on the roads of Normandy and on the beach. All costume-rental outfitters in Paris were questioned. It appeared that quite a few policeman's uniforms had been rented out, this being the season for masquerade parties. Only one had not been returned. The name and address of the client, however, could not be traced.

Lieutenant Fortunato, the White Russian taxicab driver who had taken Kutyepov home on the eve of his disappearance, had also a strange story to tell: He had awakened that Sunday at around 10 A.M. and he remembered breathing a sigh of relief upon recalling that the General did not require his services that day. For had he needed to report for duty, he would have been late. Shortly thereafter he went out. As he chanced to glance at the clock on a neighboring church steeple, he started back in surprise, for his watch was a whole hour late. Someone, during the night, had obviously crept into his hotel room and set the hands back; someone who did not know that Kutyepov had dismissed him for the day and who wished the General's trusted driver out of the way!

Equally mysterious was the case of the letter which a friend of the General's received from him in Prague, after his disappearance had already made the headlines of the European press. For though it was dated January 24, i.e., forty-eight hours *before* the kidnaping, it was postmarked January 27, i.e., twenty-four hours *after* the kidnaping, having been mailed from the post office situated Place Chopin in the Sixteenth Arrondissement.

For a while it was hoped that Kutyepov's mysterious trip to Berlin, one week before his disappearance, might yield a clue. An inspector of the Sureté was sent there to interview the two secret emissaries, only to learn that they had left for the U.S.S.R. on February 8, i.e., nearly two weeks after the outrage. He learned, however, that their presence in Berlin could be accounted for throughout the critical weeks and that they had seemed deeply shocked at the news of the General's disappearance.

As the days and then the weeks went by without any further progress being registered in the investigation of Kutyepov's fate, the mood of a section of the Paris populace became ugly. One protest meeting followed another and these were succeeded by street demonstrations. By now the voluntary contributions to the fund that had been established to assist in the investigation had reached the hitherto unheard of figure of 450,000 francs. On February 4 Soviet Ambassador Dovgalevsky lodged an official protest with the Quai d'Orsay over the ever increasing hostility of the press. On February 11 the rightist deputy Ybarnegaray moved formally in Parliament that France break off diplomatic relations with the U.S.S.R. That same evening some three thousand angry demonstrators marched on the Soviet Embassy. According to Alexander G. Graff, alias "Barmine" (in those days an official of the Soviet Trade Mission in Paris), Ambassador Dovgalevsky was so fearful that the Embassy building might be taken by storm and sacked that he ordered weapons to be distributed to all members of his staff.*

And then as suddenly as it had arisen, the storm subsided. On February 17 the French cabinet fell over a minor budgetary issue

---

* Barmine, who now heads the Voice of America's Russian Section, defected in 1937 at the height of Stalin's Great Purge. In his reminiscences, published in 1945, he shows himself curiously reticent about the Kutyepov affair (of which he was, after all, a ringside witness), dismissing it with the remark that "if Kutyepov was spirited away by the GPU, as the evidence seemed to show, the thing was carried out in total independance of official Soviet representatives in Paris."[6]

It is worth noting that on another very similar occasion—the kidnaping of General Miller—the Paris Trade Mission would be directly implicated.

and France was, once again, for a few weeks without a government. And by the time Premier Tardieu returned to power, the international situation—what with the German-Austrian Zollverein, the growing world economic crisis, Great Britain's repeal of the gold standard, and Japan's stepped-up inroads in Manchuria—had deteriorated to the point where France could no longer find any time for what was, after all, for most of her citizens, just another fascinating episode in the never-ending game of international undercover intrigue. Besides they had other fish to fry; the famous Corsican bandits were now the fashionable thing to talk about.

The exact circumstances of Kutyepov's last hours have never been fully elucidated. But more important still, it has never been possible to discover who or what lured him back to the corner of the Rue Rousselet and the Rue Oudinot at about 11 A.M. on that fateful Sunday morning.

According to one version, the operation was planned in Berlin and was then carried out by some of Michel Avatin's men, under the immediate supervision of the INU's Paris "resident" Helfand and one Ellert, an old-time agent of the OGPU, who officially held a position with the Soviet Naphtha Syndicate. Ellert left Paris together with Helfand and Yanovich immediately after the coup, only to reappear with Helfand in Berlin on February 22 as, respectively, "Hoffmann" and "Schober."

On January 19, i.e., exactly one week before Kutyepov's disappearance, a Soviet vessel, the *Spartak*, arrived at Le Havre from Ghent. It stayed there until the twenty-fifth, when it weighed anchor suddenly and put out to sea in a westerly direction. Two days later, it turned up in Antwerp (in those days the headquarters of the Comintern's maritime organization in Western Europe), only to continue that same evening on to Leningrad. It never disclosed where it had spent the intervening forty-eight hours. True, early in the morning of January 26 (the day of Kutyepov's kidnaping) a vessel answering its description had been observed cruising leisurely off the coast of Normandy near Courcevilles; the Ouistreham lighthouse-keeper reported hearing its foghorn throughout the night. The two localities lie less than thirty and twenty kilometers, respectively, west of the *Falaises des Vaches Noires,* where later that day the "policeman," the woman in beige and their companions were sighted loading their mysterious package into a waiting launch, while a ship idled out at sea.

It is not improbable that, apart from wanting to decapitate the ROVS and Kutyepov's own Combat Organization, the Kremlin also hoped that it might be able to brain-wash the General to a point where, like Savinkov before him, he would recant his past, forswear his beliefs and pledge recognition to the Soviet regime. And there is no doubt that had this plan succeeded, the moral blow dealt to the White cause would have been even greater than that caused by his physical elimination. But there is reason to think that Kutyepov never did reach the Soviet Union alive. Though a man of powerful physique, he had long suffered from a heart condition which the use of ether—and the young "policeman" had admitted to Madame Flottes on the Pont de l'Alma that it *was* being used—could well have rendered critical.[7]

6

THE MAKING OF A TRAITOR

The kidnaping of General Kutyepov was a blow from which the ROVS was never to recover.

For Lieutenant General Evgheni Karlovich Miller, his mild and kindly successor at the head of the organization, was a different person altogether. A former Tsarist military attaché abroad, he had served in World War I as chief-of-staff of an army, after which he had headed the Russian military mission to Italy. Late in 1918 he had been recalled to Arkhangelsk and put in command of the so-called "Northern White Army"—a 25,000-man-strong, poorly disciplined and relatively ineffectual Russian anti-Communist formation, which had been built up there at great pains under the aegis of the Allied Expeditionary Force. And after the debacle of that venture, he had been appointed Baron Wrangel's military representative in Paris. Eventually he had joined General Kutyepov's staff, where at the time of the latter's disappearance he was in charge of administration and finance.

Though his seniority and past experience thus made him a fairly natural first choice as Kutyepov's successor, he himself had serious misgivings about his qualifications for the post. Indeed, he seems to have accepted it only because a refusal—now that both his predecessors had perished, as it were, in action—would have been tantamount to deserting under enemy fire.

He inherited a heavy burden.

118

For if Kutyepov had looked upon the ROVS as a sort of army-in-being, which sooner or later would be thrown back into the battle against Communism, Miller—perhaps because he was a more widely educated and generally more sophisticated man and also because by temperament and training he was essentially a staff, rather than a combat, officer—was inclined to take a more sober view of his organization's prospeots.

For one thing, his past diplomatic experience made it easier for him to visualize them in their proper perspective, i.e., against the background of the general political situation in the world (something the soil-bound Kutyepov had been often averse to do). And that situation—what with the mounting economic crisis and the looming Nazi and Japanese threats—was becoming increasingly unfavorable to any renewed anti-Communist initiative on the part of the Western democracies—in Miller's view the one and only chance for a White comeback in Russia.

And then in Russia itself the situation had also changed radically in the past few years. The complete collapse of all *non*-Communist opposition to Lenin's, and later Stalin's, rule, as opposed to the mounting dissatisfaction *within* Communist party ranks, made it increasingly likely that in the future the brunt of the struggle against the Red dictator would be borne by his own ex-companions-in-arms.

Under these circumstances the wisest policy seemed to be to bide one's time until an irrevocable split developed within the Communist leadership and the Red Army stepped in as mediator or until the Western Powers, taking advantage of the ensuing chaos, intervened in their turn. Meanwhile, Miller's own duty—as he saw it—was to husband his resources (both human and material) and to concentrate his efforts on helping the rank-and-file of the ROVS pull through the period of economic crisis and mass unemployment (of which foreign workers, such as the Russian *émigrés*, were naturally the first victims) and adjust themselves, as Baron Wrangel had foreseen, to a prolonged exile abroad. And this meant necessarily also discouraging any activities which, however commendable their motives, might embarrass and therefore antagonize the authorities of their various countries of refuge.

In itself this change of accent, from spearheading the struggle against Communism in Russia to concentrating on the fight for mere physical survival, implied for many of the younger White officers—the "Young Turks" of the ROVS—a psychological and sometimes even physical adjustment which they found difficult to accept. To them, the stand taken by Miller and those who saw eye to eye with him, and whom they referred to sarcastically as the "visents" (*zubry*) —meaning, roughly speaking, "troglodytes"—smacked of a senile inertia that bordered on defeatism.

And eventually this discontent turned to open revolt.

Of the leaders of the "Young Turks," one of the most vociferous in denouncing General Miller's "inept leadership" (as they called it) and in demanding a radical reform of the ROVS, was dashing young General Skoblin, commander of the famous "Kornilov" Division.*

Major General Nikolai Vladimirovich Skoblin was a typical representative of that younger generation of Tsarist officers who had stepped, as it were, straight out of the schoolroom onto the battlefields of World War I. Having gained fame and honor there and chanced to survive the carnage, they had then returned home, only to find that the world to which they belonged had meanwhile disintegrated and the values they had been brought up to revere and stand up for, been trampled brutally underfoot: Tsarist rule had crumbled virtually without a murmur; the republic—something in itself new and untried in Russia and to the military generally unsympathetic—had done no better and only a thin line of White volunteers stood now, here and there, ready to fight the Red wave that was beginning to sweep the land.

Faced with what was both a national and a personal tragedy, even some of the older officers, those bred on and steeped in Tsarist traditions, had wavered and then—whether out of opportunism, fear or idealism—had thrown in their lot with the rising Communist tide. Too young to feel irrevocably bound by the memories, traditions and habits of a past that was no more; too ambitious, often, to allow this loss to impede their rapid advancement toward the military

* Named after General Kornilov, a founder of the Southern White Army, who had perished in action at the beginning of the Civil War.

fame and fortune to which they had become accustomed; too idealistic at times, but at others also too hardened and embittered to let
arguments of ethics and morality stand in their way, the younger
officers were placed, necessarily, before an even greater dilemma.

In any event, whether they thereupon chose (like Skoblin) to join
the White movement, or whether they decided (like Tukhachevsky,
Uborevich and Yegorov, about whom more will be heard later) to
link their fate with that of the Communist cause—and a few were to
do first the one and then the other—all these young men of Russia's
"lost generation" had certain fundamental traits in common which
set them in a category apart.

Small of stature, slight of build, with pale, cold, shifty eyes and a
modest, self-effacing manner, Skoblin had emerged from World
War I with the reputation of a reckless daredevil, whose natural
tactical flare made up for his lack of theoretical knowledge (but then
these were the typical characteristics of a good Civil War commander on whichever side he happened to fight). Partly because of
this, but also because of the fantastic losses suffered by the White
Volunteer Army, he had risen rapidly in its ranks until by 1920, at
the age of twenty-seven, he was a major general, the commander of
the crack Kornilov Division and one of the outstanding young hope-
fuls of the White military movement.

And yet already in those early days there were in his character
certain flaws—a cruelty which went beyond even the accepted
harshness of civil wars (he made it a point of taking no prisoners,
torturing and then hanging all captives), a ruthlessness bordering on
opportunism, which made him a controversial personality and helped
deny him the respect, rewards and recognition his personal courage
and gifts of leadership seemed otherwise to call for. And these flaws
had not become any less evident following his meeting with the
woman who was soon to become his wife.

Of peasant origin, Nadyezhda or "Nadya" Plevitzkaya was still a
child when she ran away from home and joined a traveling circus.
Ten years later she had become Russia's foremost folk singer, a
"Soloist of His Imperial Majesty" (the highest token of musical
recognition in Tsarist Russia) and one of the most popular and

best-paid artists in the country. The Revolution had interrupted her
career but briefly. In 1918, she had followed her husband (who had
volunteered with the Red Army) to the front, to entertain the troops
with her songs. And when presently she was captured by a patrol of
the already famous Kornilov Division, she was soon as popular with
the Whites as she had been earlier in the opposite camp. Eventually
she became the mistress of young Colonel Skoblin. In 1921 they
were married, on Gallipoli, and from that moment on Plevitzkaya
appeared invariably in the role of a typical "mother-commander,"
gay and generous in times of joy, warm and helpful in the hour of
need, the "guardian angel" of the Gallipoli veterans, without whose
presence and songs no White celebration, no regimental holiday
could be viewed as a real success. Only a few knew her for what
she was in reality: ignorant and superstitious, but at the same time
sly, shrewd, ambitious, hard-boiled and soil-bound and exercising
an iron grip over her handsome young husband.

For a few years, Plevitzkaya's world-wide success as a concert
singer had assured them a sufficiently good income to dispel any
worries they might have had about their future. But they lived and
spent lavishly and as time went by and age began to tell, her voice
weakened and the box-office returns dropped, until by 1928 it was
rumored that the Skoblins were actually hard up.

And then, all of a sudden, there appeared a change in their fortunes. In the autumn of 1929 they moved from Nice to Paris, purchased a house—a small but comfortable villa in suburban Ozoir-la-
Ferrière—as well as a car, and although Skoblin (unlike most of his
fellow White officers) was strangely reluctant to take a regular job,
being content to officiate as his wife's impresario and accountant,
it seemed that their financial worries were over.

Shortly thereafter, General Kutyepov was kidnaped. Plevitzkaya,
who had never been much of an habitué of the Kutyepov household
—indeed Kutyepov seems to have had a real dislike for Skoblin—had
for some reason seen much of the General in the weeks prior to his
disappearance and in the days that followed it, she literally never
left Mrs. Kutyepova's side. She was thus kept fully informed of the
day-to-day progress of the investigation. As for her husband, he

seems to have confined his contribution, at the councils of war that followed Kutyepov's abduction, to proposing a raid upon the Soviet Embassy (something which would have done the ROVS more harm than good). Indeed, until the great 1934-1935 debate on the subject of the ROVS' reorganization (about which more will be heard later) he appeared to show only episodic interest in higher politics, being content to concentrate his attention on building up a personal following within the influential Gallipoli Association and otherwise to hover—aloof, polite, correct, an ever present but never obtrusive shadow—in the background of his wife's more flamboyant personality.

And then, all of a sudden, a little cloud appeared on the Skoblins' otherwise so serene horizon.

On February 6, 1935, the Paris Russian language daily *Posledniye Novosti* published a news item which immediately aroused widespread interest in *émigré* circles. For according to this report, a Captain Z (who, some time before, had allowed himself to be recruited as a Soviet agent, allegedly in order to discover his employers' game) had learned, in the course of his duties, that one of the OGPU's most active agents in the White Russian emigration was a General XXX, a top leader of the ROVS. The identity of the two gentlemen, as well as the whole background of the affair, was soon an open secret.

It all began on February 22, 1932, at a regimental celebration, when a Captain Fedossenko of the Kornilov Division (General Skoblin's command) chanced to come across a Lieutenant Colonel Magdenko, a former comrade of Civil War days. They had a number of drinks and eventually Magdenko admitted that he was a Soviet agent, that he worked for a good pay for one Georghi I. Port, alias "Ivanov," Berlin head of the GRU (the Soviet Military Intelligence), and that he, Fedossenko, should do likewise. The following April Fedossenko traveled at Magdenko's invitation to Berlin, where he was introduced to this "Ivanov." The latter displayed such a disconcerting knowledge of the innermost workings of the White military organizations that Fedossenko decided to join his network then and there in order to discover the source of his information. He was recruited under the alias of "The Mole," at an initial salary of sixty U.S. dollars a month. Before going back to Paris, he had a last talk with Magdenko, who now informed him, in great secrecy, firstly that a blow was about to be struck "at the very summit of the French government," as he put it, in such a way as to cast lasting discredit on the White Russian *émigrés* in France, and secondly, that the commander of their division, General Skoblin, had since 1928 himself been an agent of the OGPU and that Fedossenko should therefore be particularly careful so as not to compromise him in any way.

Upon returning to Paris at the end of the month Fedossenko, strangely enough, did nothing about these disclosures beyond sending an anonymous warning to the head of the special Sureté detail at the Palais de l'Elysée (which was, naturally enough, not acted upon). On May 5 President Paul Doumer was assassinated at a charity bazaar by a White Russian by the name of Pavel Gorgulov (who was eventually tried and executed). Whatever his original motives in joining the Ivanov-Magdenko espionage ring, Fedossenko was now so torn by remorse that on May 11 he sought an interview with General Miller to whom he told all. Miller, surprisingly enough, was not impressed and after ordering him to break off all relations with "Ivanov" forthwith, he merely advised Fedossenko to report the whole matter to Commissioner Fauxpas-Bidet (who had conducted the investigation of General Kutyepov's disappearance).

Two weeks later, on June 2, although General Miller had given him his word that he would not repeat his story to anyone, Fedossenko was summoned "in the line of duty" before General Skoblin, who without further preamble proceeded to "grill" him as to the exact tenor of his Berlin talks with Magdenko. He seemed particularly interested to know whether, apart from forecasting President Doumer's assassination, Magdenko had let slip the names of Soviet agents within the ranks of the White para-military organizations. And when Fedossenko answered in the negative and mentioned Miller's insistence that he break with Magdenko, Skoblin replied that this was the last thing he should do, that General Miller was "afraid of his own shadow, especially in such matters" and that he should, on the contrary, stay in touch with his Berlin friends, keeping him, Skoblin, informed of all further developments.

Six weeks later, Fedossenko was without warning expelled from the ranks of the Kornilov Division; a week after that, on July 23, he received a letter from "Ivanov" informing him that the GRU had decided to "dispense with his services," and when he sought to have the circumstances of his expulsion from the Kornilov Division investigated, he was informed that he had been dropped from the ROVS, too.

Thoroughly incensed over what he could not help regarding as a "double double-cross," Fedossenko thereupon submitted a detailed report on the whole affair to his hierarchical superiors and at the same time, through a journalist friend, saw to it that the story was also leaked out to the press.

By now, adverse comments on Skoblin had reached Miller also from another source. Some eighteen months earlier, in October, 1933, Miller had requested his representative in Finland, General Dobrovol'sky, to send him a report on the work of certain Finnish agents in the U.S.S.R., a subject in which "Piotr Petrovich" (one of Skoblin's aliases) was, Miller said, greatly interested. In due course Dobrovol'sky had supplied the information, only to follow it up, in August, 1934, with the news that every one of them had, strangely enough, been recently rounded up by the NKVD.

That spring of 1935 General Miller was faced by an all-out attempt on the part of the "Young Turks" to capture the leadership of the ROVS. This may or may not account for the fact that he did nothing in connection with Captain Fedossenko's written report; nor did he follow up a warning from General Dobrovol'sky, dated August 28, to the effect that the Finns refused to continue to work with the ROVS, "inasmuch as someone in Paris and *especially in Ozoir-la-Ferrière* would surely betray them!" This was followed in December by yet another warning from Dobrovol'sky that he himself too would have nothing further to do with Skoblin.

But over and above Fedossenko's denunciation and Dobrovol'sky's warnings, there existed by now also circumstantial evidence that

should have prompted Miller to give at least some consideration to
the two men's charges. Thus in 1920, i.e., immediately after Wrangel's
evacuation of the Crimea, it had already been rumored that Plevitzkaya had urged Skoblin to make his peace with the Soviet government and return to Russia. Three years later, under the pretext
that during one of her recent concert tours to the U.S.A. she had inadvertently—or at least so she claimed—sung to a pro-Soviet audience, Kutyepov had actually relieved Skoblin of his command.

Moreover, on at least one point Magdenko's disclosures to Fedossenko had been confirmed by the Skoblins themselves: they had admitted visiting Berlin and meeting with Magdenko in 1928. They
had even admitted something else: namely that Plevitzkaya had
received at the time an invitation to give a series of concerts in the
U.S.S.R., an offer which, they said, she had of course declined. A
year later, their financial situation, until then precarious, had taken
such an unaccountable turn for the better that they had been able
to buy themselves a house and a car. Kutyepov's abduction had followed just a few months later, its circumstances pointing clearly to
the participation of someone, if not fully in his confidence, then at
least well acquainted with him. In 1930 ex-Soviet Chargé d'Affaires
Bessedovsky had published his *Reminiscences,* in which he quoted
the Chekist Yanovich's remarks to him, shortly before he himself
jumped the Embassy wall in October, 1929, to the effect that the
OGPU had a man in Kutyepov's immediate entourage thanks to
whom Kutyepov's activities were as open to the OGPU "as if they
were being watched under a glass bell."

And yet when action was finally taken on Fedossenko's report, the
initiative for such action stemmed, strangely enough, not from the
high command of the ROVS, but from Skoblin himself. Indeed, in
the autumn of 1936, when he returned to Paris from one of his wife's
longer concert tours only to find the White Russian colony still agog
with the story of Fedossenko's denunciations, Skoblin demanded
that the charges be sifted by a general's Court of Honor. The latter
convened, cross-examined Fedossenko and studied the evidence.
The key witness, Lieutenant Colonel Magdenko, however, could not
be heard as he was serving a term of imprisonment in a München

jail. Presently the court announced its findings: Skoblin was absolved of all charges "for lack of proof."

Among the para-military groups which General Miller had inherited from his predecessor, there figured a little-known but very influential organization which went by the mystery-laden name of "Inner Line."

The latter had been founded by General Kutyepov in the early days of the emigration for the dual purpose of ferreting out Red *agents provocateurs* and helping in the selection and training of those who could usefully be considered for work in the "Outer Line," i.e., in Russia itself, in the ranks of his Combat Organization.

Though its organization and history are a closely guarded secret to this day, its leading spirit at the time of which we are speaking was a Captain Klavdi A. Foss, a dry, haughty and aloof-looking cavalryman of considerable intelligence, vast ambition and outstanding organizing ability, a born intelligence officer, whose feelers stretched out from the decrepit, run-down and patched-up building in Sofia's Oborishche Street (where Foss performed officially the functions of secretary of the ROVS' Second Branch in Bulgaria) into virtually every White para-military and even many a nonmilitary group.

In time the Inner Line acquired the reputation of an omniscient and all-powerful force, capable of making or breaking an officer for reasons which could well have nothing to do with security, and also of a hotbed of intrigue that had set itself the purpose of creating, through the denunciation of allegedly "unsound" elements, a vacuum around General Miller, which could then be filled by the agency's own appointees.

Actually, this reputation was probably greatly exaggerated. But because the organization had, by its very nature, to operate along strictly conspiratorial lines, it became with the passage of time increasingly difficult to control its membership as well as their contacts, with the result that dubious characters appeared on its periphery, casting a shadow on the agency as a whole.

Kutyepov himself seems in the end to have been alive to this danger, for shortly after his return to Paris from Finland (after the Opperput affair) in the spring of 1927, he ordered a complete reorganization of the Inner Line. Some agents were transferred to other duties, others were dropped altogether and the order was given to keep Skoblin out.

Soon after Kutyepov's disappearance a Captain Nikolai D. Zakrzhevsky arrived in Paris from Bulgaria. Gay, charming, gregarious and an excellent pianist to boot, he was soon a popular figure in White Russian circles. Occasionally he would accompany Plevitzkaya at her concerts and eventually he became an habitué of the Skoblin household. All of which would have been perfectly unexceptionable, were it not for the fact that Zakrzhevsky happened also to be Captain Foss's top assistant in the Inner Line and that the primary purpose of his sojourn in France was the building up of that agency's Paris section!

This first formal contact between Skoblin and Captain Foss's office was to play its part in the ensuing drama.

By the spring of 1935 the outcome of the struggle between "visents" and "Young Turks" for the leadership of the ROVS was being watched in many quarters, inasmuch as the evolution of the political situation in the world generally and in the U.S.S.R. in particular made it a matter of more than parochial interest.

For the progress of Fascism—and to many White Russians it was essentially the anti-Communist aspect of Fascism that counted—had revived the chances of an anti-Soviet crusade, this time under German or Japanese leadership. To many of the "Young Turks," *any* rule in Russia, even that of Nazi Germany, was preferable to continuing the Stalinist dictatorship. In the first place, their patience was beginning to wear thin. Besides, they argued, foreign rule would only be temporary anyhow. And then, over and beyond its mere anti-Communist aspect, there was about Fascism many things that appealed to young Europeans at the time everywhere—its discipline, its nationalism bordering on chauvinism, its adulation of force coupled with its insistence on social justice and, last but not least, its anti-Semitism* and its denunciation of Freemasonry. The younger White émigrés, needless to say, were no exceptions.

Actually, those who held this view were apt to overlook a number of important factors. For one thing, the White Russian exiles were nearing the twentieth year of their diaspora. Of those who had fought in the ranks of the anti-Communist forces, the youngest were now approaching middle age. Absorbed by the everyday struggle for physical survival in an alien environment, most of them, even if they might not admit it, had simply little or no time for politics or heroics. And the younger generation, the White veterans' children or grandchildren (most of whom had been either born or educated abroad) felt by now, naturally, far less emotionally affected by the whole issue than their fathers or grandfathers. The need to break out of the émigré "ghetto," to adapt themselves to their new environment, to assimilate themselves with their countries of refuge, was one which few, if any, would in the long run withstand.

And this evolution of the White Russian emigration had gone apace with major changes in the Soviet Union itself. There too the psychological climate had undergone a radical transformation. It is in the nature of all political emigrations to claim to represent the true face of their countries of origin. This had been all the more so with the White Russians who, aside from their sheer numbers (some 1½ million, of whom there were 400,000 in France—100,000 in Paris alone!—150,000 in Germany, etc.), represented, unlike earlier Russian political emigrations, a veritable cross-section of the Russian nation. Moreover, in the days of Lenin and Trotsky the Soviet leaders had prided themselves in being above all internationalists, to whom the cause of world revolution had priority over the fate of the Russian people proper, except inasmuch as the latter's survival was essential to the Revolution's success. Those were the years of militant atheism,

---

* Anti-Semitic propaganda among the White Russian emigration made much of the fact, for instance, that, with a population ratio of 1.77 per cent, Jews in Lenin's Russia made up 5.2 per cent of the total party membership, 25.7 per cent of the party's Central Committee and from 36.8 to 42.9 per cent of the ruling Politbureau, while among Soviet diplomats and especially senior officials of the secret police the percentage of Jews was even greater.

when churches and other national monuments were being ransacked
or destroyed by the score, when much of the country's cultural
heritage was being plundered or auctioned off abroad in exchange
for much-needed foreign currency, when most of Russia's historic
past was systematically mocked or denounced. Under these circumstances, the White émigrés felt justified in proclaiming themselves
the real custodians of Russia's historical and cultural heritage and
the standard-bearers and spokesmen for a national Russia generally,
as opposed to the world of the Third International.

The victory of Stalin and his concept of "Socialism in One Country" was bound to change all this. Though to watchful observers it
had long been clear that there had always been a strong under-
current of nationalism even in the earliest days of militant Communism, and that the Bolshevik Revolution could actually be
regarded in some respects as the triumph of "Primeval Russia" over
"Westernized St. Petersburg," 1930 marked the official birth date of
the concept of "Soviet Patriotism." Thereafter—and even though most
measures to that effect were given a heavy coating of Marxist over-
paint—the accent in the U.S.S.R. was to be placed increasingly upon
the continuity of Russia's past and her Communist present and
future. This timely appeal to the patriotic emotions of the Russian
people was to yield handsome results in the years of trial and
suffering to come; more important still, it was bound to steal much
of the White movement's ideological thunder.

It followed from all this that any attempt on the part of a foreign
power to overthrow Communist rule by force, might conceivably
(and especially if undertaken under the racist and blatantly im-
perialistic flag of Hitler's *Drang nach Osten*) evolve into an epic
fight to the death between the foreign invader and a nation now
united against the common foe. Under these circumstances, those
White Russians who joined with the aggressors could easily find
themselves branded as foreign mercenaries (the word "quisling" had
not then yet been coined) and rejected even by those Soviet citizens
who, otherwise, shared their anti-Communist feelings.

In any event, it was now all the more imperative that the leadership of the ROVS should not fall into the hands of men capable of

committing what remained of the White movement to an adventure. Thus, when in the spring of 1935 the powerful Gallipoli Association put forward Skoblin's candidacy to the post of head of the organization's First Branch (France), General Miller countered the move by assuming this function himself. Then, paradoxically enough (though he may have wished to provide a sop for Skoblin's wounded vanity and at the same time keep a closer eye on him), he revived the Inner Line in France and appointed Skoblin his personal *rapporteur* in all matters pertaining to that organization's activities. He thereby sealed his own doom.

And yet for a while the storm seemed to have abated. Starting with 1935 there appeared to be no more loyal supporter of General Miller than the Commander of the Kornilov Division. For now, at last, Skoblin's long-standing ambition to be at the fountainhead of all White undercover activities seemed close to fulfillment. But he had hoped for bigger and better things. Thus he must soon have realized that his new post gave him but little actual insight into the Inner Line's secret operations, which rested, as before, solely in the hands of the mysterious Captain Foss.

Actually Skoblin's activities throughout the years 1935, 1936, 1937 followed no clearly defined pattern. For a while he frequented the caucuses of a conspiratorial group headed by Aleksander I. Guchkov (the Russian Provisional Government's first War Minister in 1917), at which the Soviet banker Dimitri Navashin was also a welcome visitor.* In the summer of 1935 and again in 1936 he accompanied his wife on concert tours of the Baltic states, from which he returned with vast plans for an underground network based on those countries. But none of the ROVS' representatives on the spot wished to have anything to do with him.

In July, 1936, General Francisco Franco started his sedition against the Spanish government. The "Young Turks" seized this opportunity to exercise renewed pressure upon General Miller in order that he proclaim his open support of the insurgents and encourage the mass enrollment of White Russian volunteers in

* Navashin was to die, assassinated in broad daylight in the Paris Bois de Boulogne, in January, 1937.

Franco's forces. But although Miller and most of his associates were bound to feel strong sympathy for the professed aims of the Spanish Nationalists, he refused to be swayed into committing the ROVS to the support of a foreign cause. Nor would he agree to the transfer of his headquarters to Berlin or to an open endorsement of the Nazis' anti-Soviet program, and this despite the hostile atmosphere that had prevailed in France since the advent of the Popular Front.

By the end of 1936 it seemed as though Skoblin's star too was at last on the wane. In December the post of personal *rapporteur* on the Inner Line was abolished and shortly thereafter Miller confided to Vice Admiral Kedrov, his first deputy, that he had finally come to the conclusion that he had "perhaps been wrong" to put so much trust in Skoblin. The remark probably came to the latter's notice. If so, it must have removed his last scruples, if he had ever had any. For Skoblin was by now committed to another, far more spectacular intrigue, one which, if successful, could be expected to yield the honors and financial security which, in his own and his wife's opinion, had long been so unfairly denied him.

PART TWO

THE TUKHACHEVSKY AFFAIR

7

THE IDES OF JUNE—
1. THE OFFICIAL STORY

May 1, 1937, in Moscow was a gloriously sunny day and the dense forests of scarlet silken banners glowed gaily above the heads of the troops massed in Red Square. For that year, as every year since the Communist seizure of power in Russia, the advent of spring was being heralded in by a gigantic military and civilian parade. Indeed, but for the unusual number of security personnel in and out of uniform and the absence on the government podium atop Lenin's tomb of several long-familiar faces and a feeling of tenseness in the air generally, there was—at least outwardly—little to distinguish this particular occasion from countless previous ones.

As usual, the entire high command of the Red Army was present, including the recently appointed marshals of the Soviet Union: Voroshilov, Budyonny, Yegorov and Tukhachevsky. Only Blücher was missing. But then he had to keep watch over the easternmost confines of the U.S.S.R., where the Japanese were just about to unleash their ill-fated "police action" in China. As usual, also, Tukhachevsky was among the first to arrive. General Walter Ghinsburg-"Krivitzky," in those days the NKVD's top "resident" in Western Europe, was present that day in Red Square.* He has described the scene:

> The Marshal was walking across the square. . . . He paused for a moment, glanced around . . . and then proceeded to the space in front of Lenin's tomb where the Red Army generals were accustomed to review parades. . . . He took his place and stood motionless. . . . Some time later, Marshal Yegorov came up. He did not salute Tukhachevsky, nor glance at him, but took his place beside him as if he were alone. [Another] moment passed and Assistant Defense-Commissar Gamarnik walked up. He again did not salute either of his comrades, but took the next place, as though he did not see them. Presently the line was complete. . . . The military parade flowed by. It is customary for the army generals to remain in their places for the civilian parade which follows. But this time Tukhachevsky did not stay. During the intermission between the two parades, he stepped out of line and walked away . . . through the cleared lines, out of Red Square, out of sight. . . .[1]

It was to be his last appearance in Moscow's Red Square.

On May 4 it was announced that, contrary to earlier arrangements, Tukhachevsky would not, after all, head the Soviet delegation to King George VI's coming Coronation; that this would be led by Flag Officer First Grade Vladimir M. Orlov, the head of the Red Navy.

A week went by.

On May 11 *Pravda* came out with the following terse communiqué:

> By Government decree . . . Marshal of the Soviet Union, Comrade M. N. Tukhachevsky has been appointed G.O.C., Volga Military District.

By the same decree Marshal Aleksander I. Yegorov, Chief of Staff of the Red Army, was named to succeed Tukhachevsky as First

---

* By profession an architect, Ghinsburg-Krivitzky had worked as a Soviet undercover agent abroad virtually since the first days of the Soviet regime, first with the Comintern, then with the GRU and finally with the NKVD. He it was whose missing a train connection in Breslau prevented the calling off of the bloody Communist rising in Hamburg in October, 1923. In the fall of 1937, he received orders to organize the assassination of an old friend and colleague, Ignaz Reisz, who had recently defected. He refused. On December 5 he defected in his turn. The Kremlin neither forgot nor forgave him. The man hunt lasted almost four years. On February 10, 1941, he was found in a room of the Hotel Bellevue, Washington, D.C., shot through the head.

Assistant Defense Commissar. There was still another significant command shift, though it attracted little attention at the time: Army Commander First Grade Yona E. Yakir, long-time head of the Kiev Military District, was transferred to Leningrad.

The paper reported further changes, this time in the administrative structure of the Soviet armed forces: military councils were reintroduced forthwith in all district commands and the institution of political commissars was revived.

In itself, the sudden appointment of the No. 2 man in the Red Army to a relatively obscure provincial command, however unexpected, was not necessarily a token of disgrace. In normal times such transfers could be regarded as fairly routine. Tukhachevsky himself had in the past been shifted several times back and forth from the Defense Commissariat to various field assignments. Perhaps the Volga District had grown slack and needed "tightening up"? But then these were not normal times. Less than a year before, in August, 1936, a first show trial had sent to their death Zinovyev and Kamenev and several other prominent leaders of the so-called "Left Opposition." Even more recently, in January, 1937, another trial had extended this mopping-up operation to the second-ringers of the "Old Bolshevik" opposition and, significantly, the names of both Tukhachevsky and of General Putna, one of the Red Army's brightest young stars, had cropped up for no apparent reason in the course of the proceedings. The purge was now assuming unheard-of proportions. Fresh arrests were reported daily. The Red terror, which had never actually ceased since Savinkov's mismanaged rising of July, 1918, was moving rapidly into its apogee. It was now rumored that even the Red Army would not be spared, that Stalin had hinted as much. Under these circumstances Tukhachevsky's transfer could mean only one thing: the man was in trouble.

The structural reforms of the armed forces had even more ominous implications. For the twin institutions of the military councils and political commissars dated back to the crisis years of Civil War and foreign intervention. They had been established by the then all-powerful Trotsky to watch over the many Tsarist officers with whom he had been forced to staff the Red Army in the first period of its existence and whose loyalty was, needless to say, often in doubt. But they had soon become so unpopular even with the die-hard Communist commanders that the powers of the commissars (since 1925 called "Assistant Commanders for Political Matters") had been greatly curtailed, while the councils were abolished altogether. Their revival now, of all times, when the country was literally seething with rumors of plots and counterplots, meant obviously that Stalin had lost confidence in the armed forces.

Indirectly, of course, these reforms implied also a further increase of the powers of the so-called "Main Political Administration" of the Red Army (which served as the party's eyes and ears with the armed forces) and of its long-time head, "Old Bolshevik" Jan B. Gamarnik, to whom the two institutions were subordinated. But the latter did not have much opportunity to enjoy the benefits of his enhanced position, for barely two weeks later, on June 1, *Pravda* came out with the casual announcement that "former [!] Central Committee member" Gamarnik had committed suicide for fear that "his involvement with anti-Soviet elements" was about to be exposed.

Gamarnik's sudden death barely a week after the same *Pravda* had reported with the usual fanfare his election to the Moscow District Party Committee, followed, as it was presently, by the equally mysterious disappearance of four of his principal lieutenants, pointed to the existence of a major crisis within the Soviet armed forces.

Krivitzky had left Moscow a week earlier, on May 22. Already, he says, "something like panic [had] seized the entire officer corps of the Red Army. Hourly reports came in of fresh arrests. . . ." It was rumored that the fate of Defense Commissar Voroshilov himself hung in the balance. Just before leaving, Krivitzky dropped by to have a last word with First Deputy Commissar of the Interior Mikhail P. Frinovsky, who was conducting the purge.

"Tell me," he inquired of Frinovsky. "What's going on here?"

"We've just uncovered a gigantic conspiracy in the army," Frinovsky replied excitedly. "Such a conspiracy as history has never known . . . But we've got them all!"

That same evening Krivitzky took the Stockholm express. "It was," he writes, "like leaving a city in the midst of a series of earthquakes. Marshal Tukhachevsky had been arrested. NKVD circles were already buzzing with the rumor that Gamarnik had also been arrested. . . . Stalin was offering him an eleventh hour reprieve on condition that he permit his name to be used in destroying Tukhachevsky. Gamarnik had rejected the offer. . . ." According to Krivitzky, Gamarnik did not commit suicide, but was slain in prison.[2]

Two more weeks went by.

On June 9, *Pravda* came out with the casual announcement that "by order of the People's Commissar for Defense, Marshal of the Soviet Union Voroshilov, Division Commander Efremov has been appointed G.O.C., Volga Military District." Of Tukhachevsky, there was not a word.

Finally, on June 11, the news broke. That day *Pravda* announced that:

> The investigation of the case against: M. N. Tukhachevsky, Y. E. Yakir, Y. P. Uborevich, A. I. Kork, R. P. Eidemann, B. M. Feldmann, V. M. Primakov and V. K. Putna . . . has been completed and is now before the Court. . . .

The latter—a special tribunal of the Supreme Court of the U.S.S.R. presided over by the notorious purge trial judge Vassili I. Ulrich (who had first officiated in this capacity at Boris Savinkov's trial, thirteen years earlier)—was to consist of what *Pravda* described glowingly if rather rashly—considering the subsequent fate of most of its members—as "the flower of our glorious Red Army," namely, Marshals Vassili K. Blücher and Semyon M. Budyonny; Army Commanders First Grade Boris M. Shaposhnikov and Ivan P. Byelov; Army Commanders Second Grade Jan I. Alksnis, Pavel E. Dybenko and Nikolai D. Kashirin and Division Commander Emelyan I. Goryachov. Twelve months later, only two of these eight "flowers" —Budyonny and Shaposhnikov—were still living!

The defendants were charged, significantly, not with Trotskyism (this would come later, ex post facto, at the third purge trial) but with "violating their soldiers' oath," "betraying their fatherland" and being in the service of a "foreign government that is conducting an unfriendly policy toward the Soviet Union."

All of them had until recently held top command posts in the armed forces. Tukhachevsky's fame was by now literally world-wide. Putna had served as military attaché successively in the key posts of Berlin, Tokyo and London. Primakov, Budyonny's No. 2 man in command of the Red Cavalry, had long served as Yakir's Chief of Staff. Kork, Uborevich and Yakir himself had been publicly acclaimed by none other than Stalin as the Soviet Union's top strategists. The latter two were expected to command the main groups of Soviet armies in the event of a war with Germany. To accuse all of them, and especially Yakir, Eidemann and Feldmann (who were of Jewish origin), of being agents of Nazi Germany, was to admit that the entire top leadership of the Red Army was rotten to the core!

Next day, June 12, *Pravda* went on to inform its readers that the seven defendants had acknowledged their guilt and had been condemned to death. The sentence had already been carried out and the paper concluded sanctimoniously: "To dogs, a dog's death! There is no place for murderers such as they in the Soviet order of things!"

Voroshilov's order of the day to the armed forces was even more emphatic and—in the light of later developments—even more foolhardy: "Tukhachevsky and the other lackeys of capitalism," he raved, "have been wiped off the face of the earth, their memory to be cursed and forgotten!"

These three brief official communiqués represent virtually all that the Russian people have ever been allowed to know about the so-called "Tukhachevsky Affair." True, at the last of the great show trials, that of the so-called "Right Opposition" in March, 1938, Prosecutor Andrei Y. Vyshinsky (the U.S.S.R.'s famous future Ambassador to the U.N.) attempted to weave the so-called "Generals' Plot" into the now familiar pattern of conspiracy, espionage and treason. His arguments, however, sounded at best unconvincing. Khrushchev's disclosures at the Twentieth (1956) Party Congress, so detailed and voluble when relating to the purge in the party, dismiss the Army purge with a few cryptic sentences and the latest volume of the *Great Soviet Encyclopedia,* in which the biographies of some of the purged generals appear again for the first time in twenty years, is hardly more helpful: only the dates of their deaths are given, not the cause or the circumstances. Stalin himself set once and for all the tone of what was to become for years, for Communists and fellow travelers the world over, the official version of the Great Purge:

These White-Guardist pygmies [he said in a report to the Eighteenth (1939) Party Congress] whose strength can be compared only to that of insignificant tadpoles . . . [were] chucked overboard like so much excess rubbish. . . . The Soviet people subscribed to their defeat and proceeded to the next item of business on its agenda.[3]

The implication is clear. The victims of the Great Purge were a mere handful of foreign agents, of discredited "White Guardists," of potential Fifth Columnists, whose doings had been disavowed by the broad masses of the Russian population and whose shameful end signified nothing more than the culmination of a now obsolete intra-party controversy, about which the Russian people needed to show no concern.

Nikita Khrushchev, however—and he should know!—is of a somewhat different opinion. As he pointed out to the Twentieth Party Congress:

As you know, we had before the war excellent military cadres *which were unquestionably loyal to Party and the Fatherland.** . . . Those of them who managed to survive despite the severe tortures to which they were subjected in the prisons, *showed themselves from the first days* [of the war] *real patriots and heroically fought for the glory of the Fatherland.** . . . However, many such commanders perished in camps and jails and the Army saw them no more. . . . The cadre of leaders who had gained experience in Spain and the Far East was almost completely liquidated.[4]

To what extent the official Stalin-inspired version of these events was remote from the truth can be seen from the following figures:

* All italics mine.—G.B.

By conservative estimates the Great Purge of 1936-1938* claimed
at least seven to eight million victims, of which more than 50 per
cent perished at the hands of NKVD gunmen or in prisons and
labor camps.† These included some 800,000 members of the party
(or one-third of its total membership at the time).‡ Among those
shot figured: 6 out of 13 members of the ruling Politbureau;§ 98 out
of 139 members of the Central Committee (all of whom had been
hand-picked by Stalin at the Seventeenth [1934] "Congress of Victors"); 1,109 of the 1,966 delegates to that same Congress; more
than one-third of the elected deputies to his equally hand-picked
Supreme Soviet; 14 of the 18 members of the country's Council of

* Though the phenomenon of the purge seems to be an inseparable part of
Communist party life and had become in Russia a periodic spectacle after
Lenin's death in 1924, that of 1936-1938—actually it continued at a reduced
pace until the very eve of the war in the East (June, 1941)—rightly deserves the
definition of "Great Purge" for reasons of its scale and the number of its
victims.

† By matching such disparate elements as the extent of overcrowding in the
prison cells, the number of prisons in any one town, the prisoner's average
time of detention until his execution or removal to camp, the population for
the area from which the prisoners were drawn and the length of the purge,
which had a definite relation to the degree of overcrowding, it has been possible
to make fairly reliable estimates of the proportion of arrests to the total population from one town to the other and from one district to another. Calculations
of this kind were often made by the prisoners themselves, often with the help
of ex-state attorneys or NKVD officials confined in the same cell. Such calculations showed that the numbers of prisoners during the Great Purge varied
between seven million and fourteen million, this figure including the victims
of earlier repressions, such as the kulaks, who were still lingering in jail at
the time.

According to the same calculations, the number of death sentences was
rarely more than 10 per cent of the total number of verdicts handed down, but
since as a result of the impossible conditions in the camps, their population
was usually cut by 50 per cent within two or three years, the actual death toll
was incredibly high.

‡ In his report to the Eighteenth (1939) Congress Stalin himself was to admit that "during the period under review (i.e., 1934-1939) the party has succeeded in promoting to leading state and party posts over 500,000 young
Bolsheviks."[5]

The fate of their predecessors can be easily imagined.

§ The turnover rate within the Politbureau itself is a telling image of the
precariousness of power in Stalin's Russia: thus of the 27 top party functionaries
who served on that august body at one time or another prior to the Red dictator's death in 1953, only 7 have survived to tell the tale and of the rest only 4
died apparently natural deaths. Seven were shot, 3 died "suddenly," 1 was
assassinated, 1 deported (and then murdered) and 3 disappeared.

People's Commissars; nearly all the Premiers and People's Commissars of the Federated Republics and all the provincial Party
Secretaries; most of the leadership of the Young Communist League;
countless leaders of industry, engineers, doctors, artists, writers,
musicians, etc., etc. Eventually, Stalin's avenging hand reached out
into the very ranks of those who had helped him put through the
first stages of the Great Purge. By the time the now liquidated
Lavrentii P. Beria took over the secret police from the infamous
Yezhov (December, 1938), most of the top leaders of the NKVD and
many of the rank-and-file, some five to eight thousand men all told,
had followed their recent victims to the grave.

As for the armed forces, they were literally decimated. Again by
conservative estimates, from 20,000 to 35,000 officers, i.e., some 35
to 50 per cent of the Red officers' corps were purged. Japanese
intelligence sources are even more specific. According to the latter,
the victims included:

3 Marshals (out of 5)
13 Army Commanders (out of 15)
57 Corps Commanders (out of 85)
110 Division Commanders (out of 195)
220 Brigade Commanders (out of 406)—among them:
11 Assistant Defense Commissars and
75 Members of the Supreme Military Council (out of 80)

By the winter of 1937-1938 (when the Great Purge hit its peak),
such signals as the one which the then NKVD Boss Yezhov addressed one day to his representative in Frunze (Kirghiz S.S.R.)
and which read: "You are charged with the task of exterminating
10,000 enemies of the people. Report results by signal," had become
a matter of routine, as had the reply which followed shortly thereafter and which read:

In reply to yours of such-and-such a date, the following enemies of the
people have been shot:
    1. . . . .
    2. . . . .
    3. . . . .
    etc., etc., etc.[6]

The criterion used to draw up the fatal lists was in most cases some so-called "objective characteristic," which—as was the case in 1918-1920, when the so-called "bourgeois" were systematically exterminated "as a class"—could be a man's social extraction, the past or present nature of his work, his being related or friendly to someone, his membership or activity in some official Soviet organization (such as the People's Commissariat of Transportation—the perennial black sheep of Communist Russia!), his nationality or some connection with a foreign country, or simply the generation to which he happened to belong.

Such were the "few insignificant White-Guardist tadpoles" which the Russian people had, as Stalin and his apologists wished to have it believed, "chucked overboard like so much excess rubbish"! Curiously, it seems never to have occurred to those who today continue to uphold this myth that if after twenty years of Communism the elite of the regime was made up of spies, saboteurs and traitors, what a sorry commentary this represented on Communism itself!

8

ANATOMY OF A PURGE

Why? Why did he do it? For what reason?

For close to twenty years now attempts have been made to pierce the pale of mystery and lies which Stalin in his lifetime kept lowered over the background and reasons of the Great Purge and which his successors are now clumsily trying to explain away by means of the catch-all formula of the "cult of personality." According to the testimony of survivors of the purge no question excited the inmates of Stalin's jails and slave-labor camps, whether they be party members or nonparty helots, NKVD victims or former NKVD henchmen themselves now turned victims, so much as these. Endlessly argued in the wooden cells, the "dog kennels," in which prisoners were put before and after interrogation, the words "Why? What for?" could, it appears, be found in the most unexpected places—scratched with a smuggled bit of broken glass or penciled on the inside walls of the prison van, the "Black Raven," and of the crowded, lice-infested coaches of the prison trains. Indeed, no less than seventeen distinct explanations have been advanced to date, ranging from the official version of mass "conspiracy," "treason," "espionage" and "sabotage" to the theory of divine retribution for the Russian people's sins or that of the possible effects of sunspots!

"Why? What for?"

Indeed, it seems incredible, even to such a shock-hardened generation as ours, that at the very moment when the first clouds of

war were beginning to gather again over Europe—a war in which
the U.S.S.R. could hardly fail to become involved—Stalin should
have chosen to institute a blood bath that was to end by engulfing
the whole country, shattering his administration and wrecking his
army, his main bulwark against the looming Nazi threat.

Actually there is evidence that Stalin was taken unawares, both
by Hitler's advent to power and by his retention of it. As late as
June, 1930, he had denounced in scathing terms Trotsky's warnings
from abroad about the impending Nazi threat. Yet barely three
months later, at the September elections, the Nazis had, with
6,400,000 votes and 107 deputies, become the second strongest party
in the Reichstag. On the very eve of Hitler's accession to power,
he had been still convinced that after using the *Führer* as a pawn
in order to maneuver the Catholic *Zentrum* out of the picture, Von
Schleicher and the generals would push him aside and seize power
for themselves. Indeed, even after Hitler had become *Reichskanzler,*
Stalin remained for a full year significantly silent on the subject of
Nazism, leaving it to the Comintern to fight the ideological battles.
Himself an unrepentant realist, who was never to hesitate to sacrifice
the acknowledged aims of world revolution to his more parochial
policies of "Socialism in One Country," he fully expected Hitler to
do likewise with *his* anti-Communist campaign slogans.

It is only in 1934—with Berlin's *rapprochement* with Warsaw (January) and the famous "Night of the Long Knives" (June)—that Stalin
seems to have come to the conclusion, not only that Hitler was
there to stay, but that the foreign policies advocated in *Mein Kampf*
would be carried out to the letter.

Thereafter the Soviet government was to renege on practically
every tenet it had hitherto so jealously upheld: from bitter opponent
to the League of Nations and the principle of "collective security,"
it became, at least in words, its most vocal champion; from hostility
to and periodic near-conflict with the powers of the Entente and
especially France, it moved to woo them; for its perennial enmity
toward the Social Democrats throughout the world—the "Social
Traitors," as they were known in Communist jargon—it substituted
the catch-all formula of the "Popular Front." And yet all the while,

through the channel of David N. Kandelyaki, a fellow Georgian official of his personal secretariat, whom he had appointed commercial attaché to the Berlin Embassy, Stalin kept desperately trying to "reinsure" himself with Hitler, something he was finally to achieve only in August, 1939, on the very eve of war.* This explains, in Isaac Deutscher's words, the "complex and often baffling diplomatic game" in which Moscow engaged throughout the thirties, in the course of which the U.S.S.R. and her future partners in the Grand Alliance against Nazi Germany "sold space for time and let down allies and friends, until no space was left to be sold and no time to be bought,"[1] and, we may add, no friends or allies to let down or betray.

These tactics represented essentially a policy from weakness, that stemmed not so much from an understandable fear of war and of defeat in war as from Stalin's realization that the Soviet Union was seething with discontent and that if and when war came to the U.S.S.R., the Soviet people, the Red Army, even his own party might turn against him.

Indeed, his archenemy Trotsky had predicted as much in the summer of 1927 in his famous "Clemenceau Statement," in which he had served notice that in the event of war the opposition would adopt, vis-à-vis Stalin and his faction, the same stand Georges Clemenceau had taken in France at the beginning of World War I against the Caillaux-Malvy government. In other words, that it would push for a "changing of the guard." Under any normal regime, such a statement of intentions, however vexing, would have been regarded as quite unexceptionable. The fundamental tenets of Soviet Communism, however, include the contention, not only that Communism is the inevitable and highest form of human development and that the road to world Communism and world revolution lies via the seizure of power by the "proletariat" and the dictatorship of

---

* There is evidence that one of the reasons for the murder near Lausanne in September, 1937, of top INU agent Ignaz Reisz was precisely the Kremlin's fear that he might reveal the existence of these secret negotiations. As for Kandelyaki, his fate was that of all those who had the misfortune of sharing Stalin's secrets. Banished to an arctic camp in 1938, he died there shortly thereafter, allegedly of tuberculosis.

this proletariat,* but also that the chief task of a victorious proletariat (even though this might not be explicitly admitted) is to
retain such power, whatever the means used to do so.

One of Stalin's motives in instituting the Great Purge was thus,
as Deutscher rightly points out, "to destroy the men who represented the potentiality of alternative government, perhaps not of
one, but of several alternative governments. From the outset he had
identified any attempt at creating [such] an alternative government,
and even the thought of this, with counter-revolution. The destruction of all political centers from which such an attempt might, in
certain circumstances, have emanated, was the direct and undeniable
consequence. . . ."2

In so doing, he was applying a theory of which he was not the
inventor, but which he was to bring to a peak of logical perfection,
that of so-called "Social Prophylaxis." According to this theory, the
young Soviet state, threatened from within and from without, dared
not limit itself to fighting *actual* criminal acts. It had also to guard
itself against *potential* crimes, in line with the thesis that in politics
as in disease prevention is better than cure. It was thus necessary
to identify in advance those groups in which there already prevailed, or in which one day there *might* prevail, a politically critical
mood, a skeptical frame of mind, potentially dangerous, that might
lead to the commission of real crimes. Hence the earlier-mentioned
"objective characteristics," which were in time to take the place of
a person's identity and civil status and which in the end made no
distinction whatsoever between party members and nonparty helots,
distinguished "Old Bolsheviks" and Stalinist upstarts.

In the first place, as Stalin's policies evolved, ever greater numbers
of old party members were bound to resent the fact that the structure
of his new Soviet state was assuming forms, not only often incom-
patible with the revolutionary ideals for which they had fought, but
often remote from the ideals of Marxist Socialism proper.

---

* It matters little for the point of this argument that in the course of time
the abstract concept of the "proletariat" was in Stalin's Russia to be gradually
displaced by this proletariat's self-appointed "leaders," the party, that the
party in turn would be displaced by *its* leaders, the Politbureau, and the latter
by the foremost leader of them all—Stalin.

And then there was still another reason for which the sole fact that someone was an "Old Bolshevik" became an "objective characteristic" of its own, allowing its bearer no place in Stalin's Russia. For the earlier-mentioned need to retain power, as the twin tasks of revolutionizing the economy and of shepherding the masses into a highly organized, bureaucratic system, presumed the existence of complete unity within the party, a unity based on mystical faith to his creed and blind obedience to his rule, rather than on individual judgment and individual conviction. He could expect to find neither of these qualities among the countless, meritorious, idealistic Old Bolsheviks, who had made the Revolution, won the Civil War and produced out of chaos a form of working society, but who had, nevertheless, basically more in common with the old, pre-Revolutionary man they themselves had helped destroy than with the new Soviet man whom he had appointed himself to mold and who was now beginning to graduate from his school. Indeed, one of the characteristics of the Stalin era was to be the suspicion automatically aroused by idealists and thinkers, even those whose orthodoxy was otherwise beyond dispute.

> Yon Cassius has a lean and hungry look.
> He thinks too much; such men are dangerous. . . .

But the role of terror in Stalin's philosophy of statesmanship had still a further use. The insecurity of the masses, the physical elimination of the Old Bolshevik opposition had to be reinsured through the insecurity of the governing elite, of the dictator's own entourage. The function of terror was thus twofold. As prophylactic and preventive, it helped nip in the bud any possible or foreseeable resistance. As a means of reinforcing the dictator's personal power, it helped ensure continuous circulation and periodic renewal of personnel in the ranks of the officeholders, thus making virtually impossible the formation or survival of local breeding grounds of doubt, opposition and potential resistance.

This may account in part for the extension of the purge to the Stalinist stalwarts within the party and the government apparatus. For as Bertram Wolfe has stated so well:

There is one thing that is certain about the use of total terror to solve
the complex problems of economics, politics and thought. . . . It is that
one cannot have recourse to terror on a scale sufficient to embrace all the
affairs of Society, without its spilling over into the very group that used
it. . . . The universal cruelty [in the Russia] of the early 'thirties
coarsened and brutalised the whole of life. It inured men to the idea of
using torture and death to settle what was unsettled, to make certain
what was uncertain, to silence, uproot, crush opposition, compel approval, remake men and their lives. All-encompassing torment and death
spread like a plague throughout the countryside, then into the cities,
then into the Party. . . . [Thus] it was the wholesale crimes against
nameless millions [of peasants] that created the atmosphere making possible the use of similar measures against those who merely opposed the
shedding of Communist blood, and finally against those who were, in
Khrushchev's words, merely "inconvenient" to the wielders of the shears
of Fate.[3]

Some may have still been involved in official or personal relations
with others already purged under another count; some may have
been liquidated because they displayed traces of independence in
their dealings with the supreme leader or were suspected of harbor-
ing aspirations toward personal power; still others may have fallen
victim to the snowballing system of denunciations which, like all
other aspects of Soviet life, featured plans, counterplans and quotas;
some may simply have been caught up in a veritable wave of
Caesarean persecution mania which Yezhov and the NKVD for
strictly personal reasons were, needless to say, ever eager to exploit.
"Only after the juggernaut they had created and given crushing
and irresistible momentum to, began to roll over themselves, did the
best of them begin to have second thoughts."[4]

Indeed, as the vicious circle widened, few men of importance felt
safe. Even the hitherto most reluctant ones were driven to take
action in order to stop the horrible *perpetuum mobile.*

But by then it was too late . . .

. . . Too late to bow and scrape and get down on their knees
and ground in the dirt on their bellies and denounce one another—
as Zinovyev and Kamenev and Radek had done, repeatedly. Too
late to deny, repent and threaten suicide or even commit suicide—
as Bukharin had done and as his friend Tomsky would do. It was

now necessary to kick the corpses of the fallen comrades, to shovel an additional spadeful of infamy into the latter's graves, to contribute one's own pint of comradely blood and thus become accomplices in crime, to hunt or be hunted, to head the pack or be torn to pieces, only to be later "put away," discreetly, as an accomplice. . . . That is why Kuibyshev, Kirov and Ordzhonikidze would die. . . . And Postyshev . . . And Rudzutak, and Eikhe, and Kossior, and Chubar, and the rest . . .

Thus if the looming international crisis must necessarily have played no mean part in setting the stage for the Great Purge, it would be wrong to single it out as the only or even the principal factor. Indeed, the most varied political, personal and psychological motives had their say, one of them being the very concept of Bolshevism as it had evolved, first in Lenin's and then in Stalin's Russia.

Thanks to Khrushchev's famous speech before the Twentieth Congress, we now know even the precise date when the idea of a Great Purge first took seed in Stalin's mind. For in the fateful telegram which Stalin was to address in September, 1936, from his vacation place on the Black Sea to his colleagues of the Politbureau in Moscow and in which he demanded Yagoda's replacement at the head of the NKVD by Yezhov, there figured the significant charge that the latter was "four years late" in "unmasking the Opposition."[5]

Four years late! Which brings us back to the fall of 1932, when the very fate of Communist rule in Russia hung in the balance.

By 1932, with one brief respite in the summer of 1930, Stalin's drive for the collectivization of Russia's independent farmers had raged unabated for four years. For four years the bulk of the so-called *kulaks* and *srednyaks*,* i.e., the more successful farmers, who

---

* A kulak—literally, "fist"—is according to Soviet terminology an "exploiting peasant," i.e., one who employs hired labor. But the pattern of liquidation followed no specific legal definition, since the campaign made, by Stalin's admission, some ten million victims, whereas again according to his own figures the so-called kulaks numbered on the eve of the collectivization drive only one and a half to two million. Actually the bulk of those liquidated belonged mainly to two other groups. The first consisted of the so-called srednyaks or "medium-size farmers," who, though they had not benefited from the mass redistribution

provided most of the country's agricultural output, had fought back
tooth and nail with fowling pieces, scythes and pitchforks, burning
their crops in nihilistic despair, smashing their farm implements
and slaughtering their cattle, while picked detachments of the
OGPU (the Army could no longer be trusted) roamed the countryside like the notorious *Colonnes Infernales* of 1793 in rebel Vendée,
fanning class warfare between poor peasants and rich, stripping once
flourishing districts of their last stocks of grain and seed, confiscating
the land, tools and remaining livestock, besieging, bombing, strafing
from the air or storming with tanks refractory villages, massacring
their population or simply cordoning them off and then leaving
them to die of disease, hunger or cannibalism. As one writer, by no
means unsympathetic to the Soviet regime, remarks: "Observation
in the villages suggests that this portion of the peasantry was left
to starve . . . as a more or less deliberate policy. . . . The Party
appeared less disturbed by dead kulaks than by dead cows. The
former [after all] were class enemies."*6

   This fall of 1932 the offensive against the farmers entered into
its final, most ruthless stage. By now, following two successive bad
harvests, rural Russia was in a state of desperation worse than
anything it had known since 1918. All officials were explicitly for-
bidden to keep count of the number of deaths by starvation. Even
the traditionally most prosperous provinces of the famed "Black
Earth Belt," i.e., the Ukraine, the middle Volga, western Siberia and
the northern Caucasus—in Tsarist days the "granary of Europe"—
had been combed out clean as by a swarm of locusts, while in the
Don and Kuban areas—the traditional Cossack Vendée—the popula-

---

of land in 1918, had nevertheless succeeded by their own and their family's
efforts, i.e., *without outside hired labor*, in working themselves up during the
NEP to a certain degree of prosperity (in South Russia, for instance, a peasant
counted as a srednyak if he owned more than one horse, one cow and more
than twelve acres of land). The second group consisted of those who, irrespective
of their economic status, refused or hesitated to enter a *kolkhoz* (collective
farm).
   * The losses in livestock alone between 1928 and 1933 are put at: 15 million
horses (out of 30), 42 million horned cattle (out of 70), 97 million sheep and
goats (out of 147), and 8 million hogs (out of 20). The Soviet economy has not
recovered from this staggering loss to this day.

tion had been rounded up en masse and driven away on foot or in overcrowded freight cars to the Arctic, Inner Asia and Siberia to dig the canals, lay the railways or build the industrial giants that are the U.S.S.R.'s pride today.* "That summer," Duranty wrote, describing his experiences of 1933, "I drove nearly two hundred miles across country from Rostov and Krasnodar through land that was lost to weeds and villages that were empty."[7]

A mood of despair verging on open revolt began to sweep the land, such as had not been seen since the worst days of war Communism and which the Opposition might have been expected to exploit in order to wrest power, at last, from the man who had caused all the havoc.

And yet it is not in the ranks of the Opposition that Stalin was about to come up against the most dangerous defections, but among men who had hitherto been beyond suspicion, whose spirits had not been broken in endless recantation and whose hands still gripped some of the levers of power.

Since the evolution of the official "General Line" of the party in Russia was to have an essential bearing on the crystallization of the oppositionary forces to Stalin's rule, it may be appropriate at this point to outline very briefly the course of this evolution.

Once the Communist regime had consolidated itself in power,

---

* Partly because the foreign press had so often reported signs of "acute food shortage," even in the relatively plentiful years of the NEP, that Western public opinion was becoming blasé; partly because the authorities succeeded in most cases in assuring the towns a bare minimum to eat and were thus able to confine the famine to the countryside where, with the exception of emaciated children begging for food at the railway stations, foreign travelers being shepherded about by Intourist found few *visible* signs of starvation, the Soviet government has succeeded to this day in putting across the myth that there *never was* a famine in 1932-1933 and that the trouble was merely one of "temporary local supply difficulties" due to kulak sabotage which a few show trials here and there soon put right. Actually, in the eyes of the people and even of the party, the government's responsibility for the famine, owing to the senselessly brutal enforcement of collectivization, the confiscation of available stocks of seed to make up for the shortage of grain, the continued dumping of sorely needed Russian grain abroad, and the systematic extermination of the ablest and hardest-working elements among the rural population, was to be judged far more severely than was the case in 1921, when the famine could rightly be blamed on years of war and revolution.

three principal issues became the subject of intra-party discussion, and later of intra-party strife: (1) whether the path to the world-wide triumph of Communism lay via the theory of "Permanent Revolution" or that of "Socialism in One Country," the latter to be combined with rearmament and power politics of the traditional type; (2) the question of internal party democracy; and, most important of all, (3) the rhythm of "Socialist Construction," i.e., of industrialization and of its essential corollary, collectivization.

For, although thanks to Lenin's NEP the Soviet economy had by 1927 staged a fair comeback and, on paper, the gross national product actually exceeded that of 1913—Russia's last peace year—in fact, what with consumer goods production trailing at one-third to one-half of the pre-Revolution level, a growing population, an over-swollen, inefficient bureaucracy and a running inflation that fed a veritable orgy of speculation, the ever-present "scissors" between the largely socialized industry and the still largely freeholding agriculture was bound to engender, one day, a major crisis.

It is around this basic domestic problem that positions within the party crystallized themselves. Thus, while the so-called "Left," under Grigori E. Zinovyev and Lev B. Kamenev (and to some extent Trotsky), insisted that the peasantry—for which the orthodox Marxist has never had much sympathy or understanding—should not be allowed to exercise what amounted to a stranglehold over the regime, the "Right," led by Nikolai I. Bukharin, Aleksei I. Rykov and Mikhail P. Tomsky, maintained that so long as the state retained control over the key "socialist sector" of the economy (heavy industry, banking, wholesale trade, communications, utilities, etc.), the expansion of industry should proceed in harmony with and not at the expense of peasant freehold agriculture. It is interesting to note that not even the Left, at this point, advocated forced collectivization!

For a short while following Lenin's death (January, 1924), the intra-party struggle over these issues was kept dormant. Once Trotsky's faction had been successfully disposed of, however (1925), Stalin swung sharply to the Right. After a bitter struggle that lasted well into 1927, the Left was overcome. The Right's triumph, however, was short-lived. Two years later Bukharin and his friends had been outwitted in their turn, the year 1929 marking the beginning of Stalin's absolute rule.

In the course of this process his opponents suffered more than physical defeat. For as the "General Line" of the party swung from Left to Right and back to Left again, his foes of yesterday would hasten to join the bandwagon in the illusion that, now that their past stand had to all intents and purposes been vindicated and their opponents confounded, they would once again obtain a footing on the prized Olympus and an insight and perhaps even a say in the drafting of policies. Torn between their dislike of his person and hatred of his methods—now that they themselves were exposed to them—and their psychological inability, born of their Marxist upbringing, to conceive of any other technique of revolutionary struggle; jealous in advance of the possible success the very ruthlessness of these methods might bring about and fearful lest they remain outsiders in his hour of triumph; yet equally fearful of compromising and then perishing with him were he to fail; the prey in some cases, finally, of vague remnants of personal loyalty to him, which even his cynical brutality toward them had not quite succeeded in stifling; they presented by now a picture of sorry moral weakness and ideological confusion.

Whereas those who now turned against Stalin owed him everything. He had hand-picked them, reared and raised them through the ruthless, rough-and-tumble school of intra-party politics from complete or semiobscurity to membership in a successful, triumphant elite. And for years they had repaid him with their services and unquestioning loyalty, a loyalty which he in his turn had kept steady through the skillful manipulation of his patronage, through constant promotions, demotions, mutations, from which even the members and alternate members of the ruling Politbureau were not exempt, that added a measure of insecurity to their feeling of dependence on their master's whims. Many of them had, with the average Russian's proneness to an empirical and even mystical approach to the solution of practical issues, actually started off by believing in him and his methods. In Bertram Wolfe's words:

They liked his crude simplifications of the questions of social life, his organizational moves to prepare his "ideological victories," his glorification of and skill in the use of the Party machine . . . his belief in haste and force. . . . They had laughed uproariously at his coarse jests, watched his chess moves with knowing admiration, reiterated his commonplaces as gems of wisdom, shouted down his victims when they tried to speak. . . . By their cheers and heckling, by their speeches and articles, by their reports to their "constituents," by their purges of doubters and dissenters in their own staffs and fields of work, they [had] created Stalinism and made it strong and unshakable [thus completing] the change of the Party from a multiferous human organism into something inorganic, a thing of granite, a "monolith"—his monolith and theirs.[8]

Actually the ultimate crystallization of power in the hands, first of a small clique and then of one man, had been inherent in Lenin's concept of the so-called "dictatorship of the proletariat" from the first. For as Wolfe so rightly points out:

Collective leadership, difficult at best, is impossible without democracy. Where in all fields there is dictatorship, where there are no constitutional rules binding upon the rulers, where force active or potential settles all things, where opposition, check, substitution from below, are not part of the essential game of politics but something to be eliminated and crushed, the whole momentum of the State and system drives relentlessly toward personal dictatorship. . . . The struggle may be muted and concealed, it might be compromised and blunted and delayed and each fractional dictator might repeat and repeat his pledge against it, but the whole dynamics of dictatorship would continue to cry out for a dictator . . . militarized life for a supreme commander, infallible doctrine for an infallible interpreter, infallible government for an infallible leader . . . a totalitarian party-state for a *Duce*, a *Fuehrer*, a *Vozhd'*.[9]

Yet, if Lenin had already reduced Soviet society to a land of silence, where only one party had still a voice and had then outlawed factions and rival platforms within that party, he had not yet curbed all discussion and expression of difference. It remained for the Stalinists to complete the process of silencing the party as the rest of society had been silenced. This they had done: they had made Stalin the only one to think for the party, they had made him the "Beloved Leader," little realizing that where there is doctrinal infallibility, no reversal of policy can go without its pint of sacrificial blood.

In this spirit, they had also accepted his latest assignment: to liquidate the so-called kulaks, i.e., the rich and medium-size farmers, "*as a class*," first casually, joyfully even, and then—as the havoc and suffering piled up around them—with growing uneasiness and concern, only to find themselves, presently, disavowed by their "Beloved Leader" and made the scapegoats for his mistakes.

And as a result some of them rebelled. The first stirrings had taken place at the very beginning of the collectivization drive, following Stalin's famed "Dizziness from Success" article in *Pravda*, in March, 1930, in which those who were guilty merely of obeying his orders were now blandly taken to task for "overstepping their instructions" and assailed as "opportunists," "distortionists" and "blockheads." Two of Stalin's closest associates: Serghei I. Syrtzov, Premier of the Russian F.S.S.R., and "Besso" Lominadze, First Party Secretary of the important Transcaucasian Federation, had gone so far as to circulate in party circles memoranda that stressed the need for a change, not only of the party line, but perhaps also of the General Secretary of the party, i.e., Stalin. But the Syrtzov-Lominadze cabal had encountered little support. Disavowed by the Central Committee, its spokesmen had been immediately dropped from their posts and although nothing in the party statutes proscribed action such as theirs, they had presently been arrested and exiled to Siberia, where Syrtzov soon vanished without trace, allegedly a suicide, while Lominadze, though he eventually recanted, perished a few years later, one of the first victims of the Kirov affair.*

* Lominadze's defection was a particularly severe personal blow to Stalin, for he belonged to the Red dictator's immediate entourage. A fellow Georgian and a young man of considerable resourcefulness, driving ambition, tireless vitality, great charm and few scruples, he had, by the mid-twenties, graduated together with the well-known German Communist, Heinz Neumann, to the envied position of No. 1 Stalinist trouble-shooter in the Comintern. As such, he was responsible, together with Neumann, for the ill-fated Canton rising (December, 1927). In fact, Stalin had once admitted to Neumann that Lominadze was the one man he wished as a successor!

That autumn of 1932 the Syrtzov-Lominadze affair repeated itself, but with singularly different results.

Two prominent leaders of the earlier Right Opposition: Nikolai A. Uglanov, head of the Moscow party organization and Secretary of the Central Committee and a former alternate member of the Politbureau, and Mikhail N. Ryutin, a former head of the party's Main Propaganda Office, who had in the past distinguished himself by his violent attacks against the Left, now drafted a two-hundred-page "Platform" designed to unite all Stalin's foes in the party, from the far left to the extreme right. In this document the General Secretary was denounced as the "evil genius" of the Revolution who, prompted solely by his "ambition" and "vindictiveness," had brought Russia "to the edge of the abyss" and without whose "elimination" the party and the country could not recover. Judging by the prominence it was to be given at the later purge trials, this platform must veritably have haunted Stalin.

Actually, these men were not dangerous. Both of them had been removed, together with the other leaders of the "Right," in 1929. Uglanov had since recanted; Ryutin was still in jail somewhere or in exile. Stalin, however, chose to interpret the word "elimination" as a call for his assassination. Amidst a press campaign of unprecedented violence, that called for a "decisive struggle against all and any symptoms of reconciliation and of rotten liberalism vis-à-vis anti-party views and theses," Uglanov and his friends were arrested and the OGPU was ordered to dispose of all those involved in this "cabal" in the same way Blumkin had been disposed of three years earlier.

And now the totally unexpected happened. Genrikh G. Yagoda, the efficient but cruel and ambitious Deputy Head of the OGPU and one of the most feared men in the Soviet Union, had at one point been in close touch with the "Right" Opposition, whose misgivings about the tempo of collectivization he had shared (be it only because he was in a position to know the mood of the country and also because it was on the shoulders of the OGPU that rested the main burden of reprisals). Indeed, in the spring of 1929 he, his chief, OGPU Boss Metcheslav R. Menzhinski, and INU head Trilisser had intervened personally with Stalin to slow down the drive against the kulaks; it is said that they were literally "thrown down the stairs." Later the OGPU had resigned itself to the situation and had even taken the lead in building up an industrial empire based on kulak slave labor. Nevertheless, the OGPU had remained under strong "rightist" influences. And so it now declared, all of a sudden, that it was not qualified to mete out the death penalty to party members solely on account of their oppositionist activities and that it must refer the case to the party's Central Control Commission, the competent body in matters of party discipline.*

The chairman of the Control Commission was a supposedly proven Stalinist, Tomsky's successor at the head of the Soviet Trade Unions, alternate Politbureau member Jan E. Rudzutak. He too, however, declined to go into the merits of the issue, until a decision on principle had been handed down by the Commission's parent bodies—the party's Central Committee and the Politbureau.

These two met in the last week of September, 1932, and as a result Stalin sustained a resounding defeat: his insistence that the "plotters" be executed was ignored and instead they, together with Zinovyev and Kamenev for good measure (who were guilty essentially of not having denounced them), were merely expelled from the party and exiled to Siberian "polit-isolators."

By now the Army too was stirring. General Vassili K. Blücher, Stalin's prestigeful commander in Siberia, in whom he had perhaps more faith than in any other of his military leaders, had—like the other generals—been watching with growing dismay the effect the horrors of collectivization were having on the morale of his troops. And finally he could stand it no more. Taking advantage of Japan's stepped-up inroads in northern China, he served the Kremlin with a veritable ultimatum: the farmers of eastern Siberia were to be left alone, or else. . . . The Politbureau met to consider this unheard-of situation; Blücher was backed by Stalin's old crony, War Commissar

---

* That this sudden restraint was not prompted by what Stalin called "rotten liberalism vis-à-vis anti-party views and theses" can be seen from the fact that although the death penalty had been officially abolished in the Soviet Union in 1920, the OGPU had been happily shooting nonparty "helots" by the score ever since.

Voroshilov himself, and as a result Stalin was forced to stay his hand.

Shortly thereafter Stalin suffered also a grievous personal loss. On November 9, after a party in Voroshilov's home, at which she had voiced loud indignation about the famine and growing terror, his wife, Nadyezhda S. Alleluyeva, to whom he seems to have been devoted, passed away under mysterious circumstances, allegedly from a delayed appendectomy, in all probability a suicide.

And now, on the first and possibly only occasion in his career, Stalin faltered. Victor Serge has described the scene.

It was about this time that [Stalin] rose one day in the Politbureau to tender his resignation. . . . "Maybe I have indeed become an obstacle to the Party's unity," he said. "If so, comrades, I am prepared to efface myself. . . ." The members of the Politbureau . . . glanced at one another in embarrassment. Which of them would take it upon himself to answer: "Yes, old man, that's right. You ought to leave. There is nothing better for you to do." Which one? The man who would have said such a thing without being backed up by the others would have risked a lot. Nobody stirred. At last Molotov said: "Stop it! Stop it! You have the Party's confidence!" The incident was closed.[10]

Nevertheless, the facts were there for all to see. For the first time in his career Stalin had brought what he viewed as a crucial issue to a vote and had lost. In the Politbureau itself only one man, Lazar M. Kaganovich (Uglanov's successor at the head of the Moscow party organization), had supported him; the others had either opposed him or abstained. And the alternates had done no better.* But worst of all, in this, his first major defeat, the victorious opposition had been led throughout by the scourge of all former oppositions, Left and Right alike, his closest confidant, the No. 2 man in the party, whom many looked upon already as his heir, the secretary of the powerful Leningrad party organization, Kirov.

* Stalin's memorable 1936 letter to the Politbureau demanding the appointment of Yezhov to head the NKVD in Yagoda's stead, is dated September 26, i.e., four years *to a day* after the Politbureau's crucial vote on the Ryutin-Uglanov affair. "Stalin," Bertram Wolfe reminds us, "was always a great one for remembering anniversaries."[11]

It should also be noted that of the members and alternate members of the Politbureau at the time, only one—Kalinin—was to die a natural death and only four—Molotov, Kaganovich, Mikoyan and Andreyev—are still alive.

For the next two years the struggle between these two men and the philosophies they epitomized—a muted, infinitely subtle, undercover struggle of Byzantine complexity, which even today defies all but the most careful analysis—was to constitute one of the most curious, most dramatic and at the same time least-known chapters of the Stalin era.

Short, stocky, with a square, roughly hewn face that exuded energy and vitality, Serghei Mironovich Kirov was a foremost representative of that younger, homespun, soil-bound generation of Bolshevik leaders, who were for a long time to make up the backbone of the Stalinist faction within the Soviet Communist party.

After first attracting Stalin's notice in the Civil War (where as Political Commissar of the Astrakhan front, he had often found himself at loggerheads with the then all-powerful Trotsky, in itself a guarantee of favor with the future General Secretary) he had, in 1921, participated with Stalin in the reconquest of Menshevik Georgia and had thus shared in the responsibility for its bloody aftermath, which stirred even Lenin into shocked protest. Then he had headed the important Baku party organization, long a stronghold of Caucasian nationalism. In 1925 Stalin had brought him into the Central Committee and had later that year sent him to Leningrad, to take over the fief of the now disgraced Zinovyev. And there he had remained, the master's watchful warden of the north, the only one of Stalin's proconsuls to retain his post long enough to build up a personal following. Eventually his folksy manner, his organizing ability, his gifts as an orator, his open contempt for the secret police and obvious personal fearlessness—all qualities that were becoming increasingly rare among party leaders of the new school—assured him there a popularity which the brutal, cowardly Zinovyev had never known.

Yet none had been more unquestioning or enthusiastic than Kirov in backing the collectivization drive or more ruthless in pushing it, as well as Stalin's other development plans (such as the ill-famed White Sea–Baltic Canal), through in the area under his authority. By the autumn of 1933, however senseless the policy, however criminal the methods used to carry it out, the war for meat and grain and state control of the Russian peasantry had to all intents and purposes been won, the spirit of the independent farmers had been broken and the vast majority, reduced by some ten million persons or more, had been successfully herded into the 250,000 newly formed collectives. In January, finally relenting, Stalin had allowed the Red Army's granaries to be opened and their stocks distributed among the population; large contingents of grain had also been purchased on the Baltimore exchange. That spring and summer, as if tiring of the unequal struggle, rain and sun had smiled again—for the first time in three years—upon the capricious Eurasian plains. The 1933 harvest, in which hundreds of thousands of city people were made to participate (many peasants being by now too weakened by privation to work), brought in 89.9 million tons of grain, twenty million more than the preceding year, the biggest crop since the Revolution, enough to tide the nation over into 1934, and from there into the bumper-crop year of 1935, that was to mark the end of the Soviet food crisis.*

But apart from the fact that the bombastic, jovial, optimistic Kirov was the complete opposite, temperamentally, of the remote, vindictive, brooding Stalin, the former's prolonged stay in Leningrad was bound in the long run to help him first absorb and then become willy-nilly the mouthpiece of the restive mood that has at all times characterized Russia's proudest, most Westernized, most sophisticated and most liberal-minded city.

Thus, as far as Kirov was concerned, what with the advent of Hitler, and Japan's stepped-up inroads into Manchuria and the consequent growing threat of war, the success of collectivization should make possible a relaxation of tensions and a curb on terror, with a

* Twenty years later Nikita Khrushchev was to acknowledge that, although the peasants had been beaten, they had not actually surrendered. Thus their private plots, farmed without the benefit of tractors or other state-owned machinery, were producing out of all proportion to the huge kolkhozes. Even at the time of Stalin's death, in 1953, there was less grain per capita and less cattle, even in absolute figures, than there had been in 1928, the last year of the NEP, or in 1916, the last year of Tsarism. Only now, with the famed Seven-Year Plan, is it hoped at last to overcome the effects of the 1928-1933 holocaust.

view to achieving the maximum feasible degree of national unity—
voluntary unity, so far as possible—in the face of the revived foreign
threat. In Stalin's view, the contrary held true. Both the collectivization drive itself and its consequences on the party level (the Uglanov-
Ryutin affair and the revolt of the Stalinists) had merely confirmed
the theory he had been advancing for some time now, namely, that
with Russia's successful advancement toward Socialism, resistance
to the latter would grow apace, hence the need for ever greater
"vigilance," i.e., ever greater terror. Even the newly formed kolkhozes,
he warned, were a source of possible danger, since the farmers were
now organized and could put up a solid front against the government if they were so inclined!

Bukharin, little suspecting that he himself would before long be
counted among its more spectacular victims, had upon first hearing
of it dismissed this theory contemptuously as "idiotic illiteracy."
Kirov's reaction had necessarily to be more complex. For more than
anyone else, perhaps, he had helped sow its first seeds and had
reaped its first benefits. Moreover—and this applied also to the
old opposition—what imported in his mind above all was the defini-
tive triumph of the Communist system in Russia and as matters stood
on the morrow of collectivization, there was a definite danger that
any "loss of nerve" might lead, not so much to a liberalization of the
regime, as to its collapse altogether. On the other hand, he seems to
have realized that what Stalin's theory amounted to was a Russian
Thermidor, with the Revolution devouring its offspring and so,
gradually but consistently, he now proceeded, while verbally ex-
tolling the master's virtues, to push for a relaxation of tensions from
within, through the exploitation of his own prestige and following
in the party.

In January, 1934, the party convened in its Seventeenth Congress
—which, ironically enough, considering the fate of most of its
participants, was to enter history, at Kirov's suggestion, as the "Congress of Victors"—in order to map future policies in the light of the
completion of the First Five-Year Plan. Judging by the paeans of
praise to the "Beloved Leader," that from the first day to the last

resounded through the huge vaulted meeting hall, with Kirov the seemingly enthusiastic choirmaster ("the greatest statesman of all peoples and of all times!"), an outside observer would, doubtless, never have suspected that on many, if not most issues, not Stalin but his opponents were in fact calling the tune, that this was in many respects a Congress of the Opposition, the old and the new, over 60 per cent of whose members would within the next five years be branded as "double-crossers" (*dvurushniki*) and shot out of hand by the man whose virtues they had sung.

For 1933 had seen, thanks to Kirov's and the Central Committee's persistent prodding, a continuous trickle of repentant former Left and Right oppositionists from their respective places of imprisonment and exile back to Moscow. That this repentance was in many cases, perhaps, insincere; that it may even often have formed part of a deliberate plan, recommended from abroad by Trotsky himself, to "join" those they had not been able to "beat," is irrelevant. The upshot of this situation was, at least as far as Bukharin was concerned, that for all his showings of obeisance, he immediately assumed at the Congress a leadership in ideological and foreign policy matters that matched and often even duplicated that held by Kirov, professedly as Stalin's spokesman, in the domestic field.

For as regards the principle of collectivization and of forced industrialization, there had never been any major difference between Stalin, on the one hand, and Trotsky and Zinovyev, on the other; the difference had been essentially one of timing. Bukharin was something else. He alone had evolved in his famous "Notes of an Economist"* what amounted to an alternative program, different in every way and covering the entire field of the Communist doctrine. In-

* In the fall of 1928, i.e., just as the collectivization drive was about to get under way, Bukharin had published in *Pravda* a series of articles devoted to the country's economic situation, in which he stressed that the development of industrialization should run not counter to the development to agriculture, but apace with it. This thesis, which amounted to pleading the consumer's case against those known in Russia as the "hurrah-industrializers," was to enjoy such vitality that it is still being denounced to this day by the party leadership, even though many of Bukharin's arguments seem to have been adopted by them in practice.

deed, only his theories were worthy to have been branded a heresy, an "ism" in open conflict with the official doctrine of Stalinism.

And as a result, for all Stalin's smug claims that there was now "nothing more to prove and, it seems, no one to fight" (*sic!*), the Seventeenth Congress' final decisions reflected a spirit in curious contradiction to that which had colored Stalin's policies to date.

Before adjourning, the Congress took a decision that has given rise to much speculation. In the past, one of its last steps had invariably been to confirm Stalin in the post of General Secretary of the party. This time the procedure was changed and four, coequal Central Committee secretaries—Stalin, Kirov, Kaganovich and a newcomer, the young Andrei A. Zhdanov—were appointed instead. The Politbureau elected by the Congress was also strongly weighted in favor of the "liberal" wing. Before long, however, two of the "liberals" (Kalinin and Voroshilov) would have switched, and three others (Kirov, Kuibyshev and Ordzhonikidze) would be dead and replaced by the die-hards Mikoyan and Zhdanov. The remainder would show themselves to be no match for Stalin.

And then the "victors" of the Seventeenth Congress broke up and parted to return to their various and sundry posts throughout the land. Little must they have suspected that the next time their party convened in congress, in 1939, 1,109 of the 1,966 who had attended would be dead, some of them of a natural, if "sudden" death, others shot by the foremost "victor" of them all.

Yet even in Stalin's Russia a certain amount of spadework needed to be carried out and certain legal and organizational steps taken before an operation on the scale contemplated, such as the Great Purge, could be launched with the assurance of complete success and impunity.

The Politbureau's defection at the time of the Uglanov-Ryutin affair must have come as a rude shock to Stalin. The OGPU's attitude could hardly have done so, for from the outset the relationship between the Soviet government and its secret police had been an ambiguous one.

Conceived by its founder, "Old Bolshevik" Feliks E. Dzierzhinski, as a loyal and impersonal if ruthless arm of the party in the latter's struggle against counter-revolution, the OGPU had already in Dzierzhinski's lifetime developed into a useful means of detecting and then eliminating potential opposition *within* the party.

At first, by appointing someone from its own ranks to the OGPU's "Supreme Collegium" (both Stalin and Bukharin had held this post at one time) the Central Committee had been able to exercise some measure of control over the secret police's activities. By the time Stalin had reached the point where he could justly proclaim that *"L'Etat—c'est moi!"* however, the latter had evolved into a powerful and self-contained caste, jealous of its prerogatives and privileges, a state within Stalin's state, as feared by the ordinary Soviet citizen as it was hated and despised by the Army and potentially dangerous to the man whose ascent to supreme power it had facilitated.

For some time already there had existed within Stalin's private secretariat a so-called "Special Section," whose existence was long a secret and whose function it was to keep a discreet eye on the OGPU's handling of police and security affairs. In the spring of 1933 this "Special Section" had been enlarged, reorganized into a "Special Secret Political Division of State Security" and placed under an up-and-coming young member of Stalin's Secretariat by the name of Nikolai I. Yezhov, who was destined to give his name—the *"Yezhovshchina"*—to one of the most terrible periods in all of Russia's history. When in April, 1933, the Central Committee had appointed a special commission to carry out the purge it had decreed following the Uglanov-Ryutin affair, Stalin saw to it that both Yezhov and his deputy, Mikhail F. Shkiryatov, were named to head it.[*]

The Seventeenth Party Congress, whilst endorsing Kirov's "policy of reconciliation" in other respects, had rashly strengthened Stalin's potential powers of reprisal: the Central Control Commission (which had proved so difficult to control at the time of the Uglanov-Ryutin affair) was reshuffled and split up into two more easily manageable

---

[*] This Shkiryatov, one of the most sinister figures of Stalin's Russia, seems to have enjoyed a charmed life. For after playing a key role in all the purges of the thirties he was reassigned, after the *Yezhovshchina*, to party work, where he remained, safe and sound, until his death in January, 1954.

bodies. One of them retained the original title of "Control Commission," though with reduced powers. The other received a more discreet name: it became simply the Central Committee's "Special Sector." In fact, this was merely the legalized "Special Secret Political Division of State Security" of Stalin's personal secretariat, with largely the same personnel and strictly the same leaders: Yezhov and Shkiryatov. Duplicated at all levels of the party down to and including the district organizations, these Special Sectors were to evolve eventually into *the* instrument of Stalin's rule. In his new function Yezhov acquired also an office at OGPU headquarters in Dzierzhinski (formerly Lubyanka) Square and two personal assistants from among the senior OGPU personnel: Matvei D. Berman and Yakov N. Biel'sky, both of whom happened to be personal enemies of Yagoda. The OGPU's defenses had at last been breached.

A year later the carefully contrived apparatus that was to carry out Stalin's Great Purge was further consolidated: on February 25, 1935, Yezhov replaced Kaganovich as chairman of the revamped Control Commission, thus cumulating in his one person effective supervision, under Stalin, over the entire party and administrative machine.

Meanwhile a series of legal enactments had helped to prepare the ground. In June, 1933, the office of Chief Prosecutor of the U.S.S.R. had been set up, allegedly to supervise the "legality and regularity of the actions of the OGPU." In fact, in the hands of its second incumbent, the infamous Andrei Y. Vyshinsky, it was to develop into a highly effective instrument for laying the legal bases of the Great Purge.

Early in June, 1934, two officers of the Red Air Force defected with their plane, thus providing a long-sought-for pretext for the enactment of a new treason law, that made co-responsible for a crime not only all adult relatives of the accused, but also all those who had failed to denounce them.

In July, 1934, the OGPU was abolished and its functions transferred to one of the departments of the All-Union People's Commissariat for the Interior or NKVD. Though viewed at the time as just another sign of relaxation of the dictatorship, in line with the

other liberal policies adopted at the Seventeenth Congress, this and
related measures were to lead to a still greater concentration of
power, first in the hands of Yagoda, who had been appointed to head
the new NKVD, and then in those of his successor, Yezhov, until
the NKVD became, under Stalin, the factual ruler of Russia.

There remained one last step without which the purge could not
get under way. The Politbureau was still persisting in its refusal to
sanction the death penalty for party members solely on the strength
of their oppositionist activities. And so long as Kirov was around,
it was unlikely that it ever *would* sanction it.

On or about October 15, 1934, a tall, slender, pale and intense-
looking young man by the name of Leonid V. Nikolayev was inter-
cepted by the NKVD as he sought to force his way, armed with a
revolver and a detailed chart of the premises, into Kirov's office, in
Leningrad's famed Smol'ny Palace. He was promptly released,
revolver, chart and all, on the personal orders of the Deputy Chief
of the Leningrad NKVD, Zaporozhetz.

From November 25 to November 28 Kirov was in Moscow, attending the fall session of the party's Central Committee, which
had convened in order to enact some of the liberal reforms he and his
group had sponsored at the Seventeenth Congress at the beginning
of the year. At both the Committee's February and June sessions
Kirov had been urged to quit Leningrad and return to Moscow, to
devote himself full time to his new duties as one of the Committee's
four, coequal secretaries (alongside Stalin himself, Kaganovich and
Zhdanov), but for a long time he had balked and Stalin, not un-
naturally, had not gone out of the way to press the matter.* Now
it was again brought up and this time, surprisingly enough, Kirov
assented and it was decided that he would return to Moscow within
a week, for good.

He never did get back to Moscow, for two days later he was dead,
shot in the nape of the neck at 4:30 P.M. on December 1 by that

---

* There was at the time even a persistent rumor that Stalin had been actually
called upon to resign at a plenary meeting of the Central Committee so that
Kirov could take his place.

very same Nikolayev whom Zaporozhetz had freed six weeks earlier. And by an odd coincidence, the man whom Stalin now selected to succeed him as fourth secretary of the Central Committee was none other than his protégé, the ubiquitous Yezhov.

Within hours of Kirov's death two planes took off from Moscow's airport for Leningrad. One carried NKVD Boss Yagoda, the other Stalin himself and Yezhov, who had been assigned to supervise the investigation of the outrage. The Soviet press was presently to wax eloquent over the "Beloved Leader's" grief, as with tears streaming down his cheeks he bent over and brushed with his mustachioed lips the waxen face of his murdered "Paladin." In due course eighty cities and villages would be named after Kirov, only one less than Stalin named after himself. He was now heard to vow that he would avenge Kirov's death, not only on those directly involved, but also on those whose "political agitation" had rendered them "morally responsible" for the outrage. The time had come, at last, to exact blood for blood!

That same day—the document had obviously been prepared in advance and then held in anticipation of just such an "emergency"— the Presidium of the Central Executive Committee issued under the signature of its chairman, Mikhail I. Kalinin, and of its secretary, Stalin's old crony Avel Enukidze, the following directive:

1. Investigative organs are directed to speed up the processing of all cases relating to the preparation and commission of acts of terror.
2. The judicial organs are directed not to hold up the execution of death sentences relating to crimes in this category pending the possibility of a pardon, since the Presidium of the Central Executive Committee of the U.S.S.R. does not consider it possible to entertain appeals of this nature.
3. The organs of the NKVD are directed to execute the death sentences handed down to criminals in the above-mentioned categories immediately after such sentences have been passed.

Under this directive, which has come to be known as the "Kirov Decree" and which was quoted for the first time *in extenso* by Khrushchev in his famous speech to the Twentieth Congress, the accused needed merely to be *charged* with the *preparation* of acts of terror. It also made it impossible for the accused to demand a re-

examination of the case or to disavow a confession, even if it had
been obtained under torture. The whole process, from the time the
charges were made known to that of execution, was to take no more
than ten days!*

The same decree proclaimed the duty of denouncing even one's
closest relatives and, a further innovation in legal history, provided
for the drastic punishment of all relatives of the accused, even if
they were entirely ignorant of his actions.

Stalin's "idiotically illiterate" (to quote Bukharin's words) doctrine
of the proportionate growth of "class warfare," i.e., terror, with a
country's progress toward Socialism had provided the theoretical
basis of the police state. The Kirov Decree—an act, admits Khrushchev, without parallel in the history of law—was to provide its legal
basis.

The blame for Kirov's death had first been placed on unnamed
"White Guards," who were said to have entered the U.S.S.R. from
Poland and Rumania and within twenty-four hours 103 persons, *all*
of whom had been arrested well before Kirov's assassination, had
been seized at random in the jails of Moscow, Leningrad and Kiev
and shot, while thousands of party members were rounded up hastily
in Leningrad and elsewhere and shipped to Siberia. Only one escaped: "Besso" Lominadze, the hero of the 1930 cabal against Stalin,
who shot himself as he was being brought before Yezhov for interrogation.

Then it was announced that the assassin Nikolayev had received
five thousand rubles for the deed from one of the foreign consuls in
Leningrad.† By the middle of the month, however, responsibility for
Kirov's death had been shifted to Zinovyev and the "Left" and on
December 23, he, Kamenev and their sympathizers were once again
arrested, this time for good.

Five days later, on December 28, the actual assassin, Nikolayev, as

---

* Characteristically, far from entrenching him in Stalin's favor, his participation in this judicial outrage merely sealed Enukidze's doom. Expelled from
the party in the spring of 1937, he was shot a few months later.

† Later identified as Latvian Consul Bissenek, who was eventually recalled,
without him or his government being, apparently, any the worse for the incredible accusation.

well as thirteen other party members—all of them former "Left" oppositionists—were tried *in camera* by a specially appointed Military Collegium of the Supreme Court of the U.S.S.R. presided over by our old acquaintance, Vassili V. Ulrich, All of them were condemned to death. The sentences were carried out, needless to say, on the spot. The proceedings have never been made public.

On January 15, 1935, Zinovyev, Kamenev and seventeen other former prominent "Leftists" were hauled in their turn before Ulrich's Military Collegium on charges of "moral responsibility" for Kirov's death, "of organizing an underground counterrevolutionary terrorist group," of "disorganizing the party leadership," etc. The proceedings of their trial have also never been made public. The outcome, however, considering the gravity of the charges, can be regarded as fairly anticlimactic. For Zinovyev was condemned to only ten years at hard labor, Kamenev to five, and the others to still lesser terms.

Shortly thereafter, ten senior officials of the Leningrad NKVD, including the sinister Zaporozhetz and his boss, Feodor D. Medved' (all of whom had been arrested on the day after the murder) were tried in their turn. Their responsibility was, admittedly, a far greater one, for they were charged with *having possessed information* about the preparation of the attempt" on Kirov's life and of *"taking no steps* for the timely exposure and prevention of the crime *although they had ample possibility to do so."* The leaders of the "Left" had been condemned merely on the strength of their alleged "moral responsibility" for the crime. The 103 "White Guard" hostages who had been shot were not even guilty of that; they had been executed for no reason at all, in a show of "demonstrative terror." The 150,000 to 200,000 deported party members had been exiled in the same manner. But here were men who had, allegedly, known about everything in advance, had done nothing about it and yet they were condemned to only two to ten years at hard labor, those admittedly mainly responsible—i.e., Medved' and Zaporozhetz—drawing the lightest sentences of all!

"To this day," Khrushchev explained to the Twentieth Congress, "the circumstances surrounding Kirov's murder hide many things that are inexplicable and mysterious and that require the most careful examination" and he went on to insist that "Nikolayev was assisted by someone from among the people, whose duty it was to protect the person of Kirov."[12] Whether this implies a direct accusation of Stalin may still be argued. Indeed, it is possible that Nikolayev was not just an obedient tool, but that he was actuated by personal motives, both private and political. It cannot be totally excluded that his was an expression of genuine revolt on the part of the younger generation in the party against the systematic betrayal of the latter's most cherished ideals by the present leadership, with which Kirov was naturally identified. The point, however, is that Kirov's death was a providential stroke of good fortune as far as Stalin was concerned. And Yezhov was not one to hesitate to give "good fortune" a helping hand if need be. And then, curiously enough, *none* of those who were in *any capacity* involved in the Kirov affair were to survive Stalin.

Already on the day following the murder, as Kirov's bodyguard, a Chekist by the name of Borissov, was being brought for interrogation to the Smol'ny, where Yezhov's investigating team operated, the car in which he and his Yezhov-appointed escort were driving was "hit by a truck." There was, needless to say, only one victim—Borissov.

By the end of the year the feeling that something very strange indeed was taking place in Leningrad had become so general that Valerian V. Kuibyshev, one of the top men in the Politbureau, demanded and obtained the appointment of a special investigating commission of the Central Committee to supervise the NKVD's own investigation. But this commission was stillborn, for on January 25, 1935, barely a month later, Kuibyshev himself was dead, stricken at his desk by a blood clot. Or so it was claimed at the time.

Kirov's actual assassin, Nikolayev, remains a shadowy figure to this day. There are indications that Kirov had been courting his wife; that he was himself, in fact, a protégé of Kirov's. His being allowed access to the sacred premises of the Smol'ny on two successive occasions, and armed at that, would seem to indicate that he was himself associated with the NKVD.

At his own trial, in March, 1938, each time that Yagoda sought to go into the pertinent details of the Kirov Affair—which was, after all, one of the charges for which he was standing trial—he was promptly cut short by Vyshinsky or Ulrich. The defendants and their court-appointed lawyers were, needless to say, not so tactless as to inquire into the findings of the three trials that had immediately followed Kirov's murder; neither were any of the defendants in those three trials heard, since they were by now all conveniently dead. "We can assume," Khrushchev admits candidly, "that [the NKVD officials] were shot in order to cover up the traces of the organizers of Kirov's murder."[13]

Kirov's death was to be the only *proven* crime in the whole fantastic structure of wrecking, sabotage, espionage, wholesale poison, etc., which the purge trials of the thirties were designed to expose and the Great Purge to punish. "The years of terrorist preparation," the wily Radek was to recall at his own trial, with "scores of wandering terrorist groups waiting for a chance to assassinate *some* leader of the Party. . . ."[14] And the result? This one lonely crime, for which at each of the show trials, says Trotsky, "different persons, by different means and for different political objectives, claimed the responsibility. . . ."[15] The victim? The one party leader whom the all-seeing NKVD had somehow failed to protect, who was at the same time the one man who, at this stage, could still have made the Great Purge impossible.

9

THE PLOT

Stalin's Great Purge* was so thorough, it struck at so many divers elements that were either only loosely connected or else not connected at all, that it is nowadays, on the basis of published information, still not very easy to re-establish in all its details the intricate pattern of opposition against him or even to determine precisely how the military plot fitted into this over-all pattern. Much, therefore, must remain the object of somewhat arbitrary deduction and surmise.[1]

Thus at the three great purge trials of 1936-1938 the prosecution was to spare no effort in order to picture it all as a closely knit, interlocking operation which, masterminded from abroad by Trotsky and financed first by the capitalists and then the Fascists, covered virtually the whole gamut of the various opposition groups, from Zinovyev on the Left to Bukharin on the Right, with the military playing the role of obedient handmaiden. And because of the very nature of the trials and the countless obvious inconsistencies in the evidence adduced, there has been a natural temptation not only to disbelieve this theory, but to deny the existence of an anti-Stalin conspiracy altogether.

And yet as Trevor-Roper so rightly points out: "It is in the order

* Though the Russian word "*chistka*" means literally to "clean out" or "mop up," the word "purge" has by now become the accepted term for this type of operation.

of things in the atmosphere of a police-state, that what starts as a mere heresy should eventually hatch into plot and conspiracy"[2] and that the phantom conspiracy that haunted Stalin should, as the purge progressed, begin to assume flesh and blood.

On the other hand, it should be borne in mind that the various political oppositions to Stalin were united only in their hatred and fear of the man; aside from that, there existed at all times a considerable margin of difference between the extremes to which, for instance, Trotsky or Zinovyev and the Left were willing to go to achieve the Red dictator's downfall and those which Bukharin and the Right were prepared to contemplate. Moreover, as is often the fate of underground oppositions, both wings—the Right and the Left—were obliged to pick up allies on the way with whom normally they could be expected to have little in common: the restless or ambitious generals, the disillusioned nationalists, the intrigue-prone policemen whose heads had been turned by the exercise of arbitrary power. The Left Opposition itself was torn with dissent, with Trotsky—all Prosecutor Vyshinsky's claims to the contrary—steadfastly refusing to have anything to do with the Zinovyev group, which he viewed as hopelessly discredited by their cringing opportunism and repeated capitulations to Stalin. And the approach of the politicians—Right or Left—differed, in turn, considerably from that of the military. For perhaps more than anything else, the anti-Stalin opposition within the party was inhibited by the fear that, however frightening the course his rule was taking, there was the danger of something worse still, namely the overthrow of Communism altogether. Thus the politicians seem to have been consistently wary of the potential Bonapartist threat any participation of the Army in a plot would inevitably entail. Trotsky is alleged to have maintained that Tukhachevsky might not even allow him to return to Moscow! As for Bukharin, his misgivings on the subject seem to have lasted well into the winter of 1936. Since the defeat of his group in 1929 he had staged a sensational comeback. He was now once again the most listened-to theoretician in the party. The 1934 "Congress of Victors" had been up to a point *his* congress, as much as Kirov's or Stalin's, and though his present position as editor in

chief of *Izvestya* was a relatively minor one, in fact his prestige had
rarely been higher. With a little patience he could hope to bring
about a "changing of the guard" by constitutional means, through a
vote of the Central Committee—something which to him, as a true
Bolshevik, was bound to seem infinitely preferable to a military
coup d'état. It is only after the proceedings of the first show trial
(August, 1936), and Stalin's tactics at the fall session of the Central
Committee (about which more will be heard presently) had made it
clear that the chase was on and that he and his friends had been
singled out as the next victims, that Bukharin too seems to have reluctantly resigned himself to a Red Army coup.

And this complex relationship between the various opposition
groups was, needless to say, bound to affect their tactics, no less than
Stalin's reactions thereto.

Actually, the mastermind behind the anti-Stalin conspiracy in the
Red Army in its early stages seems to have been, curiously enough,
not Tukhachevsky the soldier, but Gamarnik the Political Commissar.

Jan Borisovich Gamarnik had been appointed to the key post of
head of the Main Political Administration of the Soviet armed forces
in 1931, after having held top party positions, first in eastern Siberia,
(whence his particular interest and many contacts in that area) and
later in Byelorussia. A member of the Central Committee since
Lenin's days and head of its military and Far Eastern sections, in
which capacity he was also in charge of all Soviet intelligence
activities in that part of the world, he was considered a loyal Stalinist, devoid of personal political ambitions.

But Gamarnik was also, acknowledgedly, an idealist and a man of
integrity and as such he must have found it increasingly difficult to
bow without protest before Stalin's waxing tyranny. Moreover,
thanks to the all-pervasive intelligence network with which, on
Stalin's personal orders, he had blanketed the Soviet armed forces,
he was, more than anyone except perhaps Yagoda, aware of the
disastrous effect the war against the kulaks was having upon the
morale of the troops.

There are indications that at first he tried to open Stalin's eyes to the realities of the situation. But Stalin would not be swayed. And so presently Gamarnik reverted to other methods.

Stalin's relationship with the Red Army had long been an equivocal one. For the Army had been not his creation, but that of his archenemy Trotsky. Indeed, throughout the crisis years of Civil War and foreign intervention Stalin himself had been just one of the many political commissars who, like the *Représentants en Mission* of the French National Convention, had been appointed by the government to second and watch over the loyalty of the military commanders, and to exercise civilian authority in the rear. Even so, his role had been often a highly controversial one.

The Red Army had stayed aloof from the struggle for Lenin's succession, partly because, compared to the party, it represented in those days still a relatively unimportant element in the precarious balance of power of Soviet internal politics, partly because, during the post-Civil War debate on military organization and doctrine, Stalin had stood invariably by those who, like Tukhachevsky, championed a new, revolutionary approach, as opposed to the more tradition-bound concepts of the ex-Tsarist "mil-experts," whom Trotsky favored. And then there were two other factors which must have accounted for the Army's benevolent neutrality.

In the first place, Stalin himself was still a fairly obscure and shadowy figure at the time, so obscure that at first even Trotsky hadn't bothered to polemicize with him, who maneuvered, moreover, invariably with infinite caution and in association with other, better-known or more popular leaders and who, finally, epitomized the middle-of-the-road, "national" trend within the party, as opposed to the "internationalism" of Trotsky and his friends. Also one of the avowed purposes of Stalin's Five-Year Plans had been, after all, the strengthening of the country's war-economic potential and this, however high the cost, his policies had undeniably achieved, so that, as in the case of Hitler and *his* generals, there had seemed to exist, at least in the beginning, a definite community of interests between Stalin, his faction and the military.

Indeed, by 1936 the Soviet armed forces (not counting the troops

of the NKVD) numbered already some 1.3 million men, while the
military budget, which in 1922-1923 amounted to only 244 *million*
rubles, had risen to 14.8 *billion.*

Actually the very policies and methods that had made all this possible had at the same time sown the seeds of a discontent which was
eventually to turn into open rebellion. For the young recruits who,
starting in 1928, had begun to arrive at the depots and training
camps from their villages, still seethed with rage and indignation at
the memory of the scenes they had left behind: the deserted home-
steads; the burned crops; the slaughtered cattle; the victims of
NKVD reprisals strung up on trees and telegraph poles; the trainload after trainload of ragged, hungry, desperate peasant families—
their families—being shipped under armed guard to the slave-labor
camps of Siberia and the Arctic. And their anger soon communicated itself to their commanders (themselves often of peasant stock)
and eventually even to the political commissars.

Nevertheless, until the early thirties Stalin may well have hoped
that through the pampering and encouragement of the commanders,
the systematic infiltration of every unit with agents of Gamarnik's
Main Political Administration and with those of the NKVD's ill-
famed "Special Sections" and, more important still, through the
parallel build-up of an autonomous, self-sufficient, 250,000-man-
strong army of the NKVD, he had not only contributed to the establishment of a powerful, grateful and hence perhaps even loyal
Army, but that he had also the means to enforce this loyalty, were
it ever to come into question.

Since February, 1932, there had existed in eastern Siberia a
mysterious military formation which, although ostensibly a part of
General Blücher's "Special Red Banner Far Eastern Army," was, in
fact, responsible personally to Gamarnik. This "Special Corps" (as
it was referred to in military nomenclature), about which virtually
nothing is known outside of Russia to this day, had been set up at
Gamarnik's own suggestion, supposedly for the purpose of making
the Soviet Far Eastern forces self-supporting in terms of food and
fodder in the event of war.

For the vast logistic demands of modern warfare were expected to pose insoluble problems before the already overtaxed Siberian communications network. If war were to come again to the U.S.S.R. —and Japan was already preparing to invade the Chinese mainland— Blücher's forces would have to face the classical choice between guns and butter. The then still single-spurred Trans-Siberian railway could not carry sufficient amounts of both. It was thus essential to build up on the spot a solid supply base, which only large-scale, intensive farming methods were capable of ensuring. On the other hand, collectivization of the predominantly kulak-owned Siberian farmsteads having been banned outright by Blücher, the situation seemed well-nigh insoluble. It was then that Gamarnik came up with his suggestion, which was to institute a special formation of soldier-farmers, recruited primarily from the already overpopulated rural provinces of central Russia, staffed by expert agronomists-in-uniform and equipped with the latest farm implements and machines. Upon the completion of their regular term of military service, these men would be resettled together with their families in large farm communes, a cross between Stalin's kolkhozes and Tsar Alexander I's "Military Settlements," where they would continue to lead a semifarmer's semisoldier's existence, for which they would be provided with incentives, such as would be offered kolkhoz farmers in European Russia only many years later, i.e., a house of their own, a private plot of land, a cow, some poultry, tax exemption for ten years, reduced production quotas, etc.

Gamarnik had little difficulty in winning Blücher over to his scheme and the Politbureau's agreement followed. Moreover, since his duties brought him to Siberia several times a year, he was able personally to supervise the growth and expansion of the project. By 1936, the "Kolkhoz Corps" (as it was known to initiates) numbered some sixty thousand men, plus fifty thousand reservists who had already been resettled in farm communes in the area. Grouped in three divisions and one independent regiment, with the appropriate auxiliary services, it was headed from its inception by Corps Commander Mikhail V. Kalmykov.

Whether Gamarnik intended from the first that the "Kolkhoz

Corps" should serve as the spearhead of the anti-Stalin movement in the Red Army or whether this idea came to him only later is still debatable. In any event, he had for some time now been in close touch with one whose participation must necessarily have been regarded as crucial for the success of the venture, i.e., his colleague, First Assistant Defense Commissar, Marshal Tukhachevsky.

The scion of an old but impoverished aristocratic family that descended, reputedly, from Count Henri de Mons, grandson of Baudouin VIII, Count of Flanders; half Italian by his mother, Mikhail N. Tukhachevsky had begun his military career in one of the crack regiments of the Tsar, the Semyonovsky Foot Guards. Captured early in 1915, he had succeeded finally, after four vain attempts, in making his way out of famous Camp IX, near Ingolstadt, the Colditz of World War I, a supposedly impregnable compound reserved for incorrigible escapees (and where one of his fellow captives happened to be a young French captain by the name of Charles de Gaulle), only to find upon reaching St. Petersburg that Tsarist Russia was no more, that the Bolsheviki had just seized power and that the war was over.

He had returned to Russia stone-broke, in a tattered uniform and down-at-heel soldier's boots, a pale, haggard young man with almost no past and even fewer prospects of a future. Yet two years later he was a general officer commanding an Army group, the scourge of Czechs and Whites alike, one of the outstanding leaders of the young Red Army and the one judged best qualified to lead the Red hordes on their hoped-for conquest of Europe.

Actually, to those few persons who were privileged to know him, for he was a somewhat aloof, unsociable man, Tukhachevsky's meteoric rise in the ranks of the Revolution had not been a complete surprise. For although his background seemed to identify him far more with the old regime than with the new, he was, in fact, a typical product of revolutionary chaos, a twentieth-century version of Verkhovensky in Dostoyevsky's *The Possessed*, to whom Bolshevism appealed not so much on account of its professed ideals of social justice, as because it also promised to turn society inside out and to divert Russia from the hated, despised, "decadent" West back to her vocation as a great Eurasian empire, the greatest history has known. These were the days when the poet Aleksander Blok was penning his extraordinary *The Scythians,* when artists, writers and philosophers of the "Eurasian" school were vying with one another in rediscovering Russia's Oriental past and traditions. Indeed, Bolshevism's very cruelty and initial destructiveness were to the young guardsman so many additional points in its favor, inasmuch as they might help dig an insurmountable chasm between the Russian people and those Western values of tolerance, measure and harmony, to which in the past the best sons of Russia had always looked for guidance, but which were all equally abhorrent to Tukhachevsky's restless, intolerant, pagan spirit.

In his prison compound he had been wont to rave against St. Vladimir, who had in the tenth century converted Russia to Christianity, and one day he had even been observed sculpting a rough wooden effigy of Perun, the Slavic god of thunder, war and violence, whose idols St. Vladimir had ordered hurled into the river Dnyeper. Now, in Lenin's Bolshevism he chose to see the ancient deity's revenge over its foes, and in Lenin himself the harsh but single-minded despot such as alone could successfully rule over and be respected by a people of barbarians like the Russians.

And then, although he had always despised material wealth, Tukhachevsky was consumed by ambition. To his fellow prisoners in Camp IX he had once admitted: "War is everything to me! At thirty I will either be a general or I will be dead!"[3] His escape had come too late for him to win recognition, power and glory in the ranks of the Army of the Tsar. But the Civil War was now under way. He could, of course, have joined the White Army, as Skoblin had done. But those who had started the struggle against Communism were fighting after all for, among other things, those very Western values he most abhorred. Then too, by now he probably agreed with Napoleon: Europe was a rabbit warren—Napoleon had actually used the word "molehill"—in all truth, great empires and great revolutions could be made only in the East. That was also where Russia's future lay. And so he made his choice.

Joining the Communist party, he was first assigned to staff duties, in the Red Army's department of recruitment and training. In May, 1918, he was sent to the front, to command the 1st Army against the Czechs, who had thrown off Communist rule in the upper Volga area. Hurling them back across the river, he shortly thereafter recaptured Simbirsk from the ex-Tsarist Colonel A. N. Muravyov, the colorful first Supreme Commander of the Red Army, who had recently defected to Savinkov's SR's. Presently Muravyov himself was lured into a trap and executed.

In the spring of 1919 Tukhachevsky at the head of the 5th Red Army forced the Urals and routed the White forces of Admiral Kolchak, that had advanced as far westward as Kazan. A year later his Army Group had crushed Denikin's Southern White Army and driven it into the sea. Late in April, 1920, the Poles invaded the Ukraine and Tukhachevsky was appointed Commander in Chief of all Soviet forces on the Western front. He was twenty-seven years old. His dream had come true.

The Polish war started disastrously: General Josip Pilsudski's forces fanned out over the western Ukraine and captured Kiev. But presently the Red Army recovered and early in July launched an all-out counteroffensive which within a matter of weeks brought it before the very walls of Warsaw—the first leg on the road to the Communist conquest of Europe. Indeed, it would probably have captured that city but for the insubordination of yet another ex-Tsarist officer, Colonel Aleksander I. Yegorov, who commanded the Soviet forces on Tukhachevsky's left flank and who, encouraged by his political commissar, the then still little-known Stalin, decided, rather than back Tukhachevsky's spectacular drive on Warsaw, to reap some laurels on his own. Instead of marching northwestward and joining up with the main Red forces outside the Polish capital, he moved due west, on L'vov, and War Commissar Trotsky, backed by Lenin himself, had to threaten Yegorov and Stalin with a summary court-martial before they condescended, reluctantly, to swing around to Tukhachevsky's support. But by then it was too late. Advised by French General Maxime Weygand, Pilsudski had struck at Tukhachevsky's overextended and now exposed left flank. There followed the "Miracle on the Vistula"—Lord d'Abernon's "eighteenth decisive battle of the world"—the Red forces reeled back and presently they were in headlong flight all along the front. They were never to recover.

Tukhachevsky's own reputation emerged unimpaired from this experience. If anything it was enhanced. He was by now the acknowledged child prodigy, the *Wunderkind*, of the Red Army. Thereafter, whenever the Soviet regime seemed particularly threatened, "Misha" would be the one invariably sent to redress the situation: in March, 1921, against mutinous Kronstadt; against Ataman Antonov's peasants later in the spring. And invariably he would display the same outstanding qualities of daring, presence of mind and leadership, but also driving ambition and ruthlessness.

Trotsky's downfall (January, 1925) affected his career not at all for he had often clashed with the willful War Commissar. Moreover, his avowed hostility to the "decadent West," which stood in such marked contrast with the complex love-hate attitude of so many Old Bolsheviks toward the Western world, his chauvinism, his typically Russian distrust of England, his pragmatism and contempt for ideologues, theoreticians and other "chatterboxes" (as he called them), his eagerness to absorb all that was technically new and unorthodox, all of this was bound to create between him and the man who presided now over Russia's destinies a bond if not of sympathy, then at least of understanding. Besides, Tukhachevsky was an aristocrat and openly anti-Semitic and that too was all right as far as Stalin was concerned.

In 1931 he was appointed to the Defense Commissariat as first assistant to Voroshilov. In this new capacity Tukhachevsky was responsible for the modernization and mechanization of the largely horse-drawn and foot-worn Red Army. A violent opponent, in the past, of the idea of a regular army, he now, under the German General Von Seeckt's influence, swung over to the concept of a professional force along Prussian lines. And within little more than five years, he had welded the armed rabble that was the Soviet Army of the twenties into a highly efficient, disciplined, centralized, technologically up-to-date and in some respects, indeed, avant-garde

fighting force, wedded to a dynamic and imaginative military doctrine that drew much of its *élan* from the timely revival of the best
traditions of the old Imperial Army.

For its part the Red officers' corps, which on the morrow of the
Civil War had consisted of an odd, mutually suspicious and often
mutually antagonistic medley of sophisticated ex-Tsarist officers and
uncouth, poorly educated, though often highly talented "Red Commanders" up from the ranks, had been made into a homogeneous,
highly trained caste of professional military leaders, proud of their
traditions, old and new, confident of their future, animated by a
strong *esprit de corps*, slightly contemptuous of the party bureau-
crats from whom they were expected to take orders and openly
hostile to the political commissars appointed to watch over their
loyalty.

By the mid-thirties Tukhachevsky's star had entered into its zenith.
The acknowledged No. 2 man in the Red Army, he had become the
prestigeful leader of a whole pleiad of brilliant disciples, loyal to
him personally and devoted to his teachings. On September 22,
1935, he was elevated, together with Voroshilov, Budyonny, Blücher
and Yegorov, to the rank of Marshal of the Soviet Union. He had
arrived! Abroad, many, too many perhaps, spoke of him already as
the "Russian Bonaparte."

And yet at first glance there seemed little cause, on his part, for
discontent with the Soviet regime. Proud, arrogant, snobbish even,
he had never suffered from the Russian aristocrat's traditional guilt
complex and need for atonement vis-à-vis the "Insulted and Injured."
"The reign of justice," he used to assure his fellow captives of Camp
IX, "is not for me!"[4] If the building up of Russia's war-economic
potential required a heavy toll in terms of human life and suffering,
well, that was surely a fair price considering the results. For the same
reason he was, perhaps longer than many of his future fellow conspirators, tolerant of the steadily growing concentration of power
in Stalin's hands, just as he was openly in sympathy with the latter's
ever increasing chauvinism. Hadn't the greatest moments in Russia's
history coincided with periods of autocratic rule?

But even in the exploitation of human suffering there comes a point of diminishing returns. The Red Army of the mid-thirties was an incomparably better-trained and better-equipped force than its predecessor of five to ten years previously. From the point of view of morale, however, it had hit rock bottom. For the former it had Stalin's Five-Year Plans to thank, for the latter the absurdly precipitate and criminally ruthless manner in which they had been carried out. But there was also something else. Stalin's rule was now clearly undergoing the evolution which Lord Acton predicted in the case of any absolute power: it was corrupting itself absolutely and degenerating rapidly into a despotism, an Oriental satrapy, which threatened to grind underfoot even such hitherto loyal and habitually insensitive secondary luminaries as Tukhachevsky himself, until even they would be pushed to the wall of sedition. And in this regard the continuing presence, fifteen years after the end of the Civil War, of the political commissars (even though these were being more and more edged out of the picture by the new officer caste) and of the much more feared "Special Sections" of the NKVD, acted as a vexing reminder of the master's never-resting suspicions.

And finally there was the issue of foreign policy. It is possible that for all his open Germanophobia Tukhachevsky and his friends shared some of the illusions of their German colleagues, that they too may have believed that it lay in the best interests of the two countries and in their power to revive and perpetuate their traditional association, if necessary over the heads of the politicians or even against them.*

It is this complex of beliefs and emotions which seem to have provided the background for Tukhachevsky's accession to the anti-Stalin conspiracy. When exactly he joined it and who recruited him is not yet known. Perhaps Gamarnik . . . Perhaps Assistant Commissar of Heavy Industry Pyatakov or else Assistant Foreign Commissar Krestinsky some time early in 1934—at least that is what Krestinsky was to claim at his own trial in March, 1938! His progress

---

* Already after Hitler's advent to power, late in October, 1933, Tukhachevsky had gone out of his way, in a long talk with the Councilor of the German Embassy in Moscow, Herr Von Tvardowsky, to make it clear that "despite the lamentable political developments," the Red Army's feelings toward the Reichswehr remained unchanged.[5]

from discontent to active opposition was admittedly slow, slower perhaps than that of many of his companions. But once he had made up his mind, he seems never to have faltered.

Under Tukhachevsky's influence the conspirators' plans seem to have undergone many changes. Thus, as far as the military were concerned, it must have been obvious from the start that Stalin's overthrow could best be achieved by means of a lightning palace coup within the Kremlin, carried out by picked troops—Gamarnik, in particular, seems to have counted on the elite "Proletarian" Division of the Moscow garrison—before the NKVD forces had time to rally.*

Kirov's assassination caught the military plotters unawares. Among the first to be arrested was Corps Commander Valentin M. Primakov, Chief of Staff of the Kiev Military District, who seems to have been one of the earliest and most tireless members of the conspiracy. He was held for several weeks, questioned at length by the NKVD and finally released.

That spring of 1935 Stalin carried out a purge of his own body-guard. Two men were shot, the others, some forty Chekists in all, were sentenced to various terms of imprisonment. The episode was never made public. Shortly thereafter Zinovyev and Kamenev were again brought to trial, this time in complete secrecy, and as a result Kamenev's original five-year sentence was increased to ten. At the same time Stalin ordered certain troop dispositions taken, which indicated that he had his eye on the Army too. Thus the Second

---

* There is evidence from two different sources that at one point the coup was planned to coincide with the Seventeenth "Congress of Victors," when most of the party leaders were expected to assemble in Moscow and the regime could thus be felled at one clean sweep. Shortly before the Congress opened, however, two unexpected developments occurred, which prompted the plotters to post-pone operations: Politbureau member Kossior's brother Vladimir was condemned to ten years at hard labor for "economic sabotage" and the wife of his colleague, alternate Politbureau member Postyshev, a fellow Ukrainian, likewise got into trouble with the OGPU. Both Kossior and Postyshev had been regarded until then as die-hard Stalinists. Indeed, Kossior was in those days one of the most powerful men of the regime. Both of them had been marked out for elimination. Now, however, it was judged possible, on the contrary, to woo them over to the plot.

The weakness of this thesis is that in part, at least, it was also advanced by the prosecution at Bukharin's trial, in March, 1938.

"Triandafilov" Army Corps, upon which the plotters placed much reliance, was detached from the Moscow Military District and put under the orders of the still loyal G.O.C., Western Military District, Army Commander First Grade Yeronim P. Uborevich; the Moscow Armored Division, hitherto at the disposal of the Defense Commissariat, i.e., of Tukhachevsky, was placed under Yagoda, who in his turn lost control over the Kremlin garrison, which was taken over by Stalin's personal secretariat.

The success of a palace coup was no longer a foregone conclusion Were it to fail, a regular civil war, however brief, might be unavoidable and in that case it was imperative that the plotters should dispose of a well-equipped and well-organized insurrectional base. Siberia, huge in area (one-sixth of the whole of the U.S.S.R.), of difficult access (there were only some fifty thousand troops in the Urals area and western Siberia), strongly garrisoned (Blücher's forces numbered by now some 300,000 men and 1,500 planes), economically virtually self-sufficient, was clearly an ideal choice. Even assuming that Marshal Blücher denied the rising his personal support (which was considered unlikely), a sufficiently large number of sympathizers had infiltrated his command to take over. The "Kolkhoz Corps" could in that case serve as a first nucleus, around which the other units of Blücher's Army would then rally.

Some time in 1935 a sort of insurrectional junta was set up in Khabarovsk, the principal military and administrative center in eastern Siberia. It included some of the top civilian officials and Army commanders of the area.* Then, fearful that in the event of a failure in Moscow, a single outbreak in far-off Siberia might leave

---

* Such as Feodor M. Krutov, the tall, bewhiskered, intelligent and authoritarian Territorial Party Secretary; Corps Commander Mikhail V. Sangursky, Blücher's diminutive but brilliant Chief of Staff; his Chief of Intelligence, the Armenian-born Colonel Ter-Taïrov, whose exploits had earned him the nickname of the "Soviet Lawrence"; his Quartermaster General, Corps Commander Dzuza (who acted as liaison between the Army and Krutov) and, of course, Corps Commander Kalmykov of the "Kolkhoz Corps." All of these men had, curiously enough, two things in common: all of them had, contrary to current Stalin practice, held their present positions for many years; they thus formed a sort of clique, the "Siberians" or "Khabarovites." And all of them—with the exception of Kalmykov—were men with an obscure, or at least little known background, with which Marshal Blücher alone seemed to be acquainted.

Stalin too much room and time for a recovery; fearful also lest the mass of the people, intimidated by the local authorities, might prefer to sit things out and even offer the plotters opposition for fear of the consequences of failure, it was decided to broaden the base of the operation by setting up so-called "insurrectional islands," whose purpose it would be to disrupt the so-called "mechanical inertia of power."

By the end of 1935 the plotters had secured the complicity of five key men: Primakov's chief, Army Commander First Grade Yona E. Yakir, G.O.C. Kiev Military District; his friend and colleague Uborevich, G.O.C. Western Military District; Army Commander Second Grade Aleksander I. Kork, head of the famed Frunze Military Academy in Moscow; and Corps Commanders Boris M. Feldmann, head of the Red Army's Bureau of Personnel, and Robert P. Eidemann, head of *Ossoaviachim,* the giant Soviet Civil Defense League.* They seem also to have made contact with certain top local party leaders, such as Regional Secretaries Ivan Rumyantzov (Smolensk), Mikhailov (Kalinin) and Sedel'nikov (Tula). Presently Gamarnik made another prize recruit: Central Committee member Boris P. Sheboldayev, top party leader in the northern Caucasus and an outstanding representative of the younger generation of so-called "responsible party officials,"† while Tukhachevsky contacted Valerian M. Mezhlauk, head of the State Planning Board.

At the third purge trial, in March, 1938, the prosecution sought tirelessly to obtain from the defendants an admission that the generals were planning in the event of war to "open up the front to the enemy." Though this was done clearly with the intention of discrediting the plotters in the eyes of the nation, there is good reason to believe that, while there was no question of "opening up the front" in the actual sense of the word, the plotters did not discount the possibility of taking advantage of a conflict and of the resultant mobilization of the Red Army, in order to take over the country through a series of military coups, after which negotiations would be

---

* All of them were to be shot, together with Tukhachevsky and Putna, in June, 1937.

† Rumyantzev, Mikhailov, Sedel'nikov and Sheboldayev were all to perish in 1938 in the so-called "Purge of the *Obkoms.*"

entered into with the enemy for an immediate cease-fire, the whole operation culminating in the impeachment of Stalin and his closest collaborators by a special session of the Central Committee sitting as a tribunal (though some of the generals seem to have favored their being shot), which would then, exercising its constitutional powers, appoint a new, liberalized government.

To that end the plotters seem to have taken a further precaution. Since there was always a danger that the potential enemy, i.e., Germany, might take advantage of whatever disorders occurred in the Soviet Union to press her ill-famed *Drang nach Osten,* it was deemed advisable to put out feelers to the German General Staff. Early in 1936 Tukhachevsky traveled to London via Berlin. There are indications that he met with Generals Beck and Von Fritsch, respectively Chief of Staff and Commander in Chief of the Reichswehr, and that he received from them the necessary assurances, for both Rumanian Foreign Minister Titulescu and the well-known French journalist Geneviève Tabouis, who talked to him shortly thereafter, in London and in Paris, were struck by his openly pro-German pronouncements.

Actually, it is this step which was to seal the plotters' doom.

10

ENTER THE GESTAPO

One day in the winter of 1936-1937, a short, wiry, dapper-looking man with a neatly trimmed mustache and pale, shifty eyes, was ushered into the presence of SS-*Gruppenführer* Reinhard Heydrich, the dread Chief of the SD, the Nazi Security Service. For General Skoblin had for some time already been providing the Gestapo with occasional information on Russian affairs. This time, however, he claimed to have news of quite exceptional importance to impart.

A conspiracy against Stalin was afoot in the Red Army, he said. The plotters, who were reportedly headed by Assistant Defense Commissar Tukhachevsky himself, had gotten in touch with some of the White leaders; it was rumored that General Miller, the head of the ROVS, had actually met with Tukhachevsky and the latter's confidant, Putna, the Soviet Military Attaché in London, early that spring, during their stopover in Paris on their way back to Moscow from King George V's funeral (at which the Marshal had represented the Soviet Union). But more important still: they had also contacted the German High Command with a view to obtaining an assurance of the latter's support for their coup.

Heydrich was quick to grasp the possible implications of Skoblin's disclosures. What seems to have impressed him most, however, at this stage was not so much the news of a plot in the Red Army, as the allegation that the plotters were in touch with the Reichswehr without his knowledge.

190

For by now the long-standing rivalry between Army and SS was fast moving toward a climax. A showdown was ultimately inevitable. That same autumn of 1936 the Nazi party's attempt to undermine the Army's influence with Hitler had begun to assume a concerted form; a systematic smear campaign had been started with Heydrich and his chief, *Reichsführer*-SS Heinrich Himmler, as its most insidious spokesmen, to the effect that the generals were plotting the regime's downfall and the restoration of the Hohenzollern dynasty. But as yet the *Führer* seemed skeptical. Were it now possible to prove that the generals were also in touch with certain Soviet circles, that they were, in other words, not only disloyal but perhaps even traitorous, the SS would gain an immediate advantage over their foes.

And then Heydrich had also a personal stake in the matter. For at one point he too had worn the proud uniform of an ensign in the German Navy. Charged, however, with "conduct unbecoming to an officer and a gentleman," he had been made to resign his commission and leave the service. Ever since he had nurtured a well-nigh pathological feeling of hatred for the "brass" and thirsted for revenge.

Through Himmler he now solicited a personal interview with Hitler. The meeting was to mark a turning point in contemporary history. For if Himmler and Heydrich viewed Skoblin's report mainly from the point of view of their personal vendetta against the Army, Hitler was to regard it in a different, far broader context.

Had his Russian policy been primarily concerned with the elimination of Communism, Hitler might well have resolved, then and there, to back the Red Army plotters—assuming these were not a fiction of Skoblin's imagination—against Stalin. But the overthrow of Communism was *not* his main concern in Russia. It was purely a means to an end, this end being the conquest of the Slavic peoples of Eastern Europe and the colonization of their lands. Actually, the existence of a Communist Russia offered at least the advantage of providing him with the one cause, the one slogan that could stir the Reichswehr into accepting the idea of a war—that of "anti-Communism."

For even though he probably did not yet feel seriously endangered by the anti-Nazi mutterings of some of his generals, his faith in them as a caste and specifically in their willingness to lead his armies into the war he had now decided to wage in a not too distant future, was steadily waning. Indeed, he was discovering to his surprise and indignation that the General Staff, not content to be, in Trevor-Roper's words, "just a mighty instrument of policy . . . had a policy of its own."[1]

Because they had seen in Hitler a chance to gain, at last, mass support for their aims, the generals had at first endorsed his assumption of power. Because of this, too, they had been, at least in the beginning, even prepared to close their eyes to what Trevor-Roper has wittily described as the "incidental vulgarities" of the Nazi movement.[2] And during the period of consolidation of his power Hitler had, for his part, seemed willing to abide by this *modus vivendi*. But the honeymoon was bound to be short-lived. For what might have satisfied the generals had merely fed Hitler's self-confidence and whetted his appetite for greater might and glory. His first foreign policy coups, however desirable from the point of view of the average patriotic German, had all been carried out against the express advice of the military, "on a hunch," as it were. True, through what seemed like a veritable miracle, these daring and risky moves had passed off without a hitch. Nevertheless, this practice of "brinkmanship" *avant la lettre* could not succeed forever. Then, too, developments inside Germany were bringing the generals slowly to the realization that the price their country might have to pay for the restoration of her national dignity and armed might could well be considerably greater than the "incidental vulgarities" of the Nazi movement had at first led them to expect.

A first jolt had been dealt to their complacency on June 30, 1934, during the so-called "Night of the Long Knives," when two prominent members of their caste, Generals Von Schleicher and Von Bredow, were slaughtered in cold blood by Goering's thugs. Gradually, as they watched the evolution of Nazi diplomacy, it became increasingly clear to them that the policy of *rapprochement* with Poland, the new alignment with Japan, the recent intervention with

Italy in Spain, all headed away from the Von Seeckt-Bismarck school of thinking and toward an ultimate conflict with the Soviet Union. Only a few weeks earlier Hitler had shown his hand and actually disclosed his Grand Design, that which constituted his life's theme song, his very *raison d'être*, as he saw it, as creator and *Führer* of his much-vaunted "Thousand-year Reich." Speaking before the annual September rally of the Nazi party in Nürnberg, he had implied that the Ukraine, the Urals, yes, even Siberia were part and parcel of the so-called *Grossdeutsches Lebensraum!*

And war with Russia was one thing that the German generals were to oppose to the bitter end. Hitler's praised *Drang nach Osten* might appeal to semi-intellectuals like Alfred Rosenberg or to pseudo-mystics like Himmler, but to the generals, or at least to the majority of them, it appeared at best as a pipe dream, at worst as the most irresponsible kind of adventure that could end only in a catastrophe.

In this they were thinking not solely as practical men. For friendship with Russia, with *any* Russia, had been a cornerstone of Prussian policy ever since the 1813-1815 crusade against Napoleon. And the disastrous consequences for both nations of the "two-front war" of 1914-1918 had merely strengthened the hand of those who, like the head of the Reichwehr, General Von Seeckt, pressed after Versailles for a return to the *Ostrichtung* (as this pro-Russian policy was known).

The Soviet leaders—which at the time we are discussing meant Lenin—were actuated by no sentimental or traditional attachment to any particular policy; theirs were strictly practical considerations. Now that the hated Brest-Litovsk *Diktat* had been canceled out by Germany's defeat, they were perfectly willing to let bygones be and achieve a *modus vivendi* with the Berlin government, directed first of all against Poland, the common enemy, and then, if all went well, against the West. The main thing, as far as the Kremlin was concerned, was to prevent a reconciliation between the victors and vanquished of Versailles, on the premise that "when the Capitalist wolves are quarreling, the Communist sheep are safe." As Lenin himself put it with his habitual cynicism to the Eighth Congress of the Soviets in November, 1920: "I am not fond of the Germans but . . . Germany wants revenge and we want Revolution. . . . For the moment our aims are the same. . . . [Indeed] Germany's international position impells her even against her wishes to an alliance with the Soviet Union." And he added prophetically: "When our ways part . . . [they] will be our most ferocious foes!"[3]

In March, 1921, Karl Radek, the famous Red publicist and the Comintern's top German expert, arrived in Berlin in the company of Soviet Foreign Trade Commissar Leonid B. Krassin, one of Lenin's most influential associates. On his own authority but with the knowledge and apparent consent of the Weimar government, Von Seeckt and his alter ego, Lieutenant Colonel Kurt von Schleicher (the future general and chancellor, who in those days headed the Reichswehr's influential Department of Political Affairs), initiated highly secret negotiations with the two Soviet envoys. The result was a series of agreements which, complementing the 1922 Rapallo Treaty, had by 1923 already brought about the virtual neutralization of the forbidding military clauses of Versailles, as well as the end of the state of enforced isolation in which the powers of the Entente had hoped to keep both Germany and the U.S.S.R.

From then on, while the political and diplomatic aspects of German-Soviet relations remained the privilege of the Wilhelmstrasse, the far more important military-economic ties between the two countries were handled, under the general code name of "Operation Kama," by Task Force "R" (in German: *Sondergruppe R*), a top-secret section of the *Heeresleitung* (the Reichswehr's equivalent of the old Imperial General Staff, the latter having been officially disbanded under the Versailles Treaty) which Von Seeckt set up especially for this purpose.

In its turn, Task Force "R" established a dummy corporation by the name of GEFU (from the German initials for "Society for the Promotion of Manufacturing Enterprises") with an initial capital of 75 million Reichmarks and subordinated directly to the Reichswehr's Ordnance Department. Through its Moscow offices GEFU initialed in due course a series of specific agreements with the Soviet authorities, under which joint German-Soviet subsidiaries were set up in Soviet territory by certain German firms so as to produce for the benefit of both armies the tanks, aircraft, poison gas, heavy ordnance, submarines and other military equipment which had been banned under the Versailles Treaty. By 1924 the Junkers plant in the Moscow suburb of Fili was building several hundred all-metal aircraft annually. Soon 300,000 shells would be coming out every year from the rebuilt and modernized Tsarist arsenals of Leningrad, Tula and Zlatoust, while poison gas was manufactured by the GERSOL company at Trotzk and U-boats and pocket battleships were designed or launched in the dockyards of Leningrad and Niko-layev. By 1926 some 150 million Reichsmarks, close to one-third of the Reichswehr's annual budget, were going to cover arms and am-munition purchases from the U.S.S.R. *

Simultaneously with the designing and manufacture of prohibited war material the Reichswehr also undertook to establish training centers in the Soviet Union, where servicemen of both countries could study their practical use. Starting in 1922 a military mission was functioning permanently, if in great secrecy, in Moscow under the command of Germany's "Lawrence of Afghanistan," the famous Major (later Colonel) Oscar von Niedermayer. Under its supervision several joint schools were set up: for the Air Force in Lipetzk and Borisoglebsk, for the armored forces in Kazan, for the artillery in Luga, where Reichswehr instructors taught their German and Soviet pupils the art of modern warfare. Many of the generals who were later to gain fame in building up Hitler's Wehrmacht and leading it into battle were thus "broken in," as it were, in Soviet Russia. In return, quite a few of the Red Army's leaders in World War II, starting with the famous Marshal Georghi K. Zhukov, graduated from the German War College. By 1932, the peak year of German-Soviet co-operation in this particular field, some eight hundred German officers were training yearly in these joint German-Soviet military establishments.

---

* A fairly substantial part of this sum, however, would be promptly passed on to the Comintern, to pay for the campaign of subversion the German Com-munist party was engaged in against the very same Reichswehr!

As a result, even though the strict and sometimes ruthless security measures could not entirely conceal the fact, if not the exact scope, of the U.S.S.R.'s participation in Germany's secret rearmament, Germany was eventually able, not only to offset most of the military strictures of the Versailles Treaty and keep abreast of the latest military developments, but also to pioneer new weapons and techniques. Thus the late General Guderian, Hitler's top tank expert, first tried out his blitzkrieg tactics on those very same rolling plains of the Ukraine where some ten years later his Panzers were to put them to such devastating use.* In exchange, the massed use of parachutists was first demonstrated at the Red Army maneuvers of 1931 by the then Soviet Chief of the General Staff Tukhachevsky to an awed General Von Hammerstein-Equord (Von Seeckt's successor at the head of the Reichswehr), who promptly recommended it for adoption in Germany.

But this was not all. In due course, and despite the periodic political tensions between the two governments and the presumed social-ideological differences between the two officers' corps—of the 187 officers attached to the German General Staff Corps in 1938, fifty or roughly 30 per cent belonged to the nobility—a veritable caste camaraderie developed between them. It was to be described in eloquent terms by none other than Hitler's own War Minister, Fieldmarshal Werner von Blomberg, himself in the past a frequent "visitor" to the Soviet Union, in a memorable, if little-known, speech at the Soviet Embassy in Berlin in November, 1934, on the occasion of the sixteenth anniversary of the Bolshevik Revolution.

By then, political relations between the two countries were, to say the least, cool and military co-operation had come virtually to an end. Nevertheless, the German High Command attended the event in force. The hour was late and most of the guests had already departed, when Von Blomberg suddenly stood up and raising his glass, exclaimed: "We shall never forget all that the Red Army did

---

* General Guderian's reminiscences give, typically, only a passing indication of his ever having been in the Soviet Union. His appended service record does not mention it all. On page 144, however, he writes: "As far back as 1933—" when he was serving as Chief of Staff to the Inspector of Motorized Troops in the War Ministry—"I had visited a . . . Russian tank factory, etc."[4]

for us in our hour of need. I hope that despite the difficulties of the present moment, our gratitude may one day find concrete expression. I drink to the success and future of the great and glorious Red Army and to our comradeship-in-arms, today and tomorrow!"[5]

Hitler, of course, was only too well aware of this mood, just as he must doubtless have been informed about Von Blomberg's toast. He had done nothing about it at the time; he couldn't afford to; he was still far too insecure, too dependent on the Reichswehr for the consolidation of his recently acquired power. Nevertheless, his feelings can easily be guessed. For if these were the sentiments of a Von Blomberg, the most Nazi of all his generals, what could be the attitude toward his Russian plans of the other generals, the Von Hammerstein-Equords, the Von Fritsches, the Becks, whose hostility extended, he knew, over and above matters of diplomatic strategy to his own person, his domestic policies, his and his followers' ethics, to all, in fact, he and his movement stood for?

Then there was still a last argument, one which must have sounded particularly sweet in Himmler's and Heydrich's ears. For a successful overthrow of Stalin's dictatorship by the Red Army could well snowball into a general reaction against dictatorships everywhere; even the German generals might get ideas into their heads, if they did not—as the SS claimed—have them already.

All things considered, it seemed preferable to drive a wedge between Stalin and his armed forces, thus weakening considerably the U.S.S.R.'s armed might, whilst at the same time opening up a blood-filled chasm between Hitler's own generals and the Red Army's and in this manner canceling once and for all the pernicious effects of their past co-operation.

And so presently the *Führer* announced his decision: Whether or not Skoblin's report was true was immaterial. The main thing was that the latter should be made to *look* true. Stalin could be relied upon to do the rest.

Armed with this unequivocal hint, Heydrich now went to work. First he instructed one of his top trouble-shooters, SS Major Walter Schellenberg (who, in his capacity as head of the Unified German

Intelligence Service, was to play a flamboyant if episodic role in the negotiations that preceded Germany's capitulation at the close of World War II), to make a detailed study of past relations between the German and Soviet general staffs. Actually, since it is difficult to conceive how Heydrich, or at least Hitler, could have ignored the existence of Task Force "R," it seems likely that Schellenberg's assignment was really to ascertain the whereabouts of the Task Force "R" files.

It so happened that one of the few representatives of the German "brass" for whom Heydrich felt anything approximating friendship or at least respect, was the head of the Abwehr or Military Intelligence, Rear Admiral Wilhelm Canaris. As a young ensign in the Navy he had served on the cruiser *Berlin* under the then Lieutenant Commander Canaris' command and the two men had remained on fairly amicable terms ever since; besides, even though there was never much love lost between the Abwehr and the SD their professional interests brought them often together. All of which had not prevented Heydrich from having microphones installed in Canaris' office! Heydrich now decided, and rightly, that there was a good chance that the most important files were in the Abwehr's keeping.

Canaris, however, was both a shrewd man and a man of honor. He had a high regard for Heydrich's intelligence and ability but he also knew him for what he was—a ruthless opportunist of boundless ambition and few scruples, who could be expected to go to any extreme to achieve his ends. So when the latter now came to him, oozing cordiality, and inquired casually after the whereabouts of the files and then, virtually in the same breath, suggested that the Abwehr lend the SD the services of their best graphologist "for a matter of top-secret importance," the Admiral was immediately suspicious. For a while he tried to prod Heydrich into revealing more of his intentions, but beyond hinting that the *Führer* himself was behind the project, Heydrich refrained from giving any further details.

Whereupon Canaris informed him curtly that he could release no files without an explicit order from the Commander in Chief of the Army, General Freiherr von Fritsch, a known anti-Nazi.

But the Admiral was fighting against superior odds. Shortly thereafter, a series of small fires broke out unexplainably at Army headquarters in the Bendlerstrasse and the Abwehr's offices on Tirpitzufer. Their pattern was in all cases identical and they were soon put out. But when the firemen had departed, it was found that certain safes had been tampered with by obviously expert hands and that certain files were missing. And all of them related in one way or another to "Operation Kama" and Task Force "R."

Meanwhile, a complete laboratory had been installed in great secrecy in the requisitioned home of a Jewish dime-store tycoon— a luxurious villa in the suburb of Grünewald. Here Heydrich's experts went to work.

The Bendlerstrasse files turned out to be fairly disappointing. They consisted in the main of supply orders and delivery invoices. But the Abwehr documents were a different matter altogether. Here was the complete picture of German-Soviet secret co-operation, with countless reports, minutes, official and personal letters bearing the signatures of virtually all those, great and small, who at one time or another had been involved in "Operation Kama." In expert hands much good could be made of this. The job was done with German thoroughness, after which the whole file was mimeographed, the better to conceal possible signs of tampering or forgery. The results looked entirely convincing.[6]

At an early stage of the affair Heydrich had consulted the dean of German secret agents, one Jahnke, who had considerable experience in international intrigue. To his disappointment, however, Jahnke had reacted most skeptically to the whole plan. For all one knew, he had warned, Skoblin might be playing a double game; both he and his wife lived, reputedly, in a style that was hardly commensurate with her chance earnings as a concert singer and his occasional pay as a German informer. Did he happen to serve more than one master? And if so, who were the others? Was Stalin one of them?

But Heydrich was supremely confident. Actually, as often happens in such cases, his interest in the technique of his project had by now begun to outweigh the importance of its results; it had become in his hands a work of art which must not be destroyed through counsels of prudence. And to prevent Jahnke (whose ties with the German General Staff were well known) from committing an indiscretion, he ordered him placed under house arrest for three months.

Heydrich had long ago decided that Stalin would be all the more easily convinced of the file's authenticity if it were communicated to him by a non-German source, say by the French or better still the Czechs. Earlier in the game, therefore, his agents on the spot had been instructed to prepare the ground and by now their efforts were beginning to pay off.

Czechoslovakia was just then engaged in protracted negotiations with Germany on the subject of her possible attitude in the event of a Franco-German war. One day late in January, writes the late President Beneš in his *Memoires,* Count Trautmansdorff of the German Foreign Office hinted to Czech Ambassador Dr. Mastny that Germany might soon no longer be interested in the outcome of these talks, since she was now engaged in other negotiations with an anti-Soviet group within the Red Army, which, if successful, would radically change the whole balance of power in Europe. Dr. Mastny reported the matter forthwith to President Beneš, who, convinced that Count Trautmansdorff's hint was not a mere tactical maneuver, promptly relayed the information to the Soviet Ambassador in Prague, Aleksandrovsky, who flew off with it personally to Moscow.[7]

Just about the same time, Vladimir V. Potyomkin, Soviet Ambassador in Paris, was taken aside at a diplomatic reception by Premier Edouard Daladier, who informed him in the strictest confidence that the French government had it from a reliable source* that contacts had been established by the Germans with certain members of the Soviet High Command and that negotiations were in course,

* This "reliable source" could have been Skoblin. It could also have been the Deuxième Bureau's own agents. An entry for October, 1936(!), in Bela Fromm's diary *Blood and Banquets* notes that according to "Henry," of the French Embassy in Moscow, the French had got hold of a list of Soviet officers, all of them on Tukhachevsky's personal staff, who were at the time engaged in secret talks with the Germans. After dragging these on for some time, the latter had suddenly broken them off and sent a similar list, by roundabout ways, back to Stalin.[8]

aimed at overthrowing the Communist regime in Russia and concluding an agreement with Germany.

The ground having been thus duly laid, Heydrich proceeded to tackle the final stage of the project, namely the transmission of the incriminating dossier to the Soviet authorities. There is still considerable disagreement as to how this was actually done.

According to Schellenberg, a German agent in Prague contacted one of President Beneš's confidants, who let it be known that the material should be remitted to a certain member of the Soviet Embassy in Berlin, probably the INU's "resident" Izrailovich; Izrailovich thereupon flew to Moscow, from where he returned presently in the company of a special emissary of Yezhov and announced that he had the latter's personal authorization to negotiate the purchase of the documents.

Up to this point neither Hitler nor Heydrich had planned to make any money out of the deal. Heydrich now realized that it might appear highly suspicious to the Soviets were the offer to be declined. He therefore named at random the figure of three million rubles. Within twenty-four hours the transaction was completed and Yezhov's messenger was flying back to Moscow with the fateful dossier, which was to constitute the essence of Stalin's case against his generals. *

Thus, thanks to the complicity of such unexpected—and in some cases, perhaps, unwitting—bedfellows as Chancellor Hitler of Germany, President Beneš of Czechoslovakia, Premier Daladier of France and the renegade White Russian General Skoblin, Stalin had at long last most of the elements that he required in order to proceed with the final act of the drama.

---

* There is an ironic, Cicero-like footnote to the story. It appears that when, in the early days of the war in the East, German agents in the U.S.S.R. attempted to make use of the money which Heydrich had received from Yezhov for his pains, they were all of them apprehended. For the banknotes had been either marked or forged. Whereupon Schellenberg personally burned the remainder.

11

THE IDES OF JUNE—
2. THE TRUE STORY

The measures that immediately followed Kirov's assassination had
not at first affected a very large number of people. After the horrors
of collectivization the masses could hardly be expected to weep over
the fate of a Zinovyev or a Kamenev (who had themselves at one
point also championed these harsh measures) or of a few NKVD officials (who had helped carry them out). There was no feeling of a
slowdown and still less of a reversal of the general economic, social
and political recovery, which had set in with the end of the collectivization drive. The theme song was now Stalin's much-touted announcement that "Life is getting better! Life is getting merrier!"

Below the surface, however, under the threefold pretext of holding a population census, of holding an "open debate" on Soviet
democracy and of "verifying party cards" a gigantic process of
checking, double-checking, head-counting and cataloguing had
begun which was to end by outdoing all previous operations of the
kind and to lay the ground for the worst features of the Great
Purge. For the appeal to "class vigilance" led inevitably to a flood
of "unmaskings," whereby nothing more concrete was required than
vague accusations of "having an anti-Soviet attitude," "supporting
hostile elements," "loss of class vigilance," "moral decadence," "dis-

torting the party line," "deviationism," etc. Denunciations were as often as not motivated by personal vengeance or the desire of a junior official to oust his superior, take his place and thereby secure the material advantages that went with it. Sometimes the denunciations ended with the arrest of the victim; sometimes he merely lost his job; in all cases, however, an appropriate entry was made in his file, for future reference. The time to cash most of these "rain checks" would come two years later!

In the spring of 1936 Trotsky completed *The Revolution Betrayed,* one of his most telling denunciations of Stalin's dictatorship, in which Kirov's assassination was viewed as an act of "paramount symptomatic significance" that characterized "the sharp contradictions between the bureaucracy and the broad masses of the people." And he went on to say that since "the Soviet bureaucracy will not give up its positions without a fight," since "it can be removed only by a revolutionary force," the task of the opposition, even while it helped resist the U.S.S.R.'s external foes, should be to take advantage of a "favorable historic situation," i.e., of a military defeat, in order to place itself "at the head of the masses."[1] This was his "Clemenceau Statement" all over again, except that this time it was set against a background far more menacing than that which had prevailed in 1927.

For in March of 1936 Adolf Hitler had reoccupied the Rhineland. In July General Franco was to rise up in arms against the Spanish Republic. Within a matter of weeks this purely internal affair would evolve into a minor European war. Stalin seems to have chosen this particular juncture in order to seek, through Bukharin's intermediary, a "clarification" of Trotsky's stand. The negotiations are said to have taken place on Dutch soil. They were, needless to say, unsuccessful.

This, as far as Stalin was concerned, settled it. From now on, all Trotsky's active sympathizers in Russia, as well as those who, one day, might conceivably come to sympathize with him, were to be regarded as potential traitors and treated as such. And since in his *Revolution Betrayed* Trotsky had clumsily identified Stalin with all his entourage, thus completely ignoring the revolt of the Stalinists and the Kirov schism, Stalin was now able, at last, to extort from

204

the Politbureau and the June, 1936, session of the Central Committee that which he had so long sought.*

On August 19, Zinovyev, Kamenev and fourteen other prominent leaders of the Left went on trial before Judge Ulrich's Special Military Collegium of the Soviet Supreme Court. The charges included the organization in 1932—the year of the Uglanov-Ryutin affair!—of a "terroristic center" which, inspired from abroad by Trotsky, was designed to execute attempts upon the lives of the Soviet leaders, attempts that in one case, Kirov's, were successful. The most ominous innovation in the indictment, however, was that the defendants were accused not only of having evolved into counter-revolutionaries in the course of their careers, but of having always been in contact with foreign capitalists and Fascists with a view to preventing the Revolution and of overthrowing it, once it was successful. Theirs was the first of the great show trials that were soon, more than any of his other actions, to rip the mask off Stalin's tyranny. Yet overtly all the forms of trial procedure were observed. All the accused confessed. All of them were sentenced to be shot and their property was confiscated. Within twenty-four hours they were dead.

All of a sudden a wave of indignation swept the world. Even the leftist avant-garde was stirred into shocked protest. So long as the slaughterhouses and slave-labor camps of the OGPU had filled with expropriated kulaks or members of the "unreconstructed bourgeoisie," it had been possible to invoke sanctimoniously the argument of "historical necessity" and to quote Lenin's apocryphal pun about it being impossible to make an omelet without breaking a few eggs. But this was something else; this time the "Supreme Measure of Social Equity" was reaching out to the "revolutionary elite" itself. From now on the broken eggs would be those who *had made* the revolutionary omelet and who had so long epitomized it. Presently the sinister vision of the Moloch consuming its offspring would take the place of the long-praised image of a "daring" if at times, perhaps, a "little too single-minded" reformer.

* Trotsky himself was to offer another explanation for the first show trial: Having resolved to bury the hatchet with the Western Powers, Stalin was offering in sacrifice those who in the past had most symbolized the doctrine of "continuing Revolution."[2]

And now Stalin overreached himself. For in February, 1935, i.e.,
immediately after the series of trials that followed Kirov's assassination, the Seventh All-Union Congress of the Soviets had decided to
appoint a commission to draft the new constitution which the Kirov
group had been pushing for the past year. The Commission, which
was presided over by Stalin himself, included such repentant former
oppositionists as Bukharin and Radek. After a first draft had been
published throughout the country for open discussion, it had been
announced that a specially elected Extraordinary Congress of the
Soviets would convene in November, 1936, to approve the final text.
However, an extraordinary situation revealed itself. In some areas
and particularly in Moscow itself, of all places, the number of anti-
Stalin ballots cast in the elections to this Congress was as high as 30
per cent. And this after two years of incessant checks and purges,
that had already led to the expulsion of several hundred thousand
members! Stalin promptly decided that a new monstrous conspiracy
was brewing and since by this time all the most prominent figures of
the Left were already in jail, the "plotters" had necessarily to be
sought elsewhere, abroad in the person of Trotsky, and at home
among the Right.

In the course of their pretrial examination at the hands of Yagoda
and the latter's deputy Molchanov (with Yezhov watching their
every movement) Zinovyev and Kamenev had been induced to sign
fraudulent testimony implicating Bukharin, Rykov and the "Right"
in their own alleged intrigues with Trotsky. They had been made to
repeat these charges before a special session of the Politbureau, or
rather of an emasculated Politbureau (for only the die-hard Stalinists were invited to attend it), and had done so again in court at their
trial. On August 21, Vyshinsky formally demanded an investigation
of these charges. By the beginning of September Stalin must have
judged that he had the situation well enough in hand to risk taking
the case to the Central Committee.

The latter numbered since 1927 seventy-one full members and
sixty-eight alternates. Only full members could vote. The session was
held in the Kremlin. On the fourth day (the first three were probably
devoted to a discussion of the new constitution) the committee took

up the case of the Bukharin group. Politbureau member Andreyev,
who was in the chair, called upon "Central Committee Secretary
Yezhov, Chairman of the Party's Control Commission." Uralov's
description of the fateful meeting follows:

The man who had burst like a thunderstorm . . . over the U.S.S.R.
[he writes]—a little man, with the receding forehead of a degenerate, the
greedy eyes of a hyena and the hoarse voice of a consumptive—advanced
toward the speaker's podium with the short steps of a soldier.
He began by informing the assembly that since 1918 there had existed
a "monstrous conspiracy directed against the Party and the State . . ."
"From the information in our possession," he continued, "it is clear
beyond any doubt that the Bukharin group, in concert with the Trotskyites, have put themselves at the service of the Nazi intelligence, in
order to prepare for war against the U.S.S.R. It is now established that
Bukharin and Rykov like Trotsky, Zinoviev and Kamenev, are agents of
the Gestapo. . . ."
Yezhov followed up [these charges] by proposing a motion "already
adopted in its essentials by the Politbureau" demanding the expulsion of
Bukharin and Rykov and their impeachment on a charge of high treason.
. . .
Bukharin's reply was as logical as it was eloquent. Run off secretly on
a duplicator, it was [later] circulated under cover in Moscow. He said
that he agreed with Yezhov's main point, namely that there existed
in the country and within the Party "a monstrous conspiracy directed
against the Party and against the State." "But," Bukharin said, "two
persons are at the head of this conspiracy—Stalin, the General-Secretary
of the Party, and Yezhov. . . . Stalin's aim is to establish his personal
power . . . over the Party and the country. . . . That is why we are
to be eliminated. But in order to eliminate us, you have to resort to fraud,
lies and provocation. . . . You have a crowd of paid informers at your
disposal, from Karl Radek to common criminals. . . ." [Then] addressing
himself to the assembly as a whole, Bukharin emphasized that what was
being decided at the moment was not the "Bukharin question" but the fate
of the country. . . . "It is the NKVD," he concluded, "and not the
Party which today governs the country. It is the NKVD and not the
followers of Bukharin, which is preparing a *coup d'état*."
Bukharin's speech, which lasted three hours, created a profound impression, which was heightened by Rykov's speech. To dissipate their
effect, all the heavy artillery was brought into action. One after another
the "tried comrades of Lenin and Stalin" got to their feet. . . .
But undoubtedly the most important fact which emerged from this

assembly was the schism . . . in the Politbureau itself. Of its twelve members, five—Kossior, Postyshev, Chubar, Rudzutak and Eikhe*—supported Bukharin. . . .

The motion which had allegedly been "adopted in its essentials by the Politbureau" was lamentably defeated and by the same token, the supreme executive of the party had repudiated Stalin and Yezhov.

But Stalin kept his head. After congratulating the Committee for its "healthy criticism and self-criticism, worthy of true Bolsheviks" he assured it that he would "take note of its decision for future guidance."[3]

Barely three weeks later, on September 25, Stalin, who was vacationing with Kirov's successor, Zhdanov, in the Caucasus, sent his colleagues on the Politbureau in Moscow the famous telegram in which the NKVD was accused of being "four years behind" in the "unmasking of the Trotskyite-Zinovyevite bloc" and in which it was urged that Yezhov be appointed to head that agency in Yagoda's stead.

Two days later *Pravda* came out with a decree transferring Yagoda to the Commissariat of Posts and Telegraphs and naming Yezhov to replace him.

The *Yezhovschina* had begun. By the time it had ended, says Khrushchev, only fifteen of the 140 full and alternate Central Committee members who had attended the fateful session were still alive. And of these, eight were members of the ruling Politbureau.

Thus had Stalin "taken note of its decisions for his future guidance."

The fall session of the Central Committee had two immediate consequences. On the one hand, Bukharin's last hesitations must necessarily have been dispelled. As far as the "Right" was concerned, it was now a race against time. Whatever the dangers of Bonapartism, nothing could match the terror of a continuing Stalin tyranny.

As far as Stalin was concerned, the results were even more crucial.

* For some reason Uralov does not mention Ordzhonikidze, after Kirov's death the leader of the liberal faction within the Politbureau.

For in the fateful vote on his motion to oust the leaders of the
"Right" he had found, with the sole exceptions of his two old cronies,
Voroshilov and Budyonny, *all* the generals lined up against him for
the second time in one year. Already in March, a conference of senior
military leaders had unanimously voted a series of recommendations,
which he rightly interpreted as a bid for autonomy on the part of
the Red Army. Thus the latter was to be placed under a special
Government Commission made up of Army appointees, while the
Defense Council was revamped, three of its members to be nomi-
nated by the armed forces. Obviously a new coalition, much more
dangerous than anything he had as yet had to face, was beginning to
take shape that grouped not only the "Right," but most of the military and some of the top representatives of his own Stalinist faction
as well, one which even Yagoda's NKVD might not be strong enough
or willing to take care of.

By the end of the month Yagoda had been dismissed and Yezhov
appointed in his stead.

In the midst of the crisis, in November, 1936, Stalin promulgated
the new constitution in an address to the Eighth Extraordinary Congress of the Soviets which drew, in Deutscher's apt words, "a veil
over the guillotine in the background."[4] By the time the Supreme
Soviet convened in its first session, one-third of its newly elected
members would have been executed in their turn.

Sometime in December Yezhov established within the NKVD, but
under his personal command, a new top-secret group that was to go
by the name of "Administration of Special Tasks" (in Russian "*Spetz-
bureau*"). It is this group that was destined to carry out the more
"delicate" aspects of the Great Purge, such as the framing of Marshal
Tukhachevsky and his companions, the murder of former Chekist
Ignaz Reisz, the kidnaping of General Miller and the murder of
Trotsky. In this work Yezhov would be assisted by yet another
trusted member of Stalin's personal secretariat, *Pravda's* editor in
chief, Lev M. Mekhlis. The apparatus was now in place. The show
could begin.

One cannot help marveling at Stalin's acumen and luck when one
considers that he was at the time, apparently, still completely in the

dark as to the existence of the plot which some of the very generals
he had now marked out for extermination were at that precise
moment in the process of organizing.

On January 27, 1937, a second purge trial opened in the Great
Hall of Columns of the former Assembly of the Moscow Nobility,
now House of the Trade Unions. The seventeen accused, headed by
top Soviet economist Yuri L. Pyatakov ("Sergho" Ordzhonikidze's
long-time deputy in the Commissariat of Heavy Industry) were
charged with organizing, following the elimination of the Zinovyev-
Kamenev bloc, a so-called "Trotskyite Parallel Center" for the co-
ordination of all clandestine oppositionist activities within the
U.S.S.R.

The prima donna of the trial, however, was not Pyatakov but
Radek, until recently a member of the Commission for the drafting
of Stalin's new constitution and foreign editor of *Izvestya*, who was
now to be made to taste at first hand the Shakespearean quality he
himself had made fun of, thirteen years earlier, at another show
trial, that of Boris Savinkov. In turn humble and impertinent, ingratiating and arrogant, but whenever his own head was not at
stake the invariably eager stool pigeon, Radek's function at the trial
seems to have been essentially to help Prosecutor Vyshinsky pin-point
those elements which Stalin wished to have brought out in public.
And as a consequence he—for the time being—saved his life.*

The court proceedings of the morning of January 24 were showing
the usual ghoulish picture of treason, sabotage and crime on the
part of the "truest of the true," when Vyshinsky for no apparent
reason suddenly interrupted Radek and, referring him back to the
confession he claimed to have made at his pretrial interrogation,
early in December, invited him to explain the circumstances of a
visit which Tukhachevsky's confidant, Putna, had, allegedly, paid
him a few years earlier. Whereupon Radek obligingly confirmed that
"in 1935 . . . in January . . . Vitali Putna came to see me with
some request from Tukhachevsky. I said: 'This is no way for a

* Condemned to ten years at hard labor, Radek was to perish a year later
at the hands of a cellmate, in a prison brawl, in Siberia.

leader to act. There has been no news of the man* for six months. Get hold of him, dead or alive.' Putna promised. But when I received no answer from Putna . . ." And Radek rambled on to other subjects.

This, however, was apparently not enough. For that same afternoon Vyshinsky called Radek's attention back to his earlier testimony and the following dialogue ensued:

"Accused Radek, in your testimony you say: 'In 1935 . . . in January . . . Vitali Putna came to me with a request from Tukhachevsky. . . .' I want to know in what connection you mention Tukhachevsky's name?"

"Tukhachevsky had been commissioned by the government with some task for which he could not find the necessary material. I alone was in possession of this material. He rang me up and asked if I had this material. I had it, and he accordingly sent Putna, with whom he had to discharge the commission, to get this material from me. Of course, Tukhachevsky had no idea either of Putna's role or of my criminal role. . . ."

"And Putna?"

"He was a member of the organization, and he did not come to talk about the organization, but I took advantage of his visit to have this talk."

"So Putna came to you, having been sent by Tukhachevsky on official business having no bearing whatsoever on your affairs since he, Tukhachevsky, had no relation to them whatsoever?"

"Tukhachevsky never had any relation whatsoever to them."

"He sent Putna on official business?"

"Yes."

"And you took advantage of this in order to engage in your own private affairs?"

"Yes."

"Do I understand you correctly, that Putna had dealings with members of your Trotskyite underground organization, and that your

---

* Old-time Trotskyite Efraim Dreitzer. Charged with leading one of Trotsky's clandestine strong-arm teams in Russia, Dreitzer had been condemned to death at the first (August, 1936) show trial and executed.

reference to Tukhachevsky was made in connection with the fact that Putna came on official business on Tukhachevsky's orders?"

"I confirm that and I say that I have not had and could not have had any dealings with Tukhachevsky connected with counter-revolutionary activities, because I know Tukhachevsky's attitude to the party and the government to be that of an absolutely devoted man."[5]

And that was that.

No more was said about Tukhachevsky at the trial. It would have seemed that he had been entirely vindicated, except that in his final plea Radek again made a point of stressing that he had suggested to his fellow conspirators "that the negotiations [with the Germans] be conducted by Putna, who had connections with leading Japanese and German military circles." But to those familiar with Stalin's methods, the very mention of his name in conjunction with that of the now totally compromised Putna—and it had been mentioned all in all *twelve* times—could not be accidental; indeed, it could have but one meaning: a ring *had* been or *was* being forged around the Marshal; the preliminary steps had been taken and it was now only a matter of time before his enemies closed in on him in the open for the kill.

The trial ended on January 30. Pyatakov and eleven others were sentenced to be shot, the remainder to various terms of imprisonment.

A few weeks later the Central Committee reconvened in its spring session. By now an atmosphere of real terror was beginning to sweep the land. According to Khrushchev, the number of arrests on charges of counter-revolutionary crimes had risen ten times between 1936 and 1937.

Just a few days before the session opened, on February 18, the "liberal" camp in the Politbureau suffered another grievous loss: "Sergho" Ordzhonikidze, Stalin's one-time devoted friend and accomplice in Georgia, died "suddenly," supposedly of a heart attack, perhaps a suicide, probably murdered, after having sought in vain to save the life of his long-time colleague, Pyatakov. Ordzhonikidze had ever since Kirov's death been the acknowledged spokesman for a relaxation of the terror. He commanded immense prestige. With his death, the "liberals" found themselves virtually leaderless.

And now Stalin resumed the offensive. In a report headed *On*

*Shortcomings in Party Work and on the Methods to be Used for the
Liquidation of Trotskyite and Other Double-Crossers,* which he introduced on March 3, he again elaborated upon his favorite theory
about the parallel intensification of class warfare with the country's
advance to Socialism. For his part, Yezhov demanded official endorsement of the thesis, first expounded in Stalin's and Zhdanov's
memorable telegram to the Politbureau of the preceding autumn,
that the NKVD "was four years late in its efforts to unmask these
most inexorable enemies of the people." So long as the targets of the
attack were the universally despised and hated Yagoda and other
top henchmen of the secret police, the Committee seems to have
been fairly unanimous. Even Bukharin and his friends (who had
been escorted to the session from jail)* are said to have endorsed
their condemnation. But Stalin had used the fateful words *"and other
double-crossers"!* Whom did he have in mind? Clearly the "Right"
and perhaps not only the "Right." And so when presently both Stalin
and Yezhov broadened their offensive and demanded also the expulsion of Bukharin, Rykov and their friends, members of the Politbureau and of the Central Committee stood up, one after the other
to defend them. Khrushchev in his secret speech singled out particularly the protests of Politbureau member Postyshev, who needless to
say paid with his life for his belated courage. But this time Stalin
had the situation well in hand. Since the defection of Kalinin and
Voroshilov, the "liberals" were in a minority in the Politbureau and
this new ratio of power was bound to affect also the outcome of the
debate in the Central Committee. In the end the latter agreed to all
Stalin asked for. Bukharin and the others were expelled and four
weeks later, on April 3, Yagoda himself was finally arrested in his
turn.

It is at this point that one comes up against one of the major mys-
teries of the Tukhachevsky Affair.

For by the middle of March, 1937, both sides had, presumably,
completed their preparations; they had marshaled their forces and

---

* For the last time Bukharin's name appears in *Izvestya* in the issue of
November 16. He was arrested together with Rykov in the last week of
February.

stood now poised for the showdown. And yet almost until the very end, both would continue to act as though they were totally unaware of the inevitability and imminence of this showdown.

As far as Stalin was concerned, his case against those generals he had marked out for extermination could rest. The implication of Tukhachevsky's complicity in Pyatakov's alleged plotting with Trotsky and the "Left" had been skillfully injected into the record by the ever obliging Radek. Tukhachevsky's man Putna had been for the past four months in the hands of Yezhov; he was thus presumably "ripe," at present, for anything the latter had in mind.* In his March 3 speech before the Central Committee, Stalin himself had hinted ominously at the untold harm "a few spies within the ranks of the Red Army could do to the country." Little else was necessary to start the ball rolling. And yet fully two more months were to go by before Stalin struck and when he did so, his whole behavior would show such obvious signs of improvisation, fear, panic even, that it seems well-nigh impossible to believe that the "plot" for which Tukhachevsky and his friends were formally sent to their death on or around June 12 was the very same plot which Stalin, Yezhov and Mekhlis had been so painstakingly weaving about them for the past six or eight months.

Several explanations have been offered. Krivitzky suggests that before squaring accounts with the Army, Stalin wished to secure his rear against a possible German attack. In April, 1937, he says, David Kandelyaki (Stalin's confidential agent in Berlin) returned to Moscow with a signed draft agreement with Hitler. Three weeks later—but why *three weeks later?*—the purge of the Red Army began. The trouble about this thesis is that although there is evidence that Stalin, through Kandelyaki, had indeed been negotiating with the Nazi government and that these talks gained momentum with the arrival in Berlin, in March, 1938, of Stalin's new Ambassador to Germany, Merekalov, there is no evidence of a *written* agreement between the two dictators, however sketchy, prior to the famed August, 1939, Molotov-Von Ribbentrop Pact.

---

* Putna's arrest was first reported during the first show trial, in August, 1936. Actually, it probably did not take place before the autumn.

There *are* indications, however, that Kandelyaki traveled from Berlin to Moscow that April not alone; that he was accompanied by the INU's Berlin "resident" Izrailovich and that the latter carried Heydrich's proposal to negotiate the sale of the fateful Task Force "R" file. Shortly thereafter Mekhlis flew to Berlin and within twenty-four hours the deal was consummated.

This still does not explain the hasty, even frantic way in which the purge of the Red Army was carried out, *when* it was carried out. The explanation of *that* is, of course, that the plot with which Tukhachevsky and his friends were charged was *not* the "plot" for which they were being framed and for which it was planned that they should stand trial when the time was ripe.

There is still some doubt as to who betrayed. Some name Putna, who, unable to bear the tortures to which he had been subjected since his arrest in the fall, finally told all. Another version names Army Commander Second Grade Pavel E. Dybenko, G.O.C. Central Asian Military District. A former Tsarist sailor, who had distinguished himself during the Revolution by savagely massacring any officer he could lay hands on, only to break with Lenin and Trotsky at the time of the Kronstadt rising, Dybenko was regarded generally as an impulsive, well-meaning but incapable drunkard, whose past reputation as a "revolutionary lion" alone accounted for his present position. He had been one of the last district commanders to be contacted by the plotters. According to this version, he immediately flew to Moscow and told Stalin all. Arrests started that same night.

Tukhachevsky himself had been much in evidence throughout 1936. In January he had addressed the spring session of the Central Committee on the subject of the general political-military scene in Europe, and his speech had been very much remarked because of its violently anti-German tone, which contrasted greatly with Stalin's relatively mild statements. A few weeks later the Marshal was off to London, to represent the Soviet Union at King George V's funeral. He traveled both ways via Warsaw and Berlin which, considering the Red Army's military commitments in France and Czechoslovakia,

was in itself a somewhat peculiar choice of itinerary. Even more
unusual, however, was the whole tone of his conversation following
his stopover in the German capital, which, in the mouth of the No. 2
man in the Red Army and coming as it did only a few weeks after
his January speech, produced a positively ominous impression on
some of his listeners. Thus at one reception, turning to Rumanian
Foreign Minister Nicholas Titulescu, he said: "You are wrong,
Monsieur le Ministre, to link your career and the fate of your country to countries that are old and 'finished' such as Great Britain and
France. It is to the new Germany that we should turn. For some
time, at least, Germany will be the country that will take the lead of
the European continent."[6] While to the noted French journalist
Mme. Geneviève Tabouis he made the equally startling announce-
ment that: "They [the Germans] are already invincible, Madame
Tabouis."[7]

Yet it was no secret that, even though outwardly Stalin might show
himself more cordial than ever, there had been increasing differences
between him and Tukhachevsky over the past eighteen months.
First, there had been the mysterious death of Kuibyshev. The latter
had been a close personal friend of the Marshal's and had from the
start sponsored him in party circles. Then it was said that Stalin was
deliberately delaying Tukhachevsky's latest reform projects out of
fear that these would still further strengthen the officers' caste. The
latest clash had centered around the issue of whether the Red Army
should or should not intervene actively in Spain, the Marshal holding
that it should save itself for a worthier cause. True, on most points
Tukhachevsky seemed to have won out, yet it was noted that he was
rarely allowed to stay long at his desk in the Defense Commissariat
these days, being almost constantly sent on some tour of inspection
or other, some of which clearly did not require the presence of a
man of his rank and position.

Though the Soviet press does not usually give the names of those
who attend Central Committee sessions, only a very serious reason
could have prevented Tukhachevsky, Gamarnik, Uborevich and
Yakir from attending the Committee's June session, at which Stalin
at last obtained the Committee's reluctant consent to proceed with

the first Great Purge trial, that of the Zinovyev-Kamenev group in August.

Shortly thereafter Yakir had departed at the head of a military mission to France and Czechoslovakia, but he was back again early in September, in time for the fall session of the Committee, at which Stalin and Yezhov were so resoundingly defeated.

The second half of September and most of October, once the harvest has been brought in, is traditionally the time for the Red Army's autumn maneuvers, and presently the Soviet press was reporting the presence of the Army's top military leaders in various provincial military districts: that of Voroshilov and Tukhachevsky in Byelorussia with Uborevich's command, and later in the Ukraine with Yakir's . . . that of Gamarnik with Marshal Blücher's Far Eastern forces. . . .

That autumn the military group suffered their first casualty: Putna was arrested. By now Pyatakov (who was possibly the first civilian oppositionist to have contacted Tukhachevsky) was presumably also in jail. Knowing the methods of the NKVD, there was no guarantee that they would be able to hold out long. Clearly the plotters could no longer wait for a problematic war; they had to prepare for action now. And true enough, there is evidence that at the Eighth Extraordinary Congress of the Soviets (which endorsed Stalin's new constitution) final agreement was reached between the civilian and military groups, it being left to Tukhachevsky to work out the details of the coup and its timing.

The second purge trial in January, with its specific mention of Putna and Tukhachevsky, must have confirmed the plotters' misgivings and Stalin's remarks before the Central Committee early in March added a finishing touch. There was clearly no time to waste. And yet still they did nothing. Why?

At the third purge trial, in March, 1938, at which quite a lot was said about the military aspects of the conspiracy, the prosecution stressed the difficulties and delays involved in secret correspondence with Trotsky, with whom all orders allegedly originated, and also certain differences between Trotsky and his representative inside Russia, Assistant Foreign Commissar Krestinsky. But beyond what the prosecution chose to reveal, we know as yet nothing specific about the relations between the military and Trotsky's group, with whom only Putna is known definitely to have been in touch.

True, the military group had suffered a further serious loss in the person of Corps Commander Jan. J. Latzis, who headed the Soviet Military Railway Troops, and who had died suddenly, in the autumn of 1936, of natural causes. A role of particular importance had been assigned to these units. On the one hand, they were to facilitate the concentration and deployment of the insurgent forces; on the other, they were to hamper the movements of those units that might remain true to Stalin. Finally, in the event of a failure of the coup in Russia proper, they were to withdraw, together with all the rolling stock they could salvage, beyond the Urals into the Siberian insurrectional base.

There had been other troubles. In the fall of 1935, Blücher's Far Eastern front had been reshuffled and a new Trans-Baikal Military District had been formed at the expense of his command and placed under the orders of a loyal Stalin man, the former head of the Moscow garrison, Corps Commander Gorbachov, who thus effectively barred the Siberian plotters' way westward into Russia. It would require a heightening of the tension with Japan to correct this invidious situation. By the spring of 1937, however, this had been done and the Trans-Baikal forces were now again effectively controlled by the headquarters of Blücher's Far Eastern Front, i.e., by his Chief of Staff, Sangursky.

All this was bound to cause changes and delays in the planning. But Tukhachevsky's attitude throughout these anxious months was not only completely self-confident—he had never lacked *that*—it was positively complacent. During his spring trip to Western Europe he had not even shunned contacts with certain White *émigrés,* though he must surely have suspected that his every step was being watched and reported. And after Radek's ominous testimony of January 24 the writing on the wall must have been just as clearly visible to the Marshal as it was to everyone else. And still he did nothing. Worse, there are indications that sometime between the Pyatakov-Radek trial in January and the spring session of the Central Committee early in March, he actually took off on a vacation!

The March session of the Central Committee, which he, Gamarnik, Uborevich and Yakir of course attended, could hardly have dispelled their misgivings. On March 18, however, just as the Committee had adjourned, it was announced that Tukhachevsky would once again lead the Soviet Union's delegation, coming May, to King George VI's Coronation.

It is this announcement which, possibly, caused the plotters' downfall. For the coup was, reportedly, now planned to go off on or about May 1, when the concentration of additional military forces in the capital for the traditional May Day parade would have attracted less notice. But then came Tukhachevsky's appointment to London. Rather than arouse suspicion by requesting the appointment of someone else in his stead, it was decided to postpone the showdown for a few more weeks. . . .

Late in April Tukhachevsky was seen at a ball in the Officers' Club in Moscow. It is said that he was already then shunned by most of his colleagues. A few days later, however, he attended another reception, at the U.S. Embassy, and according to Ambassador Joseph Davies, he seemed gay and unconcerned.

May came.

All too many so-called "eyewitness accounts" of Marshal Tukhachevsky's last days have appeared in the press in the course of recent years. Most of them have to be viewed with the greatest caution for the simple reason that of the known eyewitnesses, few were fortunate enough to survive the purge, and those who did are either unwilling or unable to talk.

Thus according to one account, the news of his demotion took the Marshal by surprise. He had left Moscow for a brief vacation shortly after the May Day parade and it was while resting in one of the Red Army's sumptuous sanitaria on the shores of the Black Sea that he learned of his transfer to the Volga Military District. He immediately returned to the capital, where he was informed that the decision had been motivated by his alleged "moral depravity"—the Marshal was a renowned lady-killer—and his repeated "abuses of authority." Presently he discovered that his revolver had been removed from his desk. He was so incensed that he immediately submitted his resignation from the service and wrote a personal letter to Stalin, demanding an explanation. Stalin did not reply himself, but informed him through the Politbureau that his case "would be looked into." Gamarnik, whom Tukhachevsky had also consulted, seemed equally mystified; he promised to investigate the matter and advised the Marshal, meanwhile, to accept his new assignment. Whereupon Tukhachevsky started to prepare himself for the trip.

In the indictment, Tukhachevsky was accused of holding a number of conspiratorial meetings at his house prior to his departure for Kuibyshev. His wife, his sister and his cook are reported to have been made to testify to this effect. Actually, there is record of only one gathering in the Marshal's home, on the very eve of his departure from Moscow, and this seems to have been just an ordinary farewell party for old friends come to see him off. Nevertheless, the guest list is significant.

During the day the Marshal was visited by his successor, Marshal Yegorov; by two of his alleged future judges, Generals Shaposhnikov and Alksnis; and by one of his future fellow defendants, General Eidemann. Later that afternoon Eidemann returned in the company of Gamarnik. They seemed in a hurry and did not stay. Yegorov, Shaposhnikov and Alksnis, however, were back in time for dinner. They were joined presently by another of Tukhachevsky's fellow conspirators, General Feldmann, and by Vice-Premier Valerian Mezhlauk (who was soon to perish in his turn), as well as by the head of the Red Army's artillery, General Rogovsky, their wives and a number of nonmilitary friends of the Tukhachevsky family, such as the late Maxim Gorky's daughter-in-law, Nadyezhda Alekseyevna Peshkova. The last to arrive, reportedly, was Yagoda. As the guests were leaving, Tukhachevsky invited them gaily to a boating picnic that summer on the Volga. "Don't be silly, Misha!" Yagoda countered, laughing, and slapped him on the back. "By summertime you will be back with us here in Moscow!"[8]

The only trouble about this story (which comes to us from Tukhachevsky's sister-in-law, now living abroad) is that Yagoda had been under arrest since the first week in April and could, therefore, not possibly have attended Tukhachevsky's farewell party, which for its part could have taken place only after the Marshal's appointment to Kuibyshev on May 11!

There exist four versions of Tukhachevsky's arrest. According to one, the Marshal refused to join his new post, he was thereupon summoned by Voroshilov to the Kremlin and there apprehended. According to another version, he left Moscow docilely on May 28 and was arrested in his train compartment. According to the third, he reached his destination unharmed and had just started on an inspection of his command, when he was joined by the local head of the NKVD's Special Section, who informed him that he was being summoned back to Moscow. He was arrested on the way. By yet another account, Tukhachevsky's arrest smote the plotters like a bolt out of the blue. The Marshal offered armed resistance to the NKVD officials who came to arrest him. At the Defense Commissariat, where some of the Marshal's former associates had entrenched themselves, the police had to wage a pitched battle during which some of them were killed and several others wounded, the survivors vanishing without trace. Stalin is said to have insisted on questioning Tukhachevsky in person, and he was brought to the Kremlin on a stretcher. There followed a dramatic scene, during which the Marshal heaped abuse on his master, who finally ordered him removed.

It has never been clearly established whether the generals were ever actually brought to trial before being shot or not. According to one version, a simulacrum of a trial did indeed take place, lasting from 10 A.M. to 9 P.M. Vyshinsky officiated, as usual, as prosecutor. He had only one witness: Dybenko. The evidence, however, included the Task Force "R" file and faced with that, the defendants were speechless. When Judge Ulrich had finished reading the sentence, an NKVD officer walked up to them and ripped off their insignia of rank and decorations. After which they were driven back to the Butyrki. The next day all the streets leading to NKVD headquarters in Dzierzhinski Square were barred to the public from 9 A.M. on. Shortly after 10 A.M. two "Black Marias" drove through the steel-barred gates of No. 11 Dzierzhinski Street (in which the more important prisoners were wont to be executed) into the courtyard. The defendants descended one by one, each escorted by two armed guards, and vanished through a small door into a room off the prison yard. At 10:30 A.M. Marshal Blücher arrived and vanished into the little room in his turn. Shortly after 11 A.M., the two vans started to rev up their motors until the pitch reached a deafening roar. Meanwhile an NKVD general had been chalking out a long line across the yard, which he then proceeded to mark off with crosses, alongside each of which he wrote a name. Fifteen minutes later Blücher reappeared. His face was deathly pale. He signaled with his hand. The little door opened and first Tukhachevsky, then Putna, and then the other prisoners re-entered the courtyard. This time their arms were pinioned behind their backs. Uborevich cried out: "Farewell, comrades!" but his voice, drowned out by the roar of the motors, was all but inaudible. The condemned men were led to their respective positions along the chalked-out line and stationed with their backs to their executioners. There was a moment of hesitation. Suddenly Blücher whipped out his handkerchief. The NKVD men raised their revolvers slowly and on bringing them level with the napes of the necks of their appointed victims, pulled the triggers.

The bodies were not returned to the families, since these were themselves in custody, but were buried shortly thereafter, probably in the NKVD's favorite charnel—the ravines of Khodynka Field (where the tragic mass stampede took place at the time of Tsar Nicholas II's coronation in 1894).

And yet, however effective, the above story is hardly likely. It is far more probable that the official version, that of a formal trial preceding the execution, is fiction from beginning to end. Thus, according to Krivitzky, at least one of the members of the Military Tribunal that allegedly sat in justice over Tukhachevsky and his friends, i.e., Red Air Force Chief Jan I. Alksnis, was himself already under arrest at the time. He was to perish shortly thereafter. And Krivitzky's assertion is for once confirmed by Orlov. According to Spiegelglass, the deputy head of INU, whom Orlov questioned on the subject four months later in Paris: "That was a real conspiracy—i.e., as compared to the 'Plots' for which Zinovyev, Kamenev, Pyatakov *et alia* had been sent to their death—That could be seen from the panic which spread there at the top: all the passes to the Kremlin were suddenly declared invalid; our [i.e., the NKVD's] troops were held in a state of alarm. As Frinovsky [Yezhov's deputy] said: 'The whole Soviet Government hung by a thread. It was impossible to act as in normal times: first the trial and then the shooting. In this case we had to shoot first and try later.' "9

The Marshal and his friends were thus probably dispatched like the NKVD's other countless victims, in the cellar of No. 11 Dzierzhinski Street, of which Petrov has given the following description:

The cellar, which is really the basement of the building, is subdivided into a number of rooms, for the use of the executioners, for changing the prisoners' clothes and so on. Before execution the prisoner changes into white underclothes only; he knows that he has been sentenced and is about to be executed. He is led to the death cell, where he is shot in the back of the head by the executioner, either as he stands facing the wall, or just as he walks into the cell. The weapon used is a T.T. 8-shot automatic pistol. . . . If the first shot does not dispatch the prisoner, the executioner follows it up with others. A doctor certifies death; his certificate is the last paper placed in the victim's file. A tarpaulin is spread on the floor of the cell, and a woman is employed to clean up afterwards. The bodies are taken away and buried immediately in a common grave.10

It was only after the operation had been completed that Yezhov reportedly summoned those who had been selected to give the whole thing a semblance of legality.

Neither is there complete accord as to the date on which the plotters died. Thus, for instance, it has not yet been possible to ascertain whether the Supreme Military Council which is known to have met in Moscow from June 1 to June 4, following an intensive press campaign that denounced "political laxity" in the armed forces—the invariable preliminary to all military purges in the Soviet Union—was called specifically to consider the Tukhachevsky Affair and whether the accused were allowed to attend it and to defend themselves or whether they were already under arrest or perhaps even dead at the time. In the evening of June 5 a new Vodopyanov play *A Pilot's*

Dream (*Mechta Pilota*) opened in Moscow and among the many generals who attended it, the London *Daily Telegraph* mentions both Blücher and Tukhachevsky, who, the paper claimed, received an ovation from the public.

Krivitzky, however, had left Moscow two weeks earlier, in the evening of May 22, and according to Yezhov's first deputy, Frinovsky, to whom he spoke just prior to his departure, the plotters were by that time already under lock and key.

On the night of Tukhachevsky's execution special couriers took off on Voroshilov's personal orders for the headquarters of the various military districts. They carried with them a general order in which the condemned generals were castigated in the most violent terms. Within less than a year the entire Red officers' corps had been shaken up from the rank of battalion commander up. It is said that when one of Uborevich's successors at the head of the Byelorussian Military District—the post changed hands three times in as many months—complained to Voroshilov that he could not possibly run his command since all his assistants were in jail, the latter replied that matters were no better at the Defense Commissariat. Presently it would be possible to say without much exaggeration that one had only to add Voroshilov himself, Budyonny and one or two others, and the entire Supreme Military Council would be able to hold its meetings in the central prison of the NKVD off Dzierzhinski Square.

As for the Siberian "Insurrectional Junta," it was wiped out virtually at one sweep. Blücher himself was still in Moscow, when secret orders from Yezhov and Mekhlis brought about the arrest of Krutov (the territorial party secretary of the area), Dzyza (the Marshal's quartermaster general, who had acted as liaison officer between the military and political members of the junta), Mirin (editor of the *Tikhookeanskaya Zvezda*, the Far Eastern Front's principal daily) and, of course, Kalmykov (the commander of the "Kolkhoz Corps"). The latter unit itself was ordered disbanded, its various elements being merged with the regular Rifle Divisions stationed in the area. But it was Gamarnik's representatives, the political commissars, who fared worst of all. They were liquidated virtually to the last man.

Blücher's Chief of Staff Corps Commander, Sangursky, survived only a few weeks longer.*

With Blücher's return to Khabarovsk in August, however, an era of comparative peace descended on the territory, which, in the words of an eyewitness, contrasted oddly with the orgy of terror that was prevailing elsewhere in Russia at the time. Despite the fact that his staff had been found "rotten to the core," the Marshal seems to have retained his master's confidence for a whole year longer. And the immunity which he himself enjoyed extended, curiously, to his whole command.

Late in May, 1938, however, Gamarnik's successor at the head of the Main Political Administration of the Red Army, the sinister Lev M. Mekhlis, who had been responsible for carrying out the purge in the Army elsewhere, arrived by special train in Khabarovsk with a posse of some one hundred hastily promoted, hand-picked commissars. He was followed by Yezhov's first deputy, Mikhail Frinovsky, and a detachment of specially selected NKVD men. Before long Blücher's forces were being purged at the rate of a dozen or so officers a day.

The Marshal himself survived until August, when in the midst of the so-called "Battle of Lake Hassan" between Soviet and Japanese frontier troops (at which the future Marshal Zhukov was to first achieve prominence) he was recalled to Moscow. For a while he could be seen at the Hotel Metropole. He was nearly always drunk. And then he was seen no more.

---

* A former inmate of Irkutzk jail recalls being, late in 1939, in water-pipe communication with one of his neighbors, who gave his name as Sangursky. The latter was suffering agonies of remorse for he had, after cruel torture, he said, given away the names of roughly one thousand persons. He was now being accused of having conspired with Yezhov to "wreck" the Red Army and the party!

EPILOGUE

12

THE KIDNAPING OF
GENERAL MILLER

The complex skein of intrigue, plot and counterplot which, starting that summer of 1921 with Yakushev's arrival in Revel, had culminated in the framing of Marshal Tukhachevsky and his friends, had by now become so subtly tangled that there seemed little likelihood that it would ever be unraveled. The victims had all been silenced. Before long the executioners too would be mute. And yet nothing could be left to chance. One man was still alive who might succeed in putting the various pieces of the puzzle together. If he did so and if he then spoke up, all the carefully contrived precautions would have been vain; the whole edifice of mystery, deceit and silence would collapse. Clearly he too must need be removed.

One day early in December, 1936, a NKVD courier reported in at The Hague to Walter Krivitzky (who in those days still headed INU's Western European intelligence network). He came from Avraam A. Slutzky, the new head of INU, and carried concealed on his person a roll of undeveloped microfilm.* When the latter was processed it was found to contain the following message:

---

* This device, which has now been taken over by intelligence agents everywhere, allows for the instant destruction of compromising material through the simple process of the film roll's exposure to light.

Select from your personnel two men who can impersonate German officers. They must be impressive enough in appearance to pass for military attachés, must be accustomed to talk like army men and must be exceptionally trustworthy and bold. Assign them to me without delay. This is of extraordinary importance. Expect to see you within the next few days.

Krivitzky was just then engaged in important undercover work in Germany; his staff had suffered serious casualties at the hands of the Gestapo and he was therefore, he says, most reluctant to deplete it any further for the sake of some other operation. Nevertheless an order from Slutzky could not be ignored and so he selected from his underground personnel in Germany two men who, he thought, fitted in with Slutzky's description, after which he proceeded himself to Paris.[1]

He met Slutzky at the Café Viel in the Boulevard des Capucines and took him to lunch in a little Persian restaurant near the Opéra. Presently he asked Slutzky about his two men.

"This is no routine affair," Slutzky explained excitedly. "In fact, it involves a case of such colossal importance that I have had to drop all my other work and come here to put it through. The order is from Yezhov himself!"

For a while, says Krivitzky, he heard no more of the matter. In due course his two men reported back for duty. They had been kept idle in Paris for several weeks, they explained, and had then been suddenly dismissed with the laconic statement that "the job had been postponed."

In March, 1937, Krivitzky returned to Moscow to discuss with Yezhov the effects the Great Purge was having on Western public opinion and especially on Western Communist parties. He found there an atmosphere of grim terror. If anything, he says, the extent of the purge was greater, not less, than had been reported abroad. It was rumored that over 350,000 political arrests had been made in the six months alone since Yezhov had assumed command of the NKVD and that the number of summary executions defied any count. The wildest rumors circulated about the city. Shortly before his departure for The Hague, in the evening of May 22, he made a last visit to the

NKVD. There in a corridor he bumped into Furmanov, an old Chekist friend of his, who was at the time in charge of White Russian affairs.

"Say!" Furmanov exclaimed. "Those were a couple of first-rate men you sent us!"

"What do you mean? What men?" Krivitzky inquired, for the matter, he says, had completely escaped his mind.

"Why, those 'German officers,' *you* know!" Furmanov replied with a chuckle.

"But how do *you* happen to know about them?"

"Why, that was our case!" Furmanov retorted boastfully.

Krivitzky was at the time—though we have of course only his own word for it—still completely in the dark as to the actual nature of the "job" to which he had been instructed to assign the two men. Early in July Slutzky's deputy at INU, Mikhail Spiegelglass, arrived in Paris. Short of stature, polite, businesslike, and looking with his sandy-colored hair and pale, slightly fishlike eyes more like a Russian than a Jew, Spiegelglass had had much experience in the more malodorous type of NKVD operations abroad.* His presence at any given spot meant usually only one thing: that INU was preparing a coup. He stayed on in Paris until late in September.

On Wednesday morning, September 22, General Evgheni Miller, president of the ROVS, walked out of his office, allegedly for the purpose of meeting with "two Germans, one of them a military attaché." He was never to be seen again.

Suddenly, says Krivitzky, all was clear to him.

On Sunday, September 19, 1937, the Veterans' Association of the Kornilov Division, General Skoblin's command, held its annual celebration. Coinciding as they did with the twentieth anniversary of the White movement, this year's festivities were of a particularly

---

* On February 17, 1938, Slutzky was suddenly summoned into the office of Mikhail Frinovsky, Yezhov's deputy, who promptly accused him of being an accomplice of Yagoda (who was himself to be executed a month later and was just then being brain-washed for his coming trial). Slutzky understood his meaning immediately. Pulling out his revolver, he there and then put a bullet through his head. Spiegelglass was thereupon appointed in his place. But he survived less than a year.

solemn nature and the significance of the occasion was still further
enhanced by the presence, for the first time in years, of General
Anton I. Denikin, Baron Wrangel's ill-fated but nonetheless highly
respected predecessor as Commander in Chief of the southern
"Volunteer" Army. Skoblin acted as host at the ceremony. Many
speeches were made. Many toasts were drunk. The old-timers recalled their combat experiences. Plevitzkaya sang her favorite song:

> Thou art covered with snow, O Russia!
> Over thy icebound shrouded remains
> The cold winds wail a funeral dirge . . .

and the hauntingly sad words of this beautiful lament stirred many
a battle-hardened veteran to tears. Altogether it was a moving
occasion. The hour was late when the Skoblins suggested solicitously
to General and Mrs. Miller that they give them a lift home in their
car.

On Wednesday morning, September 22, Miller went out early,
arriving at his office, the headquarters of the ROVS at No. 29 Rue
du Colisée, at about 10:30 A.M. He seemed absent-minded, preoccupied even.

At 12:10 P.M., as he was about to go out again, he turned to
General Pavel A. Kussonsky, the elderly secretary general of the
organization (who performed functions roughly similar to that of a
chief of staff), and informed him that he had an appointment in
town, after which he would return to the Rue du Colisée. He did
not name the meeting place; nor did he say who were the persons
he was about to meet. He added, however, something very strange:

"Please do not think that I have gone out of my mind," he said.
"But if I don't happen to return, open this and read it!" And
handing Kussonsky a sealed envelope, he hurried out of the room,
down the stairs and into the street.

When in town, the Skoblins were in the habit of staying at the
Hotel Pax, a small, unpretentious-looking boardinghouse that did
not even boast a reception clerk, situated at No. 143 Avenue Victor
Hugo, near the Etoile.

That morning, Wednesday, September 22, the General and his wife rose early, for they were expecting the visit of a group of Brussels veterans of the Kornilov Division.

Around 11 A.M. the General called up his former A.D.C., Captain Grigul (who operated the canteen of the Gallipoli Association), and requested him to go to the Gare du Nord and book reservations for their friends, the Chaperon du Larré family, on the 2:15 P.M. train to Brussels.* He himself, he said, would drop by and pick up Captain and Mrs. Grigul at the Gallipoli Association at 1:30 P.M., after which they would all drive to the station to say good-by to their friends.

Shortly thereafter, the Skoblins turned up at the restaurant "Serdechnyi," a little Russian bistro they occasionally patronized at No. 64 Rue de Longchamps, close to the Place de Chaillot. They did not sit down—they were in a hurry, Plevitzkaya explained—but merely ate a couple of caviar sandwiches at the counter. The clock showed 12:30 P.M. when they departed.

They kept their car, a Peugeot sedan, in a neighboring garage at No. 123 Rue de Longchamps. Now, picking it up, Skoblin drove his wife back to the Avenue Victor Hugo, where at No. 3 her dressmaker, a Mr. Epstein, owned a store by the name of "Caroline." The General, she said later, had declined to accompany her. "I allow you no more than an hour and a quarter!" he had admonished her; meanwhile he himself would stay in the car and read the papers. Actually, says Epstein, Plevitzkaya did not seem in too great a hurry. She tried on a couple of dresses; chatted away; mentioned a couple of times that her husband was waiting for her in the car and then, at 1:40 P.M., after asking pointedly for the time, gathered up her belongings and said that she must now be off or they would be late at the station. She had not been gone five minutes, when Skoblin appeared in a great state of excitement to inquire after his wife's whereabouts. There had been something wrong with the engine of the car, he explained, and he had had to

* General Chaperon du Larré happened to be married to the daughter of General Lavr G. Kornilov, Skoblin's first regimental commander and one of the founders of the White movement.

park in a side street to see what was the matter. He seemed most put out to hear that she had left without him.

Meanwhile, at the Gallipoli Association, in the Rue de la Faisanderie, Captain and Mrs. Grigul had gone out into the street to wait for the Skoblins to pick them up, as the General had promised. Fifteen minutes passed. . . half an hour. . . . Finally, fearful that they might miss the Chaperons' train, the Griguls hailed a passing taxi and drove to the Gare du Nord on their own.

Quite a large group had assembled on the platform when they arrived, around 2:05 P.M. The Skoblins were already there. Plevitzkaya had arrived first; her husband had had some trouble with the car, she had explained gaily. But her laughter, usually so spontaneous, had sounded a little forced. Presently, Skoblin himself had appeared, slightly out of breath, as if he had been running. He too seemed a little absent-minded. Captain Grigul now turned to him with a note of reproach: "We waited and waited. . . . In fact, we hardly made it. . . . Why didn't you pick us up, as you promised?" Skoblin started and then giggled an excuse: "You know how women are. . . . They and their dressmakers . . ." Then turning to General Chaperon du Larré, he begged him to do him a favor: The Belgian visa he had requested some time ago in order to attend the Kornilov celebrations in Brussels had not yet been granted. Could the General be so kind as to inquire of the Belgian authorities and generally speed things up?

As the Chaperons' train steamed out of the station, Skoblin turned to the Griguls and to another of the officers in the group, a Captain Troshin, and suggested that they all go back to the Gallipoli Association for a drink, after which he would drive his wife home to their hotel and then the three men would go together on a round of official visits.

First they drove to Sèvres to thank General Denikin for his presence at the Kornilov festivities. Denikin had never liked Skoblin; indeed, for many years now he had been definitely suspicious of him. Nevertheless, he received them graciously. As they were about to leave, Skoblin turned to him and urged him to accept his oft-repeated invitation to drive next day with him to Brussels, in order to attend the Kornilov celebrations there. General Miller, he added with an air of contrition, would, alas, not be able to attend! But Denikin once more excused himself. He had no desire to accept any favors from Skoblin.

As they drove on to Boulogne-sur-Seine to General Miller's home, at No. 3bis Avenue Jean-Baptiste Clément, to thank the latter for *his* presence at the Kornilov celebrations, Captain Grigul wondered how Skoblin could have invited Denikin to drive with him "next day" to Brussels, when he had just complained to General Chaperon du Larré at the Gare du Nord that he had not yet received his Belgian visa!

Mrs. Miller opened the door to them. Her husband, she explained, had not yet come home. Whereupon Skoblin begged her to thank him on their behalf and kissing her hand respectfully, departed with his two companions.

Dropping Grigul off at the Gallipoli Association, Skoblin and Troshin now drove back to the Hotel Pax to pick up Plevitzkaya, after which all three of them proceeded on to Ozoir-la-Ferrière, "to feed the pets" as Plevitzkaya later explained. They did not stay there more than twenty minutes, however. By 8:30 P.M. they were back again at the Gallipoli Association, where they sat, drinking and joking with their friends, until about 9 P.M., when they got up, left the car off at their garage, hailed a cab and returned to the hotel, to bed.

All around it had been a good day!

At 5 P.M. that Wednesday afternoon (i.e., at about the time General Skoblin was paying his courtesy call at the Miller home) a group of veterans of the Northern White Army arrived at the Rue du Colisée, where they had an appointment with General Miller. An hour went by . . . then another. . . . Finally, when by 8 P.M. there was still no sign of the old man, the janitor of the ROVS, Assmolov (who lived on the premises), decided to call up his home. The telephone was answered by Mrs. Miller. No, she said, her husband had not yet returned; indeed, as far as she knew, he was still at the ROVS. To which Assmolov replied that he was indeed expected there, but that he had gone out around midday and had not been seen or heard of since.

Mrs. Miller was now seriously alarmed. Her husband was known to be a most thoughtful and considerate man; whenever he was held up or delayed he would make a point of calling up his home or leaving a message. Like Mrs. Kutyepova had done in very like circumstances seven years earlier, she now first called up the Gallipoli Association (where Skoblin, Plevitzkaya and Captain Troshin would arrive from Ozoir-la-Ferrière half an hour later), only to be told that General Miller had not been seen or heard of there all day. She then telephoned various friends and acquaintances with just as little success. Finally, at wits' end, she at 10:15 P.M. sent a message by hand to Assmolov at the ROVS, begging him to notify General Kussonsky, who should in turn alert the police.

Assmolov got through to Kussonsky about twenty minutes later and it was only then that the latter recalled, all of a sudden, that he had been since noon in possession of a sealed envelope which he had been instructed to open and read in precisely such an emergency. He had locked the fateful envelope away in a drawer of his desk and had then forgotten all about it. Now, hailing the first passing taxi, he drove back to the Rue du Colisée, hurried up the stairs into his office and unlocked his desk. The envelope was still there. Kussonsky tore it open feverishly and was for a moment speechless. For the message read:

> Today at 12:30 P.M. I have an appointment with General Skoblin at the corner of the Rue Jasmin and Rue Raffet. He is supposed to take me to a meeting with a German officer by the name of Strohman—reputedly German military attaché in one of the Balkan countries—and one Werner, of the German Embassy here. They both speak good Russian. The meeting was arranged at Skoblin's initiative. This is perhaps a trap, which is why I am in any event leaving this note.

Suddenly Kussonsky recalled Miller's words, spoken many years before, at the time of General Kutyepov's disappearance: "When one goes to a suspicious rendezvous," he had said, "one leaves behind a letter. That is also what Kutyepov should have done." He, Miller, had done just that. And yet due to the incredible negligence of his Chief of Staff, even this precaution had been of no avail. It was by now 10:50 p.m. Six valuable hours had been wasted. . . .

Pulling himself together at last, Kussonsky now called up Vice Admiral Mikhail A. Kedrov (General Miller's first deputy, who officiated also as head of the ROVS' First Branch), told him all and begged him to come immediately to the Rue du Colisée. Then he sent Assmolov off to the Gare du Nord, on the off-chance that Skoblin might have decided to see his Brussels comrades off by the night train.

Meanwhile Captain Grigul (who had learned about General Miller's disappearance at the Gallipoli Association) had on his own initiative alerted Colonel Serghei A. Matzylev, the bright and energetic young secretary of the Association. The latter now also decided to call up Kussonsky, whom he finally located at the ROVS at about 12:30 a.m.

"Where is General Miller?" he inquired.

"We have no idea. . . ."

"Should I come over?"

"Please do," replied Kussonsky. "As soon as you can!"

It was close to 1 a.m. when Matzylev arrived at the Rue du Colisée. He had as yet no knowledge of General Miller's letter and was therefore not a little surprised to hear Admiral Kedrov suggest that they go to the police. "Surely," he suggested, "nothing serious could have happened to Miller. . . ."

"On the contrary," Kussonsky answered in a quavering voice. "In fact, we fear the worst!" But before going to the police, he added, they should await the return of Assmolov, whom they had sent to Ozoir-la-Ferrière to fetch General Skoblin.

Now, for the first time, although neither Kussonsky nor Kedrov chose as yet to give him any further details, Matzylev realized that Skoblin was in some way or another involved in the affair.

"But don't you know," he exclaimed, "that on Mondays, Tuesdays and Wednesdays the Skoblins spend the night in town, at the Hotel Pax in the Avenue Victor Hugo? Why, they are probably there right now! You have sent Assmolov on a wild-goose chase!"

Kussonsky had obviously forgotten about that too. This was clearly

not his day! "Are you sure?" he queried, visibly taken aback. "Very
well then, jump into a taxi and bring Skoblin back here immediately!"

Hailing a cab at the corner of the Avenue des Champs Elysées,
Matzylev arrived before the Hotel Pax at about 1:15 A.M. The
Avenue Victor Hugo was virtually deserted at this late hour; there
was not even a light in the concierge's lodge. He could hear, however, voices echoing from a café across the street. Telling the driver
to wait, Matzylev pressed the bell button which rang hollow in the
deserted hallway. Presently, someone—the owner of the hotel—
appeared in the doorway of the café, crossed over and unlocked the
front door for him. The Skoblins, he explained in answer to
Matzylev's inquiry, occupied room No. 2, first floor front. Matzylev
bounded up the narrow, creaky stairs and knocked hurriedly at their
door. After a minute he heard the sound of shuffling feet, the door
opened and Skoblin appeared on the threshold in pajamas.

"Nikolai Vladimirovich!" Matzylev whispered excitedly. "Your
presence is required urgently at the Rue du Colisée!"

"But don't you see?" Skoblin whispered back. "I'm already in
bed. . . . Why? What's the matter? What's happened?"

"It's General Miller! . . . He's vanished!"

Skoblin took the news with surprising calm. Then, after a slight
pause: "Very well," he said. "Wait for me in the hall. I'll get dressed
and be down in no time."

A few minutes later he reappeared, hatless, an overcoat thrown
over his arm. He seemed completely unruffled as they climbed back
into the waiting cab. And indeed there was no reason why he should
be anything else. After all Matzylev himself still knew nothing about
Miller's fateful letter and could therefore give him only the barest
elements of the case. Calmly Skoblin ascended the stairs of the Rue
du Colisée. Calmly he greeted Mrs. Kedrova, who had accompanied
her husband, the Admiral, to the ROVS and who now sat in a
corner of the front office. Calmly he opened the door of General
Kussonsky's office and stepped into the room where the two gentlemen were waiting for him, while Matzylev, who had not been

invited to join them, stayed behind with Mrs. Kedrova. He could
hear voices raised as though in anger, but he could not make out
what was being said.

For Skoblin had hardly closed the door behind him, when
Admiral Kedrov exclaimed: "Where is Miller?"

"I don't know. . . ."

"When did you leave him?"

"Leave him? Why, I haven't even seen him today. . . ."

"Are you *sure?*"

"Of course I'm sure! In fact, I haven't seen him since . . . er
. . . Sunday! Yes! That's right! Sunday. . . . At the Kornilov
banquet!"

He was still completely self-possessed. Kedrov's eye narrowed.

"And you arranged no meeting between him and certain foreign
agents?"

Skoblin's gaze shifted quickly from the Admiral's face to Kussonsky's and back again.

"Of course not!" he blurted. But there had been an instant's
hesitation.

"But we know the *time* of that meeting!" Kedrov went on.

"It cannot be!"

"And we know the *place* of the meeting!" Kedrov's tone sharp-
ened.

"I tell you: it cannot be!"

"Indeed, we even know the *purpose* of the meeting!" Kedrov
pursued relentlessly. "We have *documentary proof!*" And Kedrov
picked up Miller's letter.

Suddenly Skoblin became deathly pale. He passed his hand
nervously over his brow. His voice, naturally hoarse, was even more
rasping than usual as he repeated, over and over again, desperately,
that he knew nothing, that he had heard nothing, that it was all
obviously a mistake, a misunderstanding, that at twelve-thirty that
afternoon he had been lunching with his wife at the restaurant
"Serdechnyi," that he could prove it, that there were eyewitnesses,
that it was all ridiculous, that it didn't make sense. . . .

Kedrov stood up. "Very well then," he remarked, "in that case we had best go straight to the police."

Skoblin's face lit up.

"That's right," he exclaimed eagerly. "The police . . . I'll go with you!" And opening the door, he reappeared in the front office, Kedrov and Kussonsky following closely on his heels.

"We are off to the police!" the Admiral explained to Matzylev and reached for his hat.

And now the incredible happened.

For just as Skoblin pulled open the front door and stepped out onto the landing, Kussonsky turned to Kedrov and whispering in his ear, "Odd, isn't it?" signaled that he wished to have a word with him in private. Whereupon both gentlemen stepped back into Kussonsky's office, while Matzylev again stayed behind. He could hear Skoblin's footsteps on the staircase, but being an officer of the old school, he felt that as the youngest in rank, he should also be the last to leave the room. Besides, he personally had still no reason to suspect Skoblin of anything and so when Mrs. Kedrova cried out on a sudden impulse: "Watch out! He's about to escape!" he merely stared at her uncomprehendingly. And now Kussonsky and Kedrov reappeared. "Where is Skoblin?" asked Kedrov. "In the street, waiting," replied Matzylev, and they started to grope their way down the stairs. For some reason, the lights had been switched off and so their progress was slow. When they emerged at last into the street, Skoblin was nowhere to be seen.

"The traitor!" Admiral Kedrov's voice rang out like a curse.

"But no," Matzylev exclaimed, still not understanding. "It can't be . . ." and started off running toward the Avenue des Champs Elysées. Skoblin, he reasoned, had probably not understood that when Kedrov said, "We are off to the police!" what the latter had meant was, of course, that they were all four of them to go there. He had probably simply gone home to bed. And so presently Matzylev turned back. He was soon joined by his two companions. "The scoundrel! The dirty scoundrel!" Kedrov kept muttering under his breath. This was going too far! Turning on him angrily,

Matzylev finally cried out: "But stop concealing things from me! Tell me the truth! What has happened?"

Silently Kedrov handed him Miller's fateful note. And yet even as he sought to decipher Miller's hasty scrawl by the dim light of a street lamp, Matzylev's mind refused to accept the fact of Skoblin's treachery and so when Kedrov opined that since Skoblin had fled, he was clearly guilty, and that they should report the whole matter immediately to the French police, he suggested that they first drop by at the Hotel Pax. Who knows? Perhaps Skoblin had indeed gone home and if he hadn't, his wife might know where he was.

By now they had wasted at least fifteen precious minutes. Wherever he was, the fugitive had already a good start.

When they reached the hotel, Kussonsky and Kedrov stayed in the taxicab while Matzylev went up to the Skoblins' room alone. He knocked at the door. There was no reply. Turning the handle, he walked into the room and switched on the light. Plevitzkaya lay stretched out, half-dressed, on a divan. There was no sign of Skoblin.

"Where is Nikolai Vladimirovich?" Matzylev inquired in a stern voice. "Is he back? We are looking for him!"

There was a minute of silence. Then: "No . . ." Plevitzkaya murmured dully. And then suddenly she was on her feet. "But you yourself drove off with him!" she cried out. "Where is he? Where is my husband? What have you done to Kolya?" There was a note of terror in her voice.

"He went out of the room. . . . He left us. . . . And then he vanished!"

Plevitzkaya stared at him with wild, hysterical eyes. "Tell me," she cried. "You suspect him of something? That's what it is, isn't it? But answer me!" Her tone became desperate. "You know him! If you said something to him . . . He's capable of shooting himself! . . . Oh, God! What have you done to my husband? What have you done to my Kolya?" The voice trailed off into a whimper.

Consummate actress though she was, the woman was at this point clearly speaking the truth.

"Very well then," Matzylev said. "When he gets back, mind you tell him to join us at the Commissariat de Police!" After which, turning on his heel, he ran down the stairs and jumped into the waiting cab.

"Fast!" he ordered the driver without even waiting to consult his companions. "To the Commissariat de Police of the Sixteenth Arrondissement, Place Dauphine!"

It was now past 3 A.M. General Miller had been gone almost fifteen hours.

At 4 A.M. the French police started their official investigation with the routine questioning of the various hospitals and morgues of the Paris area. By 8 A.M. General Skoblin's photograph and personalia had been circulated to all police, frontier, airport and harbor authorities of France and North Africa.

The chase was on.

Shortly after 6 A.M. French detectives, accompanied by Colonel Matzylev, returned to the Hotel Pax to question Plevitzkaya. But the interview yielded nothing: she knew or claimed to know nothing of her husband's activities, his present whereabouts or the reasons of his flight and seemed in general so genuinely distraught that after grilling her for more than an hour, the police decided to leave her alone for the time being.

About 8:30 A.M. she turned up at the Gallipoli Association in what eyewitnesses later said was an "indescribable condition." It seemed hard to believe that barely twelve hours had elapsed since she had last sat there, with her husband and their friends, joking and drinking. She kept sobbing and complaining that her husband had forsaken her, that he too had been kidnaped, that he was surely dead, that she herself was now being persecuted, that she was surrounded by enemies. . . . Soon thereafter she departed, allegedly to get a sedative from Dr. Chekunov, her physician. And again no one thought of stopping her. Indeed, it was only after lunch, after a call had been put through to the doctor and he had said that she had not yet turned up there, that her friends' concern over her sorrowful condition turned first to misgivings and then to downright suspicion. By nightfall it seemed fairly certain that she too had escaped; the police were alerted and a warrant was issued for her arrest.

Another night went by in rumors and conjecture. By now the press had been notified and the search for General Skoblin and his wife (Miller was as well as given up for lost) had assumed country-wide proportions. And then the sensational news broke: Plevitzkaya had been found! Early Friday morning, September 24, she had reappeared at the Gallipoli Association in the company of a Mr. Raigorodsky, who told the following story:

Shortly before 8 P.M., on Thursday, Mrs. Chekunova, the doctor's wife, had rung him up to inquire whether she could see him right away. She had given no further details. Shortly thereafter she had appeared in the company of Plevitzkaya, with whom he was, he said, "but slightly acquainted." At this point—or at least that is what he claimed—Raigorodsky knew only what he had read in the evening papers, namely that both Miller and Skoblin had vanished. Plevitzkaya, he said, was in a state nearing hysteria and so despite their "slight acquaintance," he suggested that she stay overnight. After reading the morning papers, however, he had realized that he was, in fact, giving hospitality to a fugitive from justice and in the end he had succeeded in convincing Plevitzkaya that the best thing she could do under the circumstances was to give herself up to the police. She had begged, however, that she be first taken back to the Gallipoli Association. Only when, on her arrival there, she learned that there was still no news of her husband and no message for her, did she finally agree to be driven to Paris police headquarters, Quai des Orfèvres.

At twelve o'clock noon, Friday, M. Meyer, Director of the Police Judiciaire and Commissioner Roche began to question her.

Meanwhile it had been possible to reconstruct the first stages of Skoblin's escape.

At about 3:45 A.M., Thursday, i.e., approximately at the time Kedrov, Kussonsky and Matzylev were telling their story to a skeptical French police officer at the Commissariat of the Sixteenth Arrondissement, he had rung the night bell of a garage situated at the corner of the Boulevard de Pressbourg and the Porte des Ternes, where his brother-in-law, a Colonel Vorobyov, worked. He was, the night watchman related afterward, pale, disheveled and visibly out of breath.

"I wish to speak to Vorobyov," he panted.

But this happened to be the Colonel's night off. Would he care to leave a message? Skoblin shook his head absently. He was clearly terribly disappointed. No . . . no . . . , he muttered, it didn't matter. . . . And turning away, he hurried off in the direction of Neuilly.

About a quarter of an hour later a Mrs. Krivosheyeva, whose husband, a captain in Skoblin's Kornilov Division, owned a bookstore by the name of "Kama" at No. 27 Avenue de Villiers in Neuilly-sur-Seine, had awakened to the sound of a cautious but insistent knocking against the window shutter.

"Who is it?" she inquired guardedly.

"It's I, General Skoblin!" replied a voice she immediately recognized as that of her husband's commander. "May I have a word with your husband?"

Mrs. Krivosheyeva explained that her husband, who started his workday by selling the White Russian morning papers at the metro station "Richelieu-Drouot," had already left.

"Could I have a glass of water then, please?"

Whereupon Mrs. Krivosheyeva had unlocked the door and invited the General to step in. He was hatless and, she said, "looked awful," and when she brought the glass of water, he gulped it down at one draught as though he hadn't drunk anything for days. But when he spoke, it was with no visible excitement, though he did seem a little nervous. A silly thing had happened to him, he explained. He had lost his wallet; he was literally without a cent; he couldn't even pay for a bus ticket home. Could she lend him a hundred francs? He would return them in the morning. Mrs. Krivosheyeva, to whom Skoblin was still the legendary Civil War hero about whom she had heard so much, answered that she had better give him two hundred; he could return the money any time. Whereupon Skoblin had thanked her effusively, kissed her hand and departed. She had seen him to the door and watched him as he hurried on his way.

The last she or, for that matter, anyone else had seen of him, he was walking at a good pace in the direction of the Boulevard Binot.

At first Plevitzkaya appeared to be too shocked and too scared to make much sense, but as the questioning proceeded, and she gradually regained her composure, she became confident, coquettish, cocky even. But she remained singularly uncommunicative. She had been, she insisted, merely the devoted wife of her dashing husband. She had never known anything, because she was simply not interested, of his political activities; in any event these could have been only of the highest order. She couldn't understand why he had forsaken her. Surely it could be only because he himself was in serious trouble or perhaps even dead! As for his having been a party to General Miller's abduction, why, that was just ridiculous! Everyone knew what a devoted friend he had always been to the old man! Besides there were countless eyewitnesses who could account for literally every minute of his time on that fateful Wednesday! And she sounded so sincere and looked so candid and naïve that in the beginning her interrogators might well have been tempted to take her at her word.

Until they recalled the episode of the notebook.

For just as she was leaving the Gallipoli Association to be driven to Police Headquarters, she had slipped a small notebook into the hand of Captain Grigul's little daughter and had whispered to her to take care of it in her absence. The child had immediately told her father about it and the latter had reported the matter to the police. When the notebook was examined, one of the last pages was found to contain two interesting entries in Skoblin's hand. One of them read:

Transmit to Miller invitation to 12:30-1 P.M. appointment to—*

---

* The original message in Russian broke off in the middle of the word "za—" By playing up the identical first syllables of the Russian words *zavtra* and *zavtrak* (which mean, respectively, "tomorrow" and "luncheon") the defense was to insist at Plevitzkaya's trial that the word "to—" meant merely a routine luncheon appointment—of which there had been many during the past weeks— and could not possibly apply to the fateful meeting at the corner of the Rue Jasmin and the Rue Raffet.

And this entry was followed by another one, a combination of Cyrillic and Latin letters plus some numbers, obviously a cipher, the meaning of which was, however, never made clear:

67 vid. . . . Г Р И

З п   J.P.V.   R.V.

Plevitzkaya had first denied any knowledge of the notebook. Then, upon being confronted with Captain Grigul's story, she had dissolved into tears, as she was in the habit of doing whenever she was too sorely pressed, and resumed her complaints that she was being framed and persecuted.

Soon, as her story was checked and counterchecked, the police grew increasingly convinced that, for all her dramatics and feigned ingenuity, they had been and indeed were continuing to be fed with a carefully planned and faithfully followed alibi, the prime purpose of which seemed to be to cover up Skoblin's whereabouts during the crucial hour or so—between 12:30 and 1:30 P.M.—that had been required in order to lure Miller to his doom. Moreover, far from being a luckless victim of circumstances beyond her knowledge or understanding—as she claimed—Plevitzkaya seemed to have been an invaluable accomplice at every stage.

Thus, according to her story, she and her husband had left the restaurant "Serdechnyi" as the clock showed 12:30 P.M. and had proceeded straight to her dressmaker. But the owner of the dress shop "Caroline," Epstein, maintained that they could not possibly have arrived there later than 11:50 A.M. since his Russian-speaking salesgirl, who went off to lunch daily at 11:45 A.M., had already left and had had to be called back off the street. And Epstein's story was confirmed, presently, by the owners of the "Serdechnyi" restaurant, who reported that their clock was fast and that the Skoblins had left, therefore, not at 12:30, as Plevitzkaya claimed, but sometime between 11:30 and 11:45. First lie.

Then Epstein recalled that while she was trying on her clothes, Plevitzkaya had casually but repeatedly mentioned that her husband was waiting for her in the car and whenever she did so, she had pointedly asked for the time. Epstein remembered glancing several times out of the window. But there had been no sign of the General or his car. True, when he had rushed in to fetch her shortly after her departure, around 1:40 P.M., Skoblin had hastened to explain that the car had had engine trouble and that he had had to park it in a side street, open the hood and see what was the matter. An expert mechanic was thereupon called upon to examine the car. He found the engine in perfect running order. Besides, the Skoblins had driven many miles later that afternoon, including a trip to the country and back, without a hitch.

In the end, for the crucial time gap between their departure from the "Serdechnyi" restaurant at 11:30 A.M. or thereabouts and Skoblin's precipitate reappearance at "Caroline's" between 1:40 and 1:45 P.M., there was only Plevitzkaya's own word for it that he was waiting in the car in, or in the neighborhood of, the Avenue Victor Hugo. And by now the police were no longer inclined to take her at her word without further proof.

For the remainder of the day Plevitzkaya's alibi was absolutely foolproof; indeed, if anything it was *too* foolproof. It was as though she and her husband had gone out of their way to enlist the testimony of as many eyewitnesses as possible of their subsequent activities that day.

One of the police's first moves had been to search the villa at Ozoir-la-Ferrière. True, on the pretext that they needed to "feed the pets"—a cat and several dogs—the Skoblins had returned to Ozoir that Wednesday afternoon, with an eyewitness, of course—Captain Troshin—and had stayed there just sufficiently long to pick up, unobserved by the still unsuspecting Captain, anything they might have wished to remove from the house before the news of Miller's disappearance broke. They had returned to Paris with a small suitcase which was later found empty at the Hotel Pax. "What did it contain?" Commissioner Roche asked Plevitzkaya. "Oh, nothing in particular. Overnight stuff . . ." was her evasive reply. Nevertheless, there was some hope that a careful search of the premises might reveal, if not a clue to the mystery of Miller's disappearance, then at least some indication as to the nature of

Skoblin's activities. And the police's expectations were to some extent rewarded.

In the first place, neighbors testified that there had been much activity on the Skoblin property in recent weeks: packing cases had been ordered, the chickens and pigs had been sold, and Skoblin himself had made no secret of the fact that they were planning to put up the house for sale. He showed particular concern over the fate of his cat!

The house was gone over from attic to cellar and some four hundred kilograms of files and documents impounded. Apart from the fact that Skoblin was found to have possessed three types of cipher and four Yugloslav passports, each in a different name, it was soon apparent that, whatever his other activities may or may not have been, he had operated a vast personal intelligence service, which ranged over a multitude of subjects, from the suicide of Swedish match king Ivar Kreuger in 1932 to the more recent murder of banker Dimitri Navashin.* Moreover, the files that related to various White Russian personalities were far too detailed and comprehensive to be accounted for exclusively by his short-lived association with the "Inner Line."

Virtually from the first day of her detention at the Petites Roquettes prison for women, Plevitzkaya had kept asking for a Bible and not just any Bible, but a particular one bound in green cloth which, she said, was a Jerusalem edition and therefore of particular sentimental value to her. For some time now the police had been hoping to find among her belongings a copy of a code or cipher, that might have helped them to understand the real meaning of two post cards which she had received in jail, shortly after her arrest. Postmarked Tallinn (where Yakushev, the founder of the Trust, had first made his appearance, sixteen years earlier), both of them enjoined her to "pray God and read the Bible." It was soon

---

* A White Russian businessman, who seemed equally at home in the Soviet Embassy and in the most exclusive émigré circles, Navashin was shot one day early in January, 1937, while walking in the Bois de Boulogne. As he was, reportedly, about to come out with a denunciation of and disclosures about the Great Purge, his death was at first imputed to the NKVD. It has since been ascertained that he was a victim of the "Cagoulards."

ascertained that the writers were unknown to the Estonian police, and the latter's French colleagues came to the conclusion that the green clothbound Bible might provide the clue to their identity. This conviction was strengthened, presently, when a second note-book of Skoblin's was found, this time at the Hotel Pax, and carefully studied. One entry read: "Green Bible. Page 20. Gospel of St. John." And true enough, when the green Bible was finally located after a long search at Ozoir-la-Ferrière, page 20 of the Gospel of St. John was seen to have been marked off with pin pricks, that showed up clearly the existence of some sort of cipher. An attempt was thereupon made to apply the cipher to the two mysterious post cards. But it produced no results.

Neither was Plevitzkaya able to give a satisfactory explanation of their financial situation. According to her, the bulk of their income all these years had come from her concert earnings, plus a small monthly allowance from an old friend and admirer, Dr. Oetington.* The work of the investigators was made no easier by the fact that the Skoblins kept no bank accounts. Nevertheless, they were able to find out that Oetington had stopped his allowance to the Skoblins after 1935. Moreover, Plevitzkaya's earnings during 1936-1937, for instance, which totaled no more than sixteen thousand francs, had clearly not sufficed to cover all their expenses, which amounted to some eighty thousand francs. Finally, although Skoblin himself claimed to be often in debt and although the mortgage on his house had not yet been completely paid off at the time of his disappear-

* This Dr. Oetington, the millionaire son of a former Berlin furrier and a well-known psychiatrist in his own right, remains to this day one of the many mystery men of the Miller affair. Well known for his charities and especially for his generous assistance to needy artists, he had also other interests. Thus it is in his house that Skoblin established his first contacts with the "Eurasian" philosophical movement—which has already been mentioned in connection with its infiltration by the Trust. Though Plevitzkaya kept insisting for a long time that she had not seen or spoken to Oetington in the past six months, it was presently ascertained that there had been throughout the month of September constant telephone calls between Ozoir-la-Ferrière and the Hotel Georges V, where the Oetingtons were staying, and that the Skoblins had, in fact, seen the Oetingtons off at the Gare de Lyon *just forty-eight hours* prior to Miller's disappearance. And again it was to Oetington's brother-in-law, Raigorodsky, that Plevitzkaya had turned in her hour of need, though he himself claimed to be but very slightly acquainted with her.

ance, he was known to have recently changed large sums of foreign currency to the tune of several hundred English pounds and several thousand dollars a month. Where did it all come from? Where did it go? Why was he broke on the night of his disappearance? And why did Plevitzkaya herself, at the time of her arrest, have 7,500 francs, 50 English pounds and 50 U.S. dollars in her purse?

Her own behavior, on hearing from Colonel Matzylev that her husband had vanished, had also been strange, to say the least. Why, for instance, had she cried out: "You *suspect him* of something?" What reason had she at that early stage, when Skoblin's complicity in Miller's disappearance was as yet far from established, to assume that her husband was suspected of anything? Had he called her at the Hotel Pax to tell her that the game was up? The proprietor was confident that he had not. Besides, her grief and despair at being left to her own devices were clearly genuine. And then he couldn't have called her, even if he had wished to. Hadn't he confessed to Mrs. Krivosheyeva that he hadn't a cent? Wasn't it far more likely that Plevitzkaya had known about his role from the start and that when Matzylev had pressed her to tell his whereabouts, she had simply put two and two together?

Neither was she able to give a satisfactory explanation as to where she had spent the day of Thursday, between her departure from the Gallipoli Association, allegedly to visit her doctor, and her arrival that evening at Mr. Raigorodsky's apartment. She herself claimed that she had simply roamed the streets all day, utterly distraught. But this story could not be checked and so it remained an open question whether she had succeeded in establishing, or at least tried to establish, contact with her husband's accomplices.

General Kutyepov's disappearance in January, 1930, had struck French public opinion literally like a bolt out of the blue. Acts of political terror—a fairly frequent occurrence everywhere at the turn of the century—were becoming increasingly rare in the Western world and in France had been virtually unknown since the infamous assassination of Socialist leader Jean Jaurès on the eve of World War I and the Anarchist attempts of 1923. Indeed, the very atmosphere prevailing in the country in the first years that followed the Versailles Peace—conservative, complacent, smug even—was such that any show of violence among foreigners enjoying the hospitality of France was bound to provoke a most indignant reaction. Because of that and also because of its strongly anti-Communist program, the Tardieu government had had no compunction in exploiting to the full the resentment which this latest outrage of the OGPU had caused in a country that had only recently condescended to recognize the U.S.S.R.

The Daladier administration, which was in office at the time of General Miller's disappearance, operated under very different circumstances. For the French electorate had since Tardieu's days swung sharply to the left, this evolution culminating in 1935-1936 in the short-lived triumph of the so-called "Popular Front"—a Communist Trojan horse, which the Socialists had accepted only reluctantly and which was soon to collapse under the joint impact of the Spanish Civil War and the Molotov-Von Ribbentrop agreement, but which still enjoyed considerable appeal at the time. In addition, since 1935 France was also bound to the U.S.S.R. by a Mutual Assistance Pact, in which the French High Command had, until the Red Army purge, put much hope.

Both for ideological reasons, therefore, and also for reasons of political expediency, there existed in France at the time of which we are speaking a powerful body of opinion that was willing to go a long way in order to save "the Russian Allies" from any unnecessary embarrassment.

And then the public was becoming blasé. Since the February, 1934, riots—a preview of the pro-De Gaulle *putsch* of May 13, 1958—and the ill-famed Stavisky affair, the French political scene had been in a state of continuous turmoil and now, what with the "Cagoulard" plot,* the Civil War in Spain and the recurrent blood baths in the Soviet Union, it reacted only briefly to arson, murders, kidnapings and other like outrages. Besides, the NKVD was not the

---

* A Fascist-type organization which had come into existence at the time of the Popular Front and which, after committing a number of political and other crimes, was finally uncovered in the fall of 1937.

only foreign agency to pursue the sordid game of political terror in
French territory. First, on January 19, there had been the murder
of Dimitri Navashin. Then had come the brutal murders, also by the
thugs of the "Cagoule," of young Loetitia Tourneaux (May 17) and
of the Roselli brothers (June 9). Less than a week before Miller's
disappearance, on September 19, a group of Italians led by a Colonel
Troncozo, the Spanish Nationalist Governor of Irun, had attempted
to seize a Loyalist submarine that was undergoing repairs in Brest.
A few days before that, the "Cagoulards" had blown up two buildings off the Champs Elysées!

Be this as it may, it was soon obvious that the French police, for
one, were acting under definite instructions to cause as little incon-
venience as possible to Moscow and the latter's Embassy in the Rue
de Grenelle.

Thus, at 4 P.M. on Thursday, September 23, i.e., on the day after
Miller's disappearance, the Commissaire de Police of Le Havre,
Chauvineau, reported to his superiors in Paris that a Soviet vessel,
the *Maria Ulyanova,* had put out to sea the night before under
mysterious circumstances, after taking aboard a large wooden case
that had been brought, presumably from Paris, by Soviet diplomatic
van that same afternoon.

The *Maria Ulyanova* had arrived at Le Havre eight days earlier
and had docked at the "Marseille" pier, in the Bassin de l'Eure. She
carried a cargo of 5,522 bales of sheepskins valued at some nine
million francs and destined for a Bordeaux importer. In return, she
was supposed to pick up the aircraft in which the famous Soviet
pilot Chkalov had just successfully completed, with two companions,
his record-making flight from Moscow to San Francisco via the
North Pole. Within the next few days, a total of 130 passengers (127
Soviets and 3 Spaniards) had come on board, most of them visitors
to the Paris World Fair. At the same time a number of Soviet diplomatic vehicles were observed coming and going between the Paris
Embassy and the "Marseille" pier at Le Havre.

On Wednesday, September 22 (the day of General Miller's disappearance), at about 3:40 P.M., a port official by the name of
Olivier Colin happened to be visiting the captain of the Soviet vessel

on a routine matter of consignment papers when, all of a sudden, a crewman rushed into the cabin and proceeded to babble something excitedly in Russian, whereupon the captain, who, until then had been perfectly calm and leisurely, began to hurry Colin to go on with the business since, he said, pulling a radiogram out of his pocket, he had that day received a message from Moscow ordering him to complete unloading operations and return to Leningrad without delay. Colin later recalled having been struck at the time by the fact that the message had been addressed to the captain direct, rather than to the company agent or broker, as is the usual procedure in such cases. The captain seemed desperately eager to get rid of him and so, presently, Colin took his leave.

It was about 4:15 P.M. when he emerged on deck. As he made his way down the gangplank, he noticed a gray Ford van carrying diplomatic license plates parked on the quay alongside the vessel. It had not been there when he arrived some twenty-five minutes earlier.

The van had been observed entering the harbor precincts by two customs officials. Its windshield and radiator grid were spattered with mud, fly markings, blood drops and bird feathers; it had obviously traveled far and fast. As it came to a halt alongside the *Maria Ulyanova*, two men (who were later identified as Soviet Vice Consul Kislov, a member of the NKVD apparatus at the Paris Embassy, and an official of the Soviet Trade Mission in Paris) jumped out and hastened aboard, while their two companions, another Soviet diplomat and one of the Embassy chauffeurs, remained seated in the van. Presently the first two individuals reappeared in the company of several Soviet crewmen, who proceeded now very gingerly to unload the contents of the van—a large and heavy wooden packing case, some six by two and a half feet—and carry it aboard. Some dockers were standing idly by; they offered to help. But they were angrily waved aside.

At 6 P.M. the *Maria Ulyanova* cast off and moved out into the outer harbor. At 7:30 P.M. the gray Ford van departed in its turn, presumably for Paris. At 8:45 P.M. the Soviet steamer raised anchor again, this time for good, and presently she had vanished from sight.

She had had time neither to take aboard Chkalov's plane, which had been, ostensibly, one of the purposes of her visit, nor even to complete the unloading of her cargo. Thus six hundred bales of sheepskins went back to Leningrad, from where they had then to be shipped to their Bordeaux consignee aboard another Soviet vessel.

The mysterious gray van, whose arrival seems to have precipitated the vessel's departure, was soon identified: an eight-cylinder, twenty-one-horsepower Ford, it had been registered on August 13, 1937, i.e., barely a month prior to General Miller's disappearance, in the name of the Soviet Ambassador in Paris, Vladimir V. Potyomkin, and was used, among other things, as a school bus for Soviet children attending the Embassy school in the Boulevard de Montmorency.

That same evening, Ambassador Potyomkin was summoned to the Hotel Matignon by French Premier Edouard Daladier, who, after pointing to the grave suspicions which weighed over the Soviet Embassy in connection with Miller's disappearance, suggested, in view of the stir this outrage had caused in French public opinion, that the Soviet government signal the *Maria Ulyanova* to return to Le Havre forthwith. An hour later, however, Marx Dormoy, the Socialist Minister of the Interior, telephoned Daladier and assured him that, according to the latest reports, the Soviet Embassy van had reached Le Havre not between 3:40 and 4:15 P.M. (as Commissioner Chauvineau had claimed on the basis of Port Inspector Colin's testimony) but at about 2 P.M. It could not possibly have left Paris later than 11:30 A.M., at which time General Miller was still sitting peacefully in his office in the Rue du Colisée. Thus the ship could in no way be involved in his subsequent disappearance. The various measures which Daladier had reportedly envisaged in order to force the *Maria Ulyanova* to return to French territorial waters, including, allegedly, even the dispatch of a destroyer, were thereupon canceled.

Only later, during Plevitzkaya's trial, was it learned that upon leaving Daladier, Potyomkin had rushed to see Minister of Justice Vincent Auriol, a future President of the Fourth Republic (who was regarded in those days as one of the Soviet Union's most faithful friends in French government circles), and urged him to use his influence with his colleagues in order to avoid a diplomatic scandal. Whereupon Auriol had telephoned his fellow Socialist Dormoy and the latter had called Daladier. It was not until the *Maria Ulyanova* was well out of reach that the French Premier learned that he had been deliberately misinformed by his own Minister of the Interior.*

Meanwhile the conscientious Commissioner Chauvineau, after being at first commended for his zeal, had got into serious trouble with his superiors. On Thursday, September 23, the day after Miller's disappearance, two high officials of the Paris Sureté, Commissioner Papin and Inspector Veyret, arrived at Le Havre and on the pretext that Chauvineau's reports contained conflicting evidence, proceeded to cross-examine all eyewitnesses anew. After which they drew up a new report that contradicted Chauvineau's findings on virtually every point.

In the first place, they said, the van had arrived not between 3:40 P.M. and 4:15 P.M. (as Chauvineau had claimed on the basis of Colin's testimony) but at 3:30 P.M. at the latest. And since the distance between Paris and Le Havre was 238 kilometers—it was, in fact, 203 kilometers!—the vehicle could not possibly have made the trip in the two and a half to three hours that had elapsed between the time of Miller's disappearance and the van's arrival alongside the *Maria Ulyanova*. As for Colin's testimony, it was ignored altogether, while the large packing case became in the Papin-Veyret report "an average size suitcase." Thus armed, the two gentlemen returned to Paris.

But this was not enough. There remained Chauvineau's original reports; they were still in the records. And so presently Messrs. Papin and Veyret were followed to Le Havre by an even more exalted person, M. Léon Ducloux, Controlleur-Général of the Sureté.

* Invited to testify on this incident at Plevitzkaya's trial, Dormoy refused. He was to die in World War II, murdered by Vichy thugs. As for the *Maria Ulyanova*, she reached Leningrad, reportedly, on September 28. The Soviet authorities were later to claim that her departure had been precipitated in order to enable her to pick up some more passengers in London. The ship, however, did not put in to London. Moreover, this time she traveled, not by way of the Kiel Canal as was her wont, but all the way around Denmark. And a last curious detail: on her following cruises she carried a new captain.

He was completely outspoken. France, he reminded Chauvineau, happened to have at present very cordial relations with the U.S.S.R. And since his first reports were liable to cause embarrassment to both governments and, consequently, harm to himself, it were best that they had never existed. The Minister, i.e., Dormoy, Ducloux added ominously, was "beside himself with fury."*

But Chauvineau was both a dogged and a courageous man. Ignoring Ducloux's transparent hints, he now determined to go to Paris and submit his case orally. He was received by the Secretary General of the Sureté, Mondanel, in person. But the latter was, if anything, even more explicit than Ducloux had been. Chauvineau's reports, he remarked dryly, could obviously not be taken seriously; they would have to be rewritten from A to Z. And as Chauvineau argued, pleaded and protested, the following incredible dialogue ensued:

"Did you see an old man?"

"No, but Colin, the two customs inspectors and the dockers saw the van parked alongside the ship. . . ."

"Did you see an old man?"

"No, but the dockers saw a large, heavy packing case being unloaded from the van."

"Did you see an old man?"

"No, but the packing case was so heavy that four sailors had to carry it. . . ."

"Did you see an old man?"

"No, but the ship departed under very mysterious circumstances. . . ."

"In other words, you did *not* see any old man. . . . In fact you did not see anything. . . . Very well, don't insist! . . . Get out!"

Shortly thereafter Chauvineau was relieved "for absenting himself from his post [i.e., his trip to Paris to see Mondanel] without prior

---

* In his recently published reminiscences—one of the avowed purposes of which, incidentally, is to clear the Sureté of charges of political opportunism and bias!—Ducloux is curiously reticent about the Miller affair. In fact, he does not even mention it. Neither does he mention the Kutyepov kidnaping (except by passing reference), although he held the key post of Chief of the Sureté's CID at the time![2]

authorization" and appointed to the much inferior position of Commissioner of the Gare St. Lazare. He thereupon resigned from the service.*

The French authorities' obvious reluctance to follow up any evidence that might point to Moscow's complicity in General Miller's disappearance made itself felt also in another connection.

Thus, unlike the Kutyepov case—which had been a complete mystery from the start—the police had at the outset at least one definite clue to work on, namely, Miller's message to the effect that he had an appointment to meet Skoblin and the two "Germans" at 12:30 P.M. that Wednesday, at the corner of the Rue Jasmin and the Rue Raffet. True, owing to old General Kussonsky's forgetfulness and his and Admiral Kedrov's inept handling of Skoblin later that night when they had him in their clutches, Miller's purpose in leaving behind his fateful last message had been largely canceled out. Nevertheless, Skoblin's precipitate flight as soon as he had been apprised of the message's existence showed that this was a trail that might be usefully followed up.

The German Embassy, which had been approached for information on the mysterious Messrs. Strohman and Werner, had of course promptly denied any knowledge of them. Indeed, the first of the two names—which taken literally means, in German, "dummy" or "puppet"—could well have been one of the things about the proposed rendezvous that had aroused the German-speaking Miller's suspicions in the first place; hence his letter.

The police then went on to investigate the site of the fateful meeting. It was soon obvious that it would have been hard to find a more discreet spot. For, with the exception of a small milk shop (which closed during the luncheon hour) and of two multistoried, modern apartment buildings, there were no stores there, no cafés from which the scene of Miller's appointment with Skoblin and the latter's companions could have been observed by any third

---

* Summoned to testify on this episode at Plevitzkaya's trial, Mondanel began by denying ever having spoken to Chauvineau. He had been too busy with the "Cagoulards" and the Ignaz Reisz affair, he said. He was shown to have lied by another official of the Sureté, who testified having seen and talked to Chauvineau as he was coming out of Mondanel's office.

person. Moreover—and this was bound to cause further embarrassment to Messrs. Auriol and Dormoy—the site that Skoblin had
chosen for the fateful rendezvous was virtually ringed by Soviet-
inhabited or Soviet-owned buildings.

Thus, one of the two modern apartment houses had long served
as a residence for transient agents of the NKVD. The INU's Paris
"resident" at the time, Dr. Chaim Biel'sky, alias "Bieletzky," who
held officially a high position with the Soviet Trade Mission in
France, lived just a couple of blocks away, at No. 85 Boulevard
Suchet.*

One block up the street from the fateful meeting place, at No. 41
Boulevard Montmorency, the Soviet Embassy owned a villa, which
Ambassador Potyomkin had leased earlier that year and which was
used, among other things, as a school for the children of Soviet
officials in Paris. Closed for the summer vacations, the house was, at
the time of which we are speaking, deserted save for an illiterate old
woman, who acted as janitor. Nevertheless, a certain amount of coming and going had been observed in and about this building in the
days immediately preceding General Miller's disappearance. The
mysterious gray Ford van had been seen parked outside the gate at
about 1 P.M. that fateful Wednesday afternoon, just two and three-
quarter hours prior to its arrival alongside the *Maria Ulyanova* at
Le Havre, with the mysterious packing case. And it was to be seen
there again in the days that followed the outrage.

At about 12:50 or 12:55 P.M. that Wednesday, a Gallipoli veteran,
who was personally acquainted with both Miller and Skoblin, happened to be standing on the terrace of a house situated just a short
way down and across the street from the Soviet villa, when he noticed three men standing on the sidewalk outside the latter's gates.
Two of them he recognized immediately. They seemed to be arguing. Skoblin kept pointing to the entrance of the villa, as if inviting

* Biel'sky had just returned, empty-handed, from Prague, where he had been
sent to induce the famous German Communist Willi Münzenberg to return to
Moscow. Münzenberg, one of the most brilliant Comintern agents of all time,
survived another three years. Having formally defected in 1939, he was in 1940
arrested and interned in a detention camp by the French authorities as an
"enemy alien." He perished shortly thereafter, shot in the back "while attempting to escape."

Miller to enter. But the old man clearly hesitated. A third individual —tall and powerfully built—stood between them, his back to the watcher. Just then the latter was called away and when he returned to the terrace, a few minutes later, there was no one in sight. Instead a gray van now stood outside the gates.

A little later, a traveling salesman by the name of Pic, who happened to be returning home for lunch, noticed two men standing at the entrance of the metro station "Jasmin," at the corner of the Avenue Mozart. They were arguing about something and gesticulating. They spoke Russian and so Pic turned away in disgust, for he disliked foreigners and especially Russians. But he had had time to notice the face of one of them. It was Skoblin.

It took the French police, curiously enough, six long weeks to get around to searching the Soviet villa at No. 41 Boulevard Montmorency and when they did so, it was on the personal instructions of President Lebrun, following a moving appeal from General Miller's widow. The Sureté was later to claim that it had required all that time in order to ascertain whether the building enjoyed diplomatic immunity! Needless to say, the search yielded nothing.

A little over a year after General Miller's disappearance, on December 5, 1938, Plevitzkaya went on trial before the Court of Assizes of the Department of the Seine. Although it had not been possible to establish the Soviets' direct responsibility in the affair, the investigation had by now yielded convincing evidence of Skoblin's participation in the outrage and of his wife's knowledge of it and complicity. The trial turned into one of the *causes célèbres* of the year. All Paris flocked to the hearings. But the proceedings brought out few facts that were not already known. At times, the defendant seemed on the verge of breaking down and telling all. But then—whether out of fear of possible reprisals, or out of loyalty to her husband and the cause they had both served—she would regain her self-control and relapse into silence. On December 9 the court announced its verdict: Plevitzkaya was found guilty of complicity in an act of "arbitrary sequestration and violence" and condemned to twenty years at hard labor. The sentence was one of the harshest ever handed down against a woman in the annals of French justice.

She never completed her sentence. In October, 1944, she died in the Rennes prison for women, taking her secret with her into the grave.

Sometime after the German occupation of Paris the Gestapo carried out a search of the premises of the ROVS, at No. 29 Rue du Colisée. To the amazement of all concerned, every room was found to be wired to a master switchboard that had been installed in the same building, in the home of a White Russian *émigré* by the name of Tretyakov (of the well-known family of Moscow millionaires who built the famous art gallery that still carries their name). Upon his arrest the latter readily admitted being a Soviet agent of many years' standing. He denied, however, having had anything to do with the Miller Affair. The Gestapo, curiously, also saw fit to seize old General Kussonsky, Miller's luckless Chief of Staff. He was to die shortly thereafter in a Nazi concentration camp in Belgium.

This discovery provides a clue to Skoblin's escape that fateful night of the twenty-second to the twenty-third of September, 1937, from the Rue du Colisée. For whereas it had until then been naturally assumed that upon stepping out of the offices of the ROVS, he had *descended* the stairs into the street and then made good his escape, it was now far more likely that he had *ascended* them and hidden out in Tretyakov's apartment until the coast was clear.

Except that it is then difficult to understand why after that he had to go all the way to Neuilly in order to borrow a couple of hundred francs from the Krivosheyevs!

On February 22, 1938, the body of a White Russian taxi driver, one Colonel Chimerin, was fished out of the Seine in suburban Levallois-Perret. He was found to have been strangled after a violent struggle. The investigation brought out that he had left his home one evening, late in January, and had not been seen or heard of since. Friends claimed that he had been terribly depressed ever since the Miller affair and that in moments of drunken candor he would insist that his days were numbered, that he was a condemned man, for he had inadvertently stumbled upon the answer to the whole mystery. At the same time he seemed strangely reluctant to go to the police with his story. The newspapers devoted half a dozen columns to *"l'Affaire du Colonel Tchimerine,"* but then they gave up and it was soon forgotten.

Apart from its understandable desire to decapitate a hostile organization such as the ROVS at a time of impending world crisis, the Kremlin's motives in ordering the kidnaping of a seventy-year-old man are not immediately apparent. For taken alone, that reason seems clearly inadequate. In the first place, though noisy and perhaps at times even bothersome, the ROVS was by now not very dangerous. Moreover, however much this may have been alleged at the time, there was virtually no chance that their man Skoblin would have succeeded Miller at the head of the organization; he was much too unpopular outside his own narrow circle. The reasons must therefore necessarily be sought elsewhere.

At least one influential Western newspaper, the *Manchester Guardian,* was prepared to discount Moscow's role altogether. Thus, writing on the morrow of the General's disappearance, it pointed out that "while it would be reckless to suggest that Miller was the victim of Right-wing extremists, it seems equally improbable that the Soviets could have had any interest in kidnaping him." And the paper went on to echo the hypothesis that the clue to the whole mystery should be sought in Spain, where, if not Miller himself, then at least some of his closest associates were known to have been in close contact with the Nationalists.

The Soviet press, needless to say, was prompt in following up this suggestion. Just a little over a week after Miller's kidnaping, on September 30, *Pravda's* well-known correspondent in Republican Spain, Mikhail Koltzov (who was himself to perish shortly in Stalin's Great Purge), published a series of letters that had allegedly been found on the body of the White Russian General, Anton Fock—a

prominent "Young Turk" who, volunteering with Franco's forces
early in the Civil War, had just been killed in action—and one of
which, from Miller, charged Fock openly with excessive Nazi
sympathies. And Koltzov went on, naturally, to conclude that Miller
had been removed by the Gestapo. But this charge, which at first
glance may have been viewed as not totally implausible, considering
Miller's persistent refusal to side with Germany, was soon invali-
dated by another Communist organ, the Comintern's *International
Press Correspondence,* which insisted in its No. 48 of November 6
that the Gestapo was guilty, not only of Miller's disappearance, but
also of Dimitri Navashin's death in the Bois de Boulogne and of the
recent Chekist defector Ignaz Reisz's murder in Lausanne. This
was rash of the Comintern, to say the least, since the NKVD's responsibility, at least in the latter case, was by now denied only in
the Communist camp!

Then another Spanish clue was taken up. It was now claimed
that at one point Russian *émigrés* with pro-Communist leanings
were encouraged to enlist with Franco's forces with a view to
building up a potential Communist Fifth Column there. Whereupon
the Nationalist Counter-Intelligence had, through the above-mentioned General Fock, invited the ROVS to help weed them out.
Miller had, allegedly, declined the invitation, thereby courting
death at the hands of the enraged Nationalists. A Captain Savin,
who was known to have made a number of trips to Nationalist Spain
at the time, purportedly at Miller's behest, was called to testify on
the matter at Plevitzkaya's trial. But it was soon ascertained that
Miller had had nothing to do with his trips. Moreover, Savin was
found to have been in suspiciously close contact with the Spanish
Count Mendés de Sevigny, a shady character who, after serving in
turn the Nationalists and the Republicans as a double agent, was in
the end recalled to Barcelona and shot there by the Spanish NKVD.

Actually, Krivitzky alone seems to have come close to the truth
when he suggests that the key to the Miller mystery should be
sought in the Tukhachevsky affair.

Indeed, the crucial month in both cases seems to have been the
month of December, 1936. For it was in December, 1936, that

Yezhov set up his "Administration for Special Tasks," which was to handle the most secret aspects of the Great Purge. It was also in December or at the latest early in January, that Karl Radek, Stalin's No. 1 stool pigeon in the first two show trials, must have been made to fabricate the evidence that linked General Putna, and through him Tukhachevsky, with the opposition, evidence which Radek then repeated in court on January 24 and 25, 1937, and which heralded the coming purge of the Red Army. Stalin's decision to speed up the liquidation of his generals must thus have gone back at least as far as that. And finally it was in December that Krivitzky himself received orders to assign two trusted agents to an affair "of such colossal importance," that INU head Slutzky had been obliged to give up all other business to see it through. Thus the plan to kidnap General Miller must also have gone back at least as far as that. Indeed, it does not seem illogical to conclude that the original purpose of Miller's kidnaping was to provide a potential witness, who could be brain-washed into testifying against the generals at their show trial. But then a hitch occurred, as a result of which Krivitzky's two men, after being made to cool their heels in Paris for a couple of weeks, were sent back to The Hague, their mission unaccomplished. What was this hitch?

The answer to this question seems to have been provided during Plevitzkaya's trial. For there it was learned that again in that fateful month of December, 1936, Miller had received General Dobrovol'-sky's explicit warning to the effect that Skoblin was, in the Finns' opinion, a Soviet double agent. And as a result Skoblin was at last dismissed from his post of "Special *Rapporteur*" on all matters pertaining to the "Inner Line," the post itself was abolished, and Miller's personal attitude toward him cooled noticeably. And since the success of the original kidnaping plan hinged largely on Miller's blind trust in Skoblin and his willingness to agree to anything the latter might suggest, the venture had now to be postponed until Skoblin had regained his chief's confidence or until an alternative plan had been worked out.

Nine months later the kidnaping attempt was successfully carried out according to the original plan.

And now two questions come to mind:

Firstly, the very fact that, upon leaving for his fateful appointment with Skoblin, Miller saw fit to leave a written warning that the meeting might be, in his own words, "a trap," goes to show that Skoblin was still suspect in the old man's eyes. In that case, why did the latter attend the rendezvous in the first place? Was he trying to atone for his past credulity by offering himself as a live decoy? But unless Skoblin could be caught *flagrante delicto* as it were—and Miller took no steps to that end beyond writing the above cryptic warning*—this sacrifice of his person made no sense. What other reason was there? We know not.

The second question is even more important from the point of view of this narrative. For by the time Miller was kidnaped, the original purpose of his kidnaping no longer held good. He could not possibly have been brain-washed into testifying against the Red generals for the simple reason that they were dead and had been dead for the past three and a half months. Which, in turn, brings up two further points.

What, in the first place, made Stalin change his mind and, instead of bringing his generals to open trial (as he had originally intended), shoot them out of hand, as it were, in mad haste, as if he hadn't a minute to lose?

Because he *hadn't* a minute to lose. For sometime between the months of December, 1936, and May, 1937, Stalin seems to have realized that he could not afford to wait any longer, for the simple reason that the premise upon which he planned to rest his case against his generals had now become a reality: they were not *potential* plotters; they *were* plotters. And by an extraordinary coincidence, this realization (whatever its origin) came at the very moment when he was being offered from Berlin the documentary evidence that would convict them in the eyes of their peers (who would presently sit in judgment over them) and hence, perhaps, of public

---

* In the first years following General Kutyepov's disappearance, General Miller would never go out unescorted. In 1935, however, he had canceled these precautionary measures for reasons of economy.

opinion. And so virtually overnight the original plan for a military show trial was scratched, the generals themselves were arrested and their case disposed of within one week.

But then, since Miller could no longer be called as a witness against them, why did the old man need to be kidnaped at all?

Because, says Krivitzky, he knew too much. Stalin, he reminds us—and Krivitzky's own fate, two years later, seems to prove his point—was not in the habit of allowing anyone to survive who had been in one way or another associated with his less "respectable" undertakings. That is why Slutzky and Spiegelglass, though they had carried out the Miller operation with signal success, themselves survived barely a year. That is why Yagoda and Molchanov, who had helped Yezhov prepare the first show trial, would perish. That is why Yezhov himself and all those who ran the Great Purge would also perish. And since Miller was the only one, outside of the Germans (and *they* could be trusted not to talk), who might know about, or at least suspect, Skoblin's role in the Tukhachevsky Affair, he too had to go.

And now we come up against the greatest mystery of all, one which for the time being, alas, will have to remain unanswered: What *was* Skoblin's exact role in the Tukhachevsky Affair?

His name as *the* betrayer of the Tukhachevsky group comes up for the first time in the October, 1938, issue of the German publication, *Deutsches Wehr*. What, in the first place, prompted the Germans to reveal that which normally should have remained a closely guarded secret? Indiscretion? A slip? Hardly. The Abwehr's desire (*Deutsches Wehr* was an Army, not a party publication) to avenge themselves on and cause embarrassment to the Gestapo? That could be, but the article makes, naturally enough, no mention of the latter's role in the affair, nor could it at that time be suspected that Skoblin was connected with the Gestapo in the first place. Or was it simply the understandable temptation on the part of the Nazi government, now that Skoblin's role in the Miller affair had been uncovered, to shift the blame from their own shoulders to those of an exposed double agent of the NKVD? Probably.

Krivitzky—who, incidentally, did not himself believe in the existence of a plot in the Red Army, claiming that the whole thing was a
concoction of the Gestapo—suggests that the incriminating material
was forged by Heydrich & Co. and passed on to Skoblin and that the
latter then forwarded it to his Moscow superiors.[3]

But this theory is in conflict with post-World War II German
sources (Schellenberg, Hoettl), who insist that it was Skoblin who
first apprised Heydrich of the existence of an anti-Stalin plot in the
Red Army, though they differ as to the exact date when this took
place.

This question of dates is, generally speaking, one of the most
puzzling aspects of the Tukhachevsky Affair. The crucial conference between Hitler, Himmler and Heydrich (at which it was decided to sell the Red generals out to Stalin) is reported to have taken
place in the fall of 1936 and at any rate before Christmas. Others
claim that the operation was completed only late in April, i.e.,
shortly before Tukhachevsky's official fall from favor.

To begin with, it is doubtful that the idea of doing away with the
generals crystallized in Stalin's mind *prior to* the September meeting of the Central Committee, when they and his foes in his own
faction ganged up against him. Likely as not, this decision was taken
shortly before Radek was made to testify against them, i.e., early in
January or late in December. It is only *after* Stalin had taken this
decision that Skoblin could have been instructed by the NKVD to
approach Heydrich. On the other hand, "late in January" (according
to Beneš) the Wilhelmstrasse was assuring Czech Ambassador
Mastny that it was "at the time" negotiating with an anti-Stalin
group in the Red Army. In other words, by late January Hitler *had
not yet* decided to side with Stalin against the Red Army. It is also
in January that Schellenberg claims to have submitted to Heydrich
his findings on Task Force "R." All in all, therefore, it seems far
more probable that the whole operation came to a head, not *before*
Christmas but sometime thereafter—in other words, that Stalin
ordered it sometime in December or January, that Skoblin approached Heydrich and that Heydrich conferred with Himmler and
Hitler sometime in February, or at the earliest late in January, that

the material was forged sometime between then and the end of April and that it was communicated to Stalin early in May, whereupon Tukhachevsky's disgrace, arrest and execution followed.

The question now arises: How, or from whom, did Skoblin first learn about the existence of a plot in the Red Army? From his fellow White Russians, from Miller or the "Inner Line"? But there is absolutely no evidence (beyond Skoblin's own alleged assurances to that effect to Heydrich) linking the plotters to the White paramilitary groups. Indeed, knowing the degree of the ROVS' infiltration by the NKVD, it seems highly unlikely that the plotters would *ever* have risked contacting them, especially when one considers the very insignificant benefits that could come from such co-operation. From whom then did Skoblin get his information? From the plotters themselves? Had *he* been in secret contact with them? Possibly. But in that case, since his primary allegiance was beyond any doubt to the NKVD, he must surely have promptly forwarded the information to Yezhov and in that case, why did Stalin wait until May, 1937, to strike? Besides, this does not explain the other question: Why did Skoblin report the fact to Heydrich? On whose orders? Moscow's? No doubt. But why? Stalin's plan to eliminate the generals did not, indeed, it *could* not have hinged on the receipt of the Task Force "R" dossier, since he could not possibly have foreseen that, rather than sympathize with and back the plotters, Hitler would betray them to him instead. The Task Force "R" file must have represented merely an additional, totally unexpected element in his case against Tukhachevsky & Co. The reason for which Skoblin was made to approach Heydrich must have been a different one, that had only indirect bearing on the Tukhachevsky affair. And here one can only surmise.

In the first place, Skoblin's report to Heydrich is said to have included also mention of the fact that "the Red Army plotters were in secret contact with the Reichswehr." In other words, it fed the already existing bad feelings between Hitler and *his* generals. Could Moscow's purpose have been to do just that? By now the Red generals were doomed; Stalin had singled them out for extermination. Radek had hinted as much; the circle was closing in on them, relentlessly; and there was absolutely nothing the generals themselves or anybody else, for that matter, could do about it, unless they struck first. And at the time of which we are speaking, Stalin could not possibly have known anything about the plot, or else *he* would have struck first, immediately, as he would strike, in May, once he *was* informed about it. Thus, by allowing Skoblin to approach Heydrich, Stalin's designs against the Army could hardly be affected. Hitler, however, might be induced thereby to take action for treasonable activities against *his* generals.

And then there is a final argument. Skoblin could not possibly have foreseen that Miller would leave his last fateful message. So far as it was humanly possible to judge, the kidnaping plot was foolproof. One day Miller would be there, the next day he would be gone, with nobody the wiser. And even though he could hardly expect to step into the old man's shoes, Skoblin would continue as one of the ROVS' top leaders. Assuming that he wished also to enhance his position in Berlin, with a view to gaining insight into some other Nazi anti-Soviet intrigue, one good way to go about it would be to go to Heydrich with his report, knowing full well that the Red generals' days were counted anyhow, and then when the ax fell, his prestige would be all the greater.

One way or the other, he could hardly fail.

But then came the collapse of the whole cunningly contrived edifice and the end of all his dreams, as Admiral Kedrov remarked that night in the dimly lit office of the Rue du Colisée: "But we *know* that you met with General Miller. . . . We know the *time* of the meeting . . . the *place* . . . we have *proof* . . . *documentary* proof. . . ."

Sometime in 1939 a former high official of the OGPU-NKVD, who called himself "Aleksander Antonov" (though this was obviously not his real name), admitted to a fellow prisoner (who later escaped abroad) that General Miller reached Soviet soil safely. For a while he was held in the prison of Chelyabinsk, in the Urals. What happened to him later, Antonov knew not.

Skoblin's fate too remains a mystery. Likely as not, he was made to share that of so many of his superiors in the NKVD who had failed in their mission—a bullet in the nape of the neck in the porcelain-tiled cellar of the Lubyanka.

As for Krivitzky, upon whose testimony so much of the available information on the Tukhachevsky and Miller affairs rests, he literally owed his life to General Miller. For shortly after the latter's disappearance, Soviet Chargé d'Affaires A. Hirschfeld was summoned to the Quai d'Orsay and told in unequivocal terms that were anything to happen to those recent Soviet defectors who had sought political asylum on French soil, the Paris government "would take the gravest possible view of the situation." Krivitzky thus gained a couple of years' respite.

POSTSCRIPT

One day, in 1941 or 1942, a visitor called to see Sergheil Voitzekhovsky, head of the White Russian Credentials Office in German-occupied Warsaw. The man—tall, middle-aged, powerfully built, with red hair and pale shifty eyes—extended his calling card. It read: "Baron Aleksander von Manteuffel." After a while, however, he admitted that this was not actually his name, but that of his mother, that he had been born and had grown up in the Soviet Union, that he now ran an antique shop in German-occupied Kiev and that he was on his way to Berlin, where he hoped to establish business contacts. Voitzekhovsky had taken an instant dislike to his visitor and he did not detain him long.

Sometime in 1943 Voitzekhovsky traveled himself to Berlin on official business. His colleague, the Berlin head of the White Russian Credentials Office, Lieutenant General Vassili V. Biskubsky, a well-known figure in the Russian emigration, had many contacts in German military circles.

"Tell me," Biskubsky remarked one day to Voitzekhovsky. "When you were in Warsaw, did you ever happen to come across a certain Baron Aleksander von Manteuffel?"

"Indeed I did," Voitzekhovsky replied, a little taken aback. "Have you met him too? Who is he?"

"Why, didn't you know?" said Biskubsky. "That was Edward Opperput, the man of the Trust. . . ."

Voitzekhovsky was instantly attentive, for at one time he had closely followed the fate of that organization.

"*Was?* Why 'was'? Has anything happened to him?"

"The Germans caught him," replied Biskubsky. "He was spying for the Reds. . . ."

"What did they do to him?"

"I don't know," Biskubsky said with a shrug. "Probably shot him. . . ."

New York, 1956-1959

NOTES AND SOURCES

Chapter 1. The Gentleman from Revel

1. Frunze, M.: *"Vrangel,"* in *Kommunist* (Petrograd), November 7, 1921; quoted by G. Orlov in *Vestnik Soyuza Gallipoliitzev* (Paris), August 1, 1938.
2. Golubev, Combrig: *"Bor'ba Krassnoi Armii na Krymskom Fronte,"* in the series *"Razgrom Vrangelya. 1920,"* Moscow, 1930, q.v. in *ibid.*
3. Nabokov, VI.: *Nabokov's Dozen,* N.Y., Doubleday, 1958, p. 79.
4. Triandafilov, V.: *"Likvidatsiya Vrangelya,"* in *Sbornik Trudov Voyenno-Nauchnogo Obshchestva,"* Moscow, 1922, Vol. II; q.v. in Orlov, G., *loc. cit.*

Chapter 2. Boris Savinkov and Sydney Reilly

1. Churchill, W. S.: *Great Contemporaries,* N.Y., Putnam, 1937, pp. 103-104.
2. Lockhart, Sir R. H. Bruce: *Memoires of a British Agent,* Harmondsworth, Penguin, 1950, p. 178.
3. Maugham, W. S.: "The Terrorist," in *Redbook* (N.Y.), October, 1943.
4. Kennan, G. F.: *Soviet-American Relations 1917-1920. The Decision to Intervene,* Princeton, 1956, pp. 11-12.
5. Lockhart, Sir R. H. Bruce: *loc. cit.,* pp. 272-273.
6. Maugham, W. S., q.v. Sayers, M. and Kahn, A.: *The Great Conspiracy. The Secret War Against the Soviet Union,* Boston, Little Brown, 1946, p. 138.
7. Reilly, S. G.: *Britain's Master Spy or the Adventures of Sydney Reilly,* London, Elkin, Mathews and Marriot, 1931, pp. 28-29.
8. Lockhart, Sir R. H. Bruce, *loc. cit.,* pp. 310-312.
9. Reilly, S. G., *loc. cit.,* p. 21.
10. Kennan, G. F., *loc. cit.* p. 461.
11. In the light of recent attempts by the present Soviet leadership to blame Stalinist terror as a departure from the Lenin school of statesmanship, it is interesting to note the following letter from Lenin to Grigori E. Zinovyev, in those days chairman of the Leningrad party organization and dated June, 1918. It reads: "Comrade Zinovyev!

Only to-day did we in the Central Committee learn that the Petersburg *workers* wanted to answer Volodarsky's assassination with mass terror and that you (not you personally, but the Petersburg members of the Central Committee and Communist Party) restrained them. I must emphatically protest. . . . This is in-ad-missible! . . . One must foster the mass-nature of the terror against the counter-revolutionaries and push it with ever greater energy, especially in Petersburg, whose example is *decisive*. Greetings! Lenin." (quoted by M. Vishnyak in *Novyi Zhurnal* (N.Y.), June, 1959, No. 57, from "*Iz Istorii Vsrossiiskoĭ Chrezvychainöi Komissii, 1917-1921, Sbornik Dokumentov,*" Moscow, 1958.

12. Engels, F., q.v. in Souvarine, B.: *Stalin. A Critical Survey of Bolshevism,* N.Y., Longmans, Green, 1939, p. 252.
13. Hill, Capt. Geo.: *Go Spy the Land,* London, Cassell, 1932, p. 244.
14. It is still a matter of speculation whether there was any substance to Reilly's plan, or whether the whole thing was not, in W. H. Chamberlin's words, just "a compound of actual advances [by Lockhart] of money, of which the *Cheka* probably found some trace, and of fanciful schemes which the *Cheka* agents laid before the too credulous and too imaginative Reilly." (W. H. Chamberlin: *The Russian Revolution, 1917-1921,* N.Y., 1935, Vol. II, pp. 68-69.) Chamberlin bases this suggestion on an interview published in *Pravda* on September 5, 1918, i.e., just a few days after all these events, in which Yakov Peters, Dzierzhinski's right-hand man, admitted that the Cheka, having become convinced that the threads of various anti-Soviet plots led to Lockhart's British Mission, "arranged a fictitious plot" and dispatched some "old and trusted Communists" to Lockhart (Berzin and Smidchen?) with an alleged plan to overthrow the regime.
15. Churchill, W. S., *loc. cit.,* p. 108.
16. Reilly, S. G., *loc. cit.,* p. 113.
17. Lockhart, Sir R. H. Bruce, *loc. cit.,* p. 178.
18. Churchill, W. S., *loc. cit.,* p. 109.
19. Churchill, W. S., *idem.,* p. 110.
20. Lockhart, Sir R. H. Bruce, *loc. cit.,* pp. 178-179.
21. Reswick, W.: *I Dreamt Revolution,* Chicago, Regnery, 1952, p. 11.
22. Bessedovsky, G. Z., *Na Putyakh k Termidoru: Iz Vospominanii Byvshago Sovyetskago Diplomata,* Paris, 1931, Vol. II, pp. 69 *et seq.*
23. Duranty, W., *The Curious Lottery,* N.Y., Coward-McCann, 1929, pp. 128 *et seq.*
24. Reswick, W., *loc. cit.,* pp. 8-11.
25. *Pravda* (Moscow), May 12, 1925.
26. Duranty, W., *loc. cit.,* p. 132.

27. Q.v. in Sayers, M. & Kahn, A., *loc. cit.*, p. 138.
28. *Ibid.*, p. 139.
29. Churchill, W. S., *loc. cit.*, 110.
30. Reilly, S. G., *loc. cit.*, pp. 169 *et seq.*
31. *Ibid.* p. 186.
32. *Ibid.* pp. 194-195.
33. *Ibid.* p. 213.
34. Q.v. in *Ibid.*, p. 214.

Chapter 3. Opperput

1. *Uusi Suomi* and *Huvustadbladt* (Helsinki), April 24 and 26, 1927.
2. Hill, Capt. Geo., *loc. cit.*, pp. 257-258.
3. Even then, said Opperput—though again we have only his own word
   for it—Yakushev set down in writing the terms on which he was willing
   to co-operate with the OGPU. Thus, while his anti-Communist convictions remained unchanged and he would therefore have nothing to
   do with the OGPU's struggle against the opponents of the regime *inside*
   the country, he felt that the Whites had sold themselves out to the
   enemies of Russia and was consequently willing to help neutralize
   them.

   However implausible all this may seem, even granting that there was
   in the early NEP days of the Soviet era considerable flexibility in the
   Kremlin's policies toward its various enemies, there exists, in fact, no
   clear-cut evidence of duplicity on the part of Yakushev prior to his
   arrest in the fall of 1921. True, *Lesso-Export*, the giant Soviet lumber
   trust on whose behalf he had traveled to Oslo that summer, was already then closely tied in with the Cheka, which was eventually to
   supply most of the slave-labor manpower for the exploitation of
   Russia's forest resources.

   Neither is it clear to this day whether the MUCR ever existed as a
   bona fide anti-Communist underground or whether it was created by
   the Cheka especially for the purpose of furthering Commissar Kiakowski's master plan. According to one version, it started off under the
   former Tsarist General Zayonchkovsky's leadership as a genuine
   clandestine group late in 1921, holding its first secret congress in
   Moscow in February-March, 1922, but presently it was betrayed to
   the Cheka, which forced Zayonchkovsky to "co-operate" by seizing his
   daughter as hostage. Yakushev seems to have been released late in
   January or early in February, 1922, after which he was rearrested and
   again released, this time for good, in April. As he figures on the list of
   the MUCR's charter members, it is not impossible that it was he who
   sold the organization out to the Cheka in the first place.

4. *Posledniye Novosti* (Paris), June 18, 1927.
5. Brunovsky, VI.: *The Methods of the OGPU*, London, Harper, 1931, pp. 195-198; also *idem*. in *Segodnya* (Riga), September 21, 1927, No. 37.

Chapter 4. The End of the Trust

1. Hill, Capt. Geo.: *loc. cit.*, pp. 195-196.
2. Larionov, Capt. V.: q.v. in Amfiteatrov, A.: *"Vzryv na Moike,"* in *Vozrozhdenie* (Paris), 1935, No. 4011 *et seq*.
3. Q.v. in Chebyshev, N.: *"Trust. Istoriya Odnoi Leghendy*. Part IX,"* in *Vozrozhdenie* (Paris), 1935, No. 3740.
4. Q.v. in Kichkassov, N.: *Byelogvardeiskii Terror Protiv S.S.S.R.*, Moscow, 1928.
5. A historico-philosophical outgrowth of the once famous Slavophile movement, with a strong injection of Spengler-Kayserling ideas, the "Eurasian" (in Russian *Yevraziiski*) doctrine, which enjoyed a considerable vogue in certain Russian intellectual circles at the beginning of the century, held that the Western creative genius was rapidly wilting and that its product, Romano-Germanic civilization, was therefore in a profound state of crisis. All past attempts to revive it had failed, because all of them had rested on the equally fallacious twin cornerstones of Law and Economic Materialism, which lay at the root of its original decline.

Russia, however, never having belonged, properly speaking, to Western Europe, did not have to share in this—to quote Spengler— "catastrophe of contemporaneousness." Indeed, the 1917 Revolution had provided her with a unique opportunity to cast off the dead weight of Western cultural tradition, that had made her for centuries a foster child of the West, and to recover her true identity, which was neither with the West nor with the East, but somewhere in between, as "Eurasia." Thus Russia could become the "ideological fulcrum of the world," the cradle of a new civilization that would substitute the purely Russian concept of "truth" (*pravda*) to the now obsolete Western concept of "law" (*pravo*).

As for Communism, the "Eurasians" were inclined to regard it as a last materialistic attempt to revive Western civilization, a transitory if necessary evil, foredoomed to failure like all earlier ones, but through which Russia had need to pass in order to rediscover her real destiny.

From this to the acceptance of Soviet rule and then even its active promotion, there was but a step—which the Soviet leadership early realized. Starting in 1924, therefore, the OGPU proceeded to infiltrate the "Eurasian" movement and by 1926, it had already done so well,

that the Chekist Langovoy—himself one of the founders of the Trust
—had become *persona grata* in *émigré* "Eurasian" circles (where he
played much the same role as his friend and colleague Yakushev did
in Kutyepov's entourage), and it had become generally difficult to
determine where genuine philosophy ended and Communist propaganda began.

Chapter 5. The Kidnaping of General Kutyepov

1. Reilly, S., *loc. cit.*, p. 120.
2. Plekhanov, G., q.v. in Souvarine, B., *loc. cit.*, p. 186.
3. Maugham, W. S.: "The Terrorist," *loc. cit.*, p. 186.
4. Alekseyev, N.: "*Razoblacheniya Predatelya. GPU i Emigratziya,*" in
   Vozrozhdenie (Paris), 1927, No. 1626.
5. Bessedovsky, G.: *loc. cit.*, p. 245.
6. Barmine, A.: *One Who Survived. The Life Story of a Russian under
   the Soviets*, N.Y., Putnam, 1945, p. 186.
7. Though the authenticity of M. Litvinov's *Notes for a Diary* (N.Y.,
   William Morrow, 1955) has been very much disputed, some of the
   entries have an undoubtedly genuine ring. One of these, dated March,
   1930 (pp. 134-138) quotes the INU's Paris "resident" Helfand's
   version of the Kutyepov affair. "The case is now closed for ever,"
   Helfand is alleged to have said, "Some of [our] agents among the
   émigrés had a finger in it, but they won't talk. . . . Two of these
   agents are well-known White generals. This third is an ex-White
   minister. They had no direct part in the abduction. They acted only
   in the preparatory stages. The job itself was done by our agents who
   were sent from here [i.e., from Russia] to France. They have returned
   to the U.S.S.R. . . . Kutyepov will never be found. He has disappeared one hundred meters down. . . ." But then a later entry
   quotes the OGPU's Counter-Intelligence Chief Artuzov as saying that
   Helfand himself had no hand in the business!

Chapter 7. The Ides of June—1. The Official Story

1. Krivitzky, W. (pseud. for Walter Ghinsburg): *In Stalin's Secret Service*,
   N.Y., Harper, 1939, pp. 227 *et seq.*
2. *Ibid.*, p. 230.
3. Stalin, J.: *Problems of Leninism*, Moscow, 1945, pp. 620 *et seq.*
4. Q.v. in Wolfe, B.: *Khrushchev and Stalin's Ghost*, N.Y., Praeger, 1957,
   p. 176.
5. Stalin, J., *loc. cit.*, pp. 620 *et seq.*
6. Petrov, VI. and E.: *Empire of Fear. Their Own Story*, N.Y., Praeger,
   1956, p. 73

278   THE CONSPIRATORS

Chapter 8. Anatomy of a Purge

1. Deutscher, I.: *Stalin. A Political Biography,* N.Y. & London, Oxford, 1949, p. 417.
2. *Ibid.,* p. 375.
3. Wolfe, B.: *loc. cit.,* p. 169. Typically, when one of his followers, Boris Souvarine, came out in 1929 with the demand that the OGPU be abolished—the latter had just summarily shot one of its own officials, the Trotskyite Yakov Blumkin (one of the assassins, in 1918, of German Ambassador Count Mirbach), on the sole charge of contacting Trotsky abroad—Trotsky himself, in an unsigned editorial in his *Bulleten' Oppositzii* (q.v. in Wolin, S. and Slusser, Robert M.: *The Soviet Secret Police,* N.Y., Praeger, 1957, p. 46, fn. 67), retorted icily that "The OGPU is an organ of self-defense of the proletarian dictatorship. Inasmuch as the October Revolution is still surrounded by a world of enemies, it cannot give up such organs—the dictatorship cannot cease to be a dictatorship. . . . Only liberals and liberalizing Social-Democrats can put the question on a formal basis. We put it on a class basis: *In whose name* is repression being applied? *Against whom* is it being applied? . . . It is a matter of revolutionary expediency and not of super-class justice. . . ." Which was as good a justification of mass terror as any Stalin was as yet to offer.
4. Wolfe, B.: *loc. cit.,* p. 243.
5. *Ibid.,* p. 130.
6. *Passim,* Maynard, Sir J., *Russia in Flux,* N.Y., Macmillan, 1948.
7. Duranty, W.: *Stalin & Co., the Politbureau, the Men Who Run Russia,* N.Y., Sloane, 1949, p. 77.
8. Wolfe, B., *loc. cit.,* p. 239.
9. *Ibid.,* p. 19.
10. Serge, V.: *Portrait de Staline,* Paris, Grasset, 1940, pp. 94-95.
11. Wolfe, B.: *loc. cit.,* pp. 129-131.
12. Souvarine, B.: *loc. cit.,* p. 483.
13. Wolfe, B.: *loc. cit.,* pp. 129-131.
14. Q.v. Radek's testimony in *Sudebnyi Otchet Po Dyelu Anti-Sovyetskago Trotzkistkago Tzentra,* Moscow, 1937, q.v. in Dewár, Hugo: *Assassins at Large,* London, Wingate, 1951, p. 545.
15. Q.v. in Dewar, Hugo, *loc. cit.,* p. 158.

Chapter 9. The Plot

1. The latest version, published on May 14, 1956, in *Life* magazine alongside a denunciation of Stalin as a former agent of the Tsarist secret police, stems from the pen of one "Aleksander Orlov."

   By his real name Aleksander Nikol'sky (though he seems to have carried at various times other aliases), Orlov, an old-time Chekist, was dispatched in the summer of 1936 by the Kremlin to Spain, to advise and assist in the building up of a Spanish Communist secret police. It is the latter which was later responsible for such exploits as the liquidation of the POUM and the murder of the famous Spanish Trotskyite leader, Andrès Nin—a decisive step toward the Communist infiltration of Republican Spain. In time he seems to have acquired such an unsavory reputation that two of the top Soviet advisers in the country, General Jan Berzin, long-time head of the Soviet Military Intelligence and now Chief of the Red Army's mission, and Artur Stashevsky, Soviet Trade Representative in Barcelona and in fact the Central Committee of the CPSV's secret agent in Spain, insisted that he be recalled. But this was 1937, the "Year of the Long Knives," when Yezhov's minions could get away with literally anything. And so it was Berzin and Stashevsky who were recalled instead. They disappeared shortly thereafter. In March, 1938, however, the Great Purge began to reach out into the ranks of the NKVD itself. One after the other, those who had so eagerly helped organize the holocaust were now themselves dragged away to the death cellars of the Lubyanka. This brought about a mass defection of NKVD agents abroad and in July of that year, Orlov "chose freedom" in his turn. Fleeing first to Paris and then to the U.S.A., he eventually published a sensational volume of reminiscences, *The Secret History of Stalin's Crimes* (London, Jarrolds, 1954) in which most of his former fellow henchmen of the NKVD are depicted, needless to say, as well-meaning victims of their "sense of duty," their loyalty to Communism and circumstances generally.

According to Orlov, the anti-Stalin conspiracy originated not with the Red Army or the party opposition, but in the NKVD of all places, following Yagoda's discovery of old Tsarist files that showed Stalin to have been at one point a police spy. This discovery caused, allegedly, such consternation in the NKVD and in party circles generally, that a group of top officials, including Ukraine party boss Stanislav V. Kossior, Kiev NKVD Chief Victor A. Balitzky and the local Army Commander, General Yona E. Yakir, banded together with Tukhachesky, Gamarnik and others to overthrow their "fallen idol." Which is tantamount to claiming that, so long as Stalin confined himself to slaughtering off the Russian peasantry, chaining the workers to their lathes and exterminating all opponents to his personal tyranny, his generals were willing to go along with him, but that when it became known that all this was being done by a former Tsarist stool pigeon, their consciences rebelled. In the first place, the charge that

Stalin was once a Tsarist agent is not a novel one; many years ago, it was offered to Trotsky as a weapon in his epic struggle for Lenin's succession, but he had turned it down for lack of proof. But then, even were this charge to prove one day true, it could hardly have been the prime reason for an anti-Stalin movement in the Red Army or elsewhere. It was not Stalin's past errors, but his present crimes—in which the NKVD was playing so sinister a part—that must have made his continuing rule intolerable, even to some of his former stalwart supporters.

2. Q.v. Trevor-Roper, H. R.: *The Last Days of Hitler,* London, Macmillan, 1947.
3. Gul', R.: *Tukhachevsky, Krassnyi Marshal,* Berlin, p. 42.
4. Fervacque, P.: *Le Chef de l'Armée Rouge. Mikaïl Toukatchevski,* Paris, 1928, p. 29.
5. Hilger, Gustav: *Wir und der Kremlin. Deutsch-Sovjetische Beziehungen 1918-1941,* Frankfurt am/Main, Metzner, 1955, p. 259.

Chapter 10. Enter the Gestapo

1. Trevor-Roper, H. R., *loc. cit.,* p. 7.
2. *Ibid.,* p. 8.
3. *Ostinformation* (Berlin), No. 81, December 4, 1920, q.v. in Wheeler-Bennett, J. W.: *The Nemesis of Power. The German Army in Politics, 1918-1945,* N.Y., St. Martin's Press, 1954, pp. 126-127.
4. Guderian, Gen. Heinz: *Panzerleader,* N.Y., Dutton, 1952, p. 144.
5. Vid. "*O Moskovskikh Protzessakh,*" in *Posev* (Frankfurt am/Main), February 3, 1949, which in its turn quotes an article by Horst Falkenhagen in *Die Neue Zeitung.* Fairly abundant material is now available on German-Soviet military and economic co-operation in the twenties and early thirties, generally, and on the activities of Task Force "R," in particular. Cf. Wheeler-Bennett; J. W., *loc. cit.;* Hilger, Gustav, *loc. cit.;* Melville, Cecil F.: *The Russian Face of Germany. An Account of the Secret Military Relations between Germany and the Soviet-Russian Governments,* London, 1932; Berndorff, H. R.: *General zwischen Ost und West,* Hamburg, 1951; Wollenberg, E.: "*Der Apparat. Stalin's Fünfte Kolonne,* in *Ostprobleme,* 1951, No. 19; Freund, Ger.: *Unholy Alliance. Russian-German Relations from Brest-Litovsk to Berlin (1918-1926),* London, Chatto & Windus, 1957, to name only a few.
6. Maxim Litvinov's *Notes for a Diary, loc. cit.,* pp. 20, 98-99, 105, contain a curious passage which, if true, would cast additional light on this particular aspect of the Tukhachevsky Affair.

Some time in December, 1928, the passage reads, three Russian generals, Tukhachevsky, Yakir and Uborevich—all of whom were to perish in the 1937 Red Army purge—arrived in Berlin from Moscow and asked to see generals Von Seeckt and Von Hammerstein, both of them prime champions of the afore-mentioned *Ostrichtung* in German military circles.

Though it had, at the time, recovered from its 1927 war scare, the U.S.S.R. was still fearful lest the Dawes reparations plan with its corollary, the Allied evacuation of the Ruhr, might lead to a *rapprochement* between the victors of Versailles and Germany—the perennial bogey of the Kremlin. In itself, the Red generals' visit to Berlin was in no way sensational. There was in those days a constant coming and going of top civilian and military people between the two capitals. To their German hosts, however, the Soviet visitors now revealed the existence of a Red Army plot to overthrow Stalin's budding dictatorship and to replace it by a military junta with which Germany might wish to have close ties. Needless to say, the Russian generals said, this plan could succeed only if there was peace; any threat to Russia on the part of the Western Powers would lead necessarily to the banding together of all Russian patriots, whatever their political convictions.

Von Seeckt (who, though retired, still wielded considerable influence) promptly relayed the information to Reichswehr Minister Gröner, urging him to prevail upon the Weimar Government to steer clear of any anti-Soviet involvement with the West, in which Germany would surely be made to play but a secondary role anyway, since she might shortly be in a position, through timely support of a successful military *putsch* in Russia, to achieve there a position of exclusive influence that would immeasurably strengthen her bargaining powers vis-à-vis the West.

In due course the Reichswehr agreed to advance the Russian generals 500,000 marks from its secret funds, which sum was deposited in Yakir's name with a Vienna bank.

The Soviet Military Intelligence, the famous GRU, however, soon got wind of the mysterious transaction. Indeed, General Berzin, the GRU's able chief, took such a serious view of the matter that he decided to report it personally to Stalin. To his surprise, instead of being complimented on his agency's watchfulness, he was ordered curtly immediately to recall the agent responsible for the discovery. On his arrival in Moscow, the latter was arrested by the OGPU at the station and was never seen or heard of again, the GRU being advised not to inquire into the man's whereabouts.

According to the *Notes*, these talks continued off and on until the spring of 1930, when the growing economic crisis must have made it clear to Stalin that the threat of a Western-led coalition against the U.S.S.R. had receded.

Assuming that this story is true and that some mention of these talks had survived in the Task Force "R" files, Heydrich's task must have been greatly facilitated. For little forgery would have been necessary; by merely changing a few dates here and there and substituting a few names elsewhere, the whole story of the 1928-1930 Von Seeckt-Tukhachevsky talks could have been made to look as of much more recent vintage. According to Schellenberg, the job was done in four days, which would seem to imply that Heydrich's team worked largely with already existing material.

7. Beneš, Ed.: *Memoires,* London, Allen & Unwin, 1954, p. 19, fn. 47; see also Churchill, W. S.: *The Gathering Storm,* Boston, Houghton Mifflin, 1948, pp. 288-289.
8. Q.v. in Bela Fromm: *Blood and Banquets. A Berlin Social Diary,* N.Y., Harper, 1942.

Chapter 11. The Ides of June—2. The Real Story
1. Trotsky, L.: *The Revolution Betrayed,* N.Y., Doubleday & Doran, 1937, pp. 287-288, 165-166.
2. Q.v. in Trotsky, L.: *La Bureaucratie Stalinienne et l'Assassinat de Kirov,* Paris, 1935.
3. Uralov, Aleksander (pseud. of Avtorkhanov): *The Reign of Stalin,* London, The Bodley Head, 1953, pp. 44 *et seq.*

Though contrary to usage, no official mention has ever been made in the U.S.S.R. of a fall, 1936, session of the Central Committee, there can nowadays no longer be any doubt that such a session did indeed take place. Under the party statutes, as adopted at the Fourteenth (1925) Congress and amended at the Seventeenth (1934) Congress, the Central Committee was supposed to meet at least once every four months. Sessions of the Congress of the Soviets or of the party Congress were also inevitably preceded by Central Committee meetings, be it only to draft the agendas of these congresses.

A first draft of Stalin's new constitution had been approved at the June, 1936, session of the Central Committee (when the fateful decision had also been taken to bring Zinovyev & Co. to trial), after which it had been made public for open discussion. As a result, thousands of amendments had been suggested and 43 of them had been incorporated in the final draft for endorsement by the Extraordinary Congress of the Soviets that had been called into session early in the coming November. By whom had these amendments been accepted and incorporated? Obviously by the Central Committee. And when? Also obviously between the June session of the Central Committee and the beginning of the Congress of the Soviets' session in November.

On September 10 Pravda came out with the somewhat surprising announcement that "the investigation of the charges against comrades Bukharin and Rykov has been dropped." It seems safe to conclude, therefore, that the fateful session of the Central Committee (which is of such crucial importance in this narrative) took place shortly after the conclusion of the first show trial, i.e., after August 21 (when Vyshinsky demanded a formal sifting of the charges against the leaders of the Right) and before September 10 (when these charges were dropped). The official silence which covers this session to this day is, surely, merely an additional proof that its outcome was unfavorable to Stalin.

4. Deutscher, I.: *loc. cit.*, p. 381.
5. "*Sudebnyi Otchet Po Dyelu Anti-Sovyetskago Terroristickeskago Tzentra*," *loc. cit.*, pp. 105, 135, 545.
6. Shahanan Essez, E.: q.v. in Sayers, M. and Kahn, A.: *loc. cit.*, p. 293.
7. Tabouis, G.: *Ils l'ont appelé Cassandre*, N.Y., 1942, p. 248.
8. Nord, L.: "*Eshche o Tukhachevskom*," in *Chassovoy* (Brussels), 1951, No. 306.
9. Orlov, A.: *The Secret History of Stalin's Crimes*, London, Jarrolds, 1954, p. 237.
10. Petrov, Vl. and E., *loc. cit.*, p. 71.

Chapter 12. The Kidnaping of General Miller

1. Krivitzky, W., *loc. cit.*, p. 213.
2. V.d. Ducloux, L.: *From Blackmail to Treason. Political Crime and Corruption in France, 1920-1940*, London, Deutsch, 1958.
3. As Spiegelglass, INU head Slutzky's deputy, boasted to Krivitzky: "We have information from Germany too, from inside sources. Ours doesn't come from salon conversations, but from within the Gestapo itself. . . . As a matter of fact, we've been receiving material from Germany on Tukhachevsky, Gamarnik and all their clique for a long time." (Krivitzky, W., *loc. cit.*, p. 234 *et seq.*)

GLOSSARY

"ARTUZOV" (alias for Renucci): Italian-born head of the Cheka's Counter-Intelligence Department (KRO).

BESSEDOVSKY, G. Z.: one-time Soviet Chargé d'Affaires in Paris. Defected 1929.

BLÜCHER, MARSHAL V. K.: long-time G.O.C., Soviet armed forces in eastern Siberia. Purged in 1938.

BUDYONNY, MARSHAL S. M.: long-time G.O.C., Soviet cavalry.

BUKHARIN, N. I.: top Communist theoretician after Lenin. One-time member of the Politbureau and head of the Comintern. Leader of the "Right" opposition to Stalin. Purged in 1937.

CANARIS, R.-ADM. W.: head of the German Abwehr (Army Counter-Intelligence). Hanged by Hitler in 1945.

CHEKA (alias OGPU, alias NKVD): literally "Extraordinary Commission for Combating Counter-Revolution and Sabotage." First name of the Soviet political police.

CHEKIST: an official of the Cheka.

DZIERZHINSKI, F. E.: founder and long-time head of the Cheka. Died 1926.

EIDEMANN, GENERAL R. P.: a fellow conspirator of Tukhachevsky. Head of OSSO-AVIACHIM, the Soviet Civil Defense League. Purged in 1937.

"EURASIANS": followers of the "Eurasian" (in Russian: *Yevraziiski*) philosophical movement.

FEDOSSENKO, CAPTAIN: White double agent. Was the first to denounce Skoblin as a Soviet double agent.

FELDMANN, GENERAL B. M.: a fellow conspirator of Tukhachevsky. Head of the Red Army's Administration and Personnel Department. Purged in 1937.

284

FRINOVSKY, COMMISSAR GENERAL M. P.: top aide of NKVD Boss Yagoda. In charge of the first stage of the Great Purge. Then G.O.C., Soviet Frontier Troops. Purged in 1938.

GALLIPOLI ASSOCIATION: White Russian organization grouping White Army veterans. Prominent in émigré politics.

GAMARNIK, JAN B.: a fellow conspirator of Tukhachevsky. Long-time head of the Red Army's Main Political Administration. Murdered or committed suicide in 1937.

HELFAND, L. B.: Soviet Chargé d'Affaires in Paris in 1930. Reputedly responsible for the organization of General Kutyepov's kipnaping.

HEYDRICH, SS-Gruppenführer Reinhard: head of the German SD (Gestapo). Assassinated in 1941.

HILL, CAPT. G.: British intelligence agent in Russia in 1918. A friend of Sydney Reilly.

"INNER LINE": secret group within the ROVS. Was at one time headed by Skoblin.

INU: Foreign Department of the Cheka-OGPU.

"OPERATION KAMA": code name for German-Soviet military-economic co-operation prior to the denunciation of the Versailles Treaty.

"KAMENEV," L. B. (alias for Rosenfeld): one-time member of the Politbureau, Vice-Premier, head of the Moscow Communist party organization. A leader of the Left opposition to Stalin. Purged in 1936.

"KIAKOWSKI," V. (alias for Stetskevich): official of the Cheka's KRO. The founding father of the Trust.

KIROV, S. M.: member of the Politbureau. Head of the Leningrad Communist party organization. Assassinated in 1934.

KOLKHOZ: Collective farm.

KORK, GENERAL A. I.: a fellow conspirator of Tukhachevsky. Head of the Frunze Military Academy. Purged in 1937.

"KRIVITZKY," W. (alias for Ghinsburg): one-time head of the Western European section of the NKVD's Foreign Department. Defected in 1937. Murdered in 1941.

KULAK: wealthy peasant.

KUSSONSKY, GENERAL P. A.: General Miller's Chief of Staff. Responsible for Skoblin's escape.

KUTYEPOV, GENERAL P. A.: White Russian military leader. Headed the ROVS. Kidnaped in 1930.

LARIONOV, CAPTAIN V. A.: prominent White Russian terrorist.

LOCKHART, SIR R. B.: one-time British agent in Russia.

LUBYANKA: synonym for the Cheka-OGPU, from its location in Moscow's Lubyanka Square.

MEKHLIS, L. M.: prominent member of Stalin's Secretariat. Editor in chief of *Pravda*. Succeeded Gamarnik at the head of the Main Political Administration of the Red Army. Prominent actor in the Red Army purge.

MILLER, GENERAL E. K.: White Russian military leader. Succeeded Kutyepov at the head of the ROVS. Kidnaped in 1937.

MUCR: "Monarchist Union of Central Russia." Original name of the Trust.

NEP: Lenin's "New Economic Policy."

NIHILIST: late nineteenth-century anti-Tsarist revolutionary.

NIKOLAYEV, L. V.: Kirov's assassin.

OGPU: successor name of the Cheka.

"Old Bolshevik": pre-1917 member of the Communist party.

"OPPERPUT," E. (alias for Upeninsch, "Staunitz," etc.): top double agent of the Trust.

ORDZHONIKIDZE, G. K.: member of the Politbureau. Commissar of Heavy Industry. Committed suicide or murdered in 1937.

PILAR VON PILHAU, BARON R. A.: top Chekist. Figured prominently in the capture of both Savinkov and Reilly.

PLEVITZKAYA, N. V.: General Skoblin's wife. Convicted for her role in the kidnaping of General Miller. Died in prison in 1944.

Politbureau: top echelon of the Communist party; the virtual government of the U.S.S.R.

POTAPOV, GENERAL: Yakushev's deputy in the Trust.

PRIMAKOV, GENERAL V. M.: one of Tukhachevsky's fellow conspirators. Marshal Budyonny's deputy as head of the Red cavalry. Purged in 1937.

PUTNA, GENERAL V. K.: one of Tukhachevsky's fellow conspirators. Soviet military attaché in London. Purged in 1937.

"Task Force R": a top-secret section of the German General staff in charge of "Operation Kama."

"RADEK," KARL (alias for Sobelson): top Soviet journalist, active in Comintern affairs, purged as a Trotskyite in 1937.

RADKOVICH, G. N.: White Russian terrorist. Maria Schultz's husband.

REILLY, CAPTAIN S. G.: British intelligence agent in Russia in 1918. Lured back to the U.S.S.R. and shot in 1926.

ROVS: for *Russkii Obsche-Voyenskii Soyuz* (Russian Armed Forces' Union), principal. White Russian para-military group. An emanation of the White armies, it was headed successively by Generals Baron Wrangel, Kutyepov and Miller.

RUDZUTAK, JAN E.: alternate member of the Politbureau. Tomsky's successor at the head of the Soviet trade unions. Purged in 1938.

RYKOV, A. I.: Lenin's successor as Soviet Premier. One-time member of the Politbureau. Prominent member of the Right opposition to Stalin. Purged in 1938.

RYUTIN, M. N.: prominent member of the Right opposition to Stalin.

SAVINKOV, B. I.: top anti-Tsarist and later anti-Communist terrorist. Lured back to the U.S.S.R. in 1924, where he perished shortly thereafter, murdered or a suicide.

VON SEECKT, GENERAL H.: founder and long-time head of the German Reichswehr. An ardent champion of a German-Soviet alliance.

SKOBLIN, GENERAL N. V.: White Russian military leader and Soviet double agent. Sold out Marshal Tukhachevsky and General Miller.

SLUTZKY, A. A.: head of the NKVD's INU at the time of General Miller's kidnaping.

SPIEGELGLASS, M.: Slutzky's deputy and successor as head of INU.

SR: A Socialist Revolutionary. Boris Savinkov's party.

"STAUNITZ": one of Opperput's many aliases.

TOMSKY, M. P.: long-time head of the Soviet trade unions. A leader of the Right opposition to Stalin. Committed suicide in 1936.

TRILISSER, M. A.: long-time head of the Cheka-OGPU's INU. Purged in 1938.

TROTSKY, L. D.: founder of the Red Army and long-time Commissar of War. Stalin's No. 1 enemy in the party. Banished in 1929. Assassinated in Mexico City in 1940.

Trust: the cover name of the OGPU's most successful infiltration of the White Russian emigration.

TUKHACHEVSKY, MARSHAL M. N.: top Soviet military leader. When purged in 1937 was First Vice Commissar of Defense.

UBOREVICH, GENERAL I. P.: One of Tukhachevsky's fellow conspirators. When purged in 1937, was G.O.C., Byelorussian Military District.

UGLANOV, N. A.: one-time alternate member of the Politbureau and head of the Moscow party organization. A leader of the Right opposition to Stalin.

ULRICH, V. I.: top Soviet purge-trial judge.

VOROSHILOV, MARSHAL K. E.: long-time Soviet Commissar of Defense. An old crony of Stalin. Now President of the U.S.S.R.

VYSHINSKY, A. Y.: long-time chief Soviet prosecutor. One of the foremost artisans of the purge trials. Later Minister of Foreign Affairs and then Soviet Ambassador to the U.N.

WRANGEL, GENERAL BARON P. N.: last commander in chief of the White Russian armies. Founder of the ROVS.

CAPTAIN "X": Yakushev's first contact with White Russian circles.

YAGODA, G. G.: long-time head of the OGPU-NKVD. After helping to organize the first stage of the Great Purge, was himself purged in 1938.

YAKIR, GENERAL Y. E.: One of Tukhachevsky's fellow conspirators. When purged in 1937, was G.O.C., Kiev Military District.

YAKUSHEV, A. A.: the Trust's front man with the White Russian emigration.

"YANOVICH," A.: wife of General Kutyepov's kidnaper and herself a top agent of the OGPU.

"YANOVICH," V. B. (alias for Volovich): General Kutyepov's kidnaper. Husband of the above.

YEGOROV, MARSHAL A. I.: long-time Chief of Staff of the Red Army. When purged in 1938, was First Vice Commissar of Defense.

YEZHOV, N. I.: Stalin's top henchman in conducting the Great Purge. When himself purged in 1938, was head of the NKVD.

Yezhovshchina: the name by which the Great Purge is commonly known in the U.S.S.R.

ZAKHARCHENKO-SCHULTZ, M. V.: top White agent in the U.S.S.R. and their long-time contact with the Trust.

"ZINOVYEV," G. Y. (alias for Radomysl'sky): long-time member of the Politbureau and head of the Leningrad party organization. Leader of the Left opposition to Stalin. Purged in 1936.

BIBLIOGRAPHY

D'Abernon, Viscount E.: *An Ambassador of Peace. Pages from the Diary of . . . (1920-1926)*, London, Hodder & Stoughton, 1929-30.

————: *Portraits and Appreciations*, London, Hodder & Stoughton, 1931.

Abshagen, K. H.: *Canaris, Patriot und Weltbürger* [*Canaris, Patriot and Citizen of the World*], Stuttgart, Union D. Verlagsgesellschaft, 1949.

Agabekov, G. S.: *Cheka za Rabotoï* [*The Cheka at Work*], Berlin, 1930.

————: *G.P.U., Zapiski Chekista* [*With the G.P.U., Reminiscences of a Chekist*], Berlin, 1930.

"Agricola" (pseud. for A. Bauermeister): *Der Rote Marschal Tukhachevsky's Aufstieg und Fall* [*The Rise and Fall of the Red Marshal Tukhachevsky*], Berlin, Die Wehrmacht, 1939.

Albert-Petit, A.: *"De quoi s'agit-il?* [What Is It All About?]" in *Journal des Débats* (Paris), February 7, 1930.

"Aleksandrov" (pseud. for Mikhel'son): *Kto Upravlyayet Rossiyeï: Bol'shevistskii Partiinopravitel'stvennyi Apparat i "Stalinism." Istoriko-Dogmaticheskii Analiz* [*Who Rules Russia: the Bolshevik Party and State Machine and "Stalinism." A Historical-Dogmatic Survey*], Berlin, 1933.

Amfiteatrov, A.: *"O Treste* [Regarding the Trust]," in *Vozrozhdenie* (Paris), 1935, No. 3962 *et seq.*

————: *"Vzryv na Moike* [The Bombing Attempt on the Moika]," in *idem.*, 1935, No. 4011 *et seq.*

Andreyev, G.: *"Byl-li Zagovor?* [Was There a Plot?]," in *Posev* (Limburg), 1950, No. 32.

Barmine, A.: *One Who Survived. The Life Story of a Russian under the Soviets*, New York, Putnam, 1945.

Bartz, K.: *Die Tragödie der Deutschen Abwehr* [*The Tragedy of the German Abwehr*], Salzburg, Pilgrim, 1953.

Basily, N. de: *Russia under Soviet Rule. Twenty Years of Soviet Experiment*, London, Allen & Unwin, 1938.

Bazhanov, B.: *L'Enlèvement du Général Koutiepoff* [*The Kidnaping of General Kutyepov*], Paris, Spes, 1930.

Beck, F. and Godin, W.: *Russian Purge and the Extraction of Confession*, London, Hurst & Blackett, 1951.

Beneš, E.: *Memoires*, London, Allen & Unwin, 1954.

Berndorff, H. R.: *Diplomatische Unterwelt* [*The Diplomatic Underworld*], Stuttgart, Dieck, 1930.

————: *General zwischen Ost und West* [*A General's Dilemma: 'twixt East and West*], Hamburg, Hoffmann u. Campf, 1951.

Bessedovsky, G. Z.: *Na Putyakh k Termidoru: Iz Vospominanii Byvshago Sovyetskago Diplomata* [*The Road to Thermidor: from the Reminiscences of a Former Soviet Diplomat*], Paris, Mishen', 1931.

Billotey, P.: *"Autour de l'Affaire Koutiepoff* [In Connection with the Kutyepov Affair]," in *Annales Politiques et Littéraires* (Paris), March 1, 1930.

Bobrov, M.: *"Zagovor ili Revoliutziya* [Plot or Revolution]," in *Sotzialisticheskii Vestnik* (Paris & New York), 1947, No. 10.

Bol'shaya Sovyetskaya Entzyklopediya [*The Great Soviet Encyclopedia*], 2d. edition, Moscow, 1948–

Brunovsky, Vl.: *The Methods of the OGPU*, London, Harper, 1931.

Brzezinski, Z. K.: *The Permanent Purge, Politics in Soviet Totalitarianism*, Cambridge, Mass., Harvard, 1956.

Buber-Neumann, M.: *Von Potzdam nach Moscau* [*From Potsdam to Moscow*], Stuttgart, D. Verlagsanstalt, 1957.

Burtzev, Vl.: *Bol'shevistskiye Gangstery v Parizhe* [*The Bolshevik Gangsters in Paris*], Paris, Obshcheye Dyelo, Paris, 1939.

————: *Boritess' s GPU* [*Fight the GPU*], Paris, Obshcheye Dyelo, 1932.

————: *"Ispoved' Savinkova* [Savinkov's Confession]," in *Illyustrirovannaya Rossiya* (Paris), October 26, 1927.

————: *"V Syetyakh GPU* [In the GPU's Net]," in *idem.*, October 8, 1927.

————: *V Zashchitu Pravdy* [*In Defense of the Truth*], Paris, Obshcheye Dyelo, 1931.

Carr, E. H.: *The Bolshevik Revolution, 1917-1923. History of Soviet Russia*, London & New York, Macmillan, 1951-1953.

Chamberlin, W. H.: *The Russian Revolution, 1917-1921*, New York, Macmillan, 1935.

————: *Russia's Iron Age*, Boston, Little Brown, 1934.

Chebyshev, N.: *"Istoriya Odnoĭ Leghendy* [The Story of a 'Legend'],"
in *Vozrozhdenie* (Paris), 1935, No. 3702 *et seq*.

Cheka. *Materyaly po Deyatel'nosti Chrezvychainykh Komissii* [*The
Cheka. Data Relating to the Activities of the Extraordinary Commissions*], ed. by V. Chernov, Berlin, 1922.

Chernov, V.: *"Savinkov v Ryadakh Partii Sotzialistov-Revolyutzionerov*
[Savinkov in the Ranks of the S.R. Party]," in *Volya Rossii* (Prague),
1924, Nos. 14-15.

Churchill, W. S.: *Great Contemporaries*, New York, Putnam, 1937.

————: *The Gathering Storm*, Boston, Houghton Mifflin, 1948.

Ciliga, A.: *The Russian Enigma*, London, Routledge, 1940.

Colvin, Ian: *Chief of Intelligence*, London, Gollancz, 1951.

Coulondre, R.: *De Stalin à Hitler. Souvenirs de Deux Ambassades, 1936-
1939* [*From Stalin to Hitler. Reminiscences about Two Missions,
1936-1939*], Paris, Hachette, 1950.

Crankshaw, Ed.: *"The Men Around Khrushchev," in the Atlantic Monthly*
(Boston), July, 1959.

Dallin, D.: *The Real Soviet Russia*, New Haven, Yale, 1947.

————: *Soviet Espionage*, New Haven, Yale, 1955.

Davies, J.: *Mission to Moscow*, New York, Simon & Schuster, 1941.

Denikin, Gen. A.: *The Russian Turmoil; Memoires, Military, Social and
Political*, London, Hutchinson, 1921.

————: *The White Army*, London, Cape, 1930.

Deutscher, I.: *Stalin. A Political Biography*, New York & London, Oxford,
1949.

————: *The Prophet Armed, 1879-1921*, New York & London, Oxford,
1954.

Dewar, H.: *Assassins at Large*, London, Wingate, 1951.

Dewey, John: *The Case of Leon Trotzky; Report of the Hearings on the
Charges Made Against Him in the Moscow Trials by the Preliminary
Commission of Enquiry,"* New York & London, Harper, 1937.

Dickhoff-Daehrenthal, A.: *"Der Kampf Gegen die Bolsheviki* [The Struggle Against the Bolsheviks]," in *Vaterländische Nachrichten* (Berlin), November 24, 1918.

"Die Sovjetunion auf dem Wege zum Bonapartismus [The Soviet Union's
Progress Toward Bonapartism]," in *Deutsche Wehr* (Berlin), October 27, 1938.

"Die Wahrheit über den Fall Tukhachevski [The Truth about the Tukhachevsky Affair]," in *Die Welt* (Hamburg), March, 1956.

Ducloux, L.: *From Blackmail to Treason. Political Crime and Corruption
in France, 1920-1940*, London, Deutsch, 1958.

Dukes, Sir P.: *Red Dusk and the Morrow. Adventures and Investigations in the Red Russia*, Garden City, New York, Doubleday, Page & Co., 1922.

————: *The Story of S.T.25. Adventures and Romance in the Secret Intelligence Service in Red Russia*, London, Cassell, 1938.

Duranty, W.: *Stalin & Co., the Politbureau, the Men Who Run Russia*, New York, Sloane, 1949.

————: *The Curious Lottery*, New York, Coward-McCann, 1929.

————: *Duranty Reports Russia*, New York, Viking, 1934.

————: *Red Economy*, Boston, Houghton Mifflin, 1932.

Dyelo Borisa Savinkova Pered Voyennoï Kolleghieï Verkhovnago Suda S.S.S.R. [*The Case of Boris Savinkov Before the Military Collegium of the Supreme Court of the U.S.S.R. Official Transcript*], Moscow, 1924.

Fainsod, Merle: *How Russia Is Ruled*, Cambridge, Mass., Harvard, 1953.

Falls, C.: "Tukhachevsky Sups in Montmartre," in *The London Illustrated News* (London), August 16, 1952.

Fedotoff-White, D.: *The Growth of the White Army*, Princeton, 1944.

Fervacque, P.: *Le Chef de l'Armée Rouge: Mikaïl Toukatchevski* [*The Red Army's Head: Mikhail Tukhachevsky*], Paris, Fasquelle, 1928.

Fischer, R.: *Stalin and German Communism: A Study in the Origins of the State Party*, Cambridge, Mass., Harvard, 1948.

Freund, Ger.: *Unholy Alliance. Russian-German Relations from Brest-Litovsk to Berlin, 1918-1926*, London, Chatto & Windus, 1957.

Fromm, Bela: *Blood and Banquets. A Berlin Social Diary*, New York, Harper, 1942.

Guderian, Gen. H.: *Panzerleader*, New York, Dutton, 1952.

Gul', R.: *Tukhachevsky, Krassnyi Marshal* [*Tukhachevsky, the Red Marshal*], Berlin.

Henon de Lavault: *L'Affaire Koutiepoff* [*The Kutyepov Affair*], Paris, 1943.

Hilger, G.: *Wir und der Kremlin. Deutsch-Sovjetische Beziehungen 1918-1941* [*We and the Kremlin. German-Soviet Relations, 1918-1941*], Frankfurt am Main, Metzner, 1955.

Hill, Capt. Geo.: *Dreaded Hour*, London, Cassell, 1936.

————: *Go Spy the Land*, London, Cassell, 1932.

History of the Communist Party of the Soviet Union (Bolsheviks). A Short Course, Moscow, 1952.

Hoettl, W.: *The Secret Front*, London, Weidenfeld & Nicholson, 1954.

Istoriya Dilpomatii [*A History of Diplomacy*], ed. by Vl. Potyomkin, Moscow, 1944-1945.

Istoriya Grazhdanskoï Voïny, 1917-1922 [*A History of the Civil War,*

1917-1922], ed. by Gorky, Kirov, Molotov, Stalin and Zhdanov, Moscow, 1938-1948.

Kennan, Geo.: *Soviet-American Relations 1917-1920. The Decision to Intervene*, Princeton, 1956.

Kichkassov, N. N.: *Byelogvardeiskii Terror Protiv S.S.S.R.* [*White Guardist Terror Against the U.S.S.R.*], Moscow, 1928.

Kirov, S.: *Izbranniye Statii i Ryetchi* [*Selected Articles and Speeches*], Moscow, 1944.

Koestler, A.: *Darkness at Noon*, London, Cape, 1941.

Kritzky, M.: *Kornilovskii Udarnyi Polk* [*The Kornilov Shock Regiment*], Paris, 1936.

"Krivitzky, W." (pseud. for Ghinsburg): *In Stalin's Secret Service*, London & New York, Harper, 1939.

General A. P. Kutiepov. Sbornik Stateï [*General A. P. Kutyepov. An Anthology of Articles*, Paris, 1934.

Lebedev, V.: "*Konetz Savinkova* [Savinkov's End]," in *Volya Rossii* (Prague), 1926, No. 5, 14-15.

————: "*Taïna Possmertnago Rasskaza 'V Tyur'me' Borisa Savinkova* [The Secret of Boris Savinkov's Posthumous Story 'In Jail']," in *idem.*, 1926, No. 11.

***: "*Leghenda i Deistviltel'nost'* [Legend and Reality]," in *Vozrozhdenie* (Paris), 1951, Nos. 14-15.

Leites, Nathan C. and Bernaul, Elsa: *Ritual of Liquidation: The Case of the Moscow Trials*, Glencoe, Ill., 1954.

Leverkühn, P.: *German Military Intelligence. A First-Hand Account of the Wehrmacht's Secret Service in the Second World War*, New York, Praeger, 1954.

Liddell Hart, B. E.: *The Red Army*, New York, Harcourt Brace, 1956.

Litvinov, M.: *Notes for a Diary*, New York, William Morrow, 1955.

Lockhart, Sir R. H. Bruce: *Memoires of a British Agent*, Harmondsworth, Penguin, 1950.

Lüdecke, W.: *Behind the Scenes of Espionage. Tales of the Secret Service*, London, Harrap, 1929.

Maugham, W. S.: "The Terrorist," in *Redbook*, New York, October, 1943.

Maynard, Sir J.: *Russia in Flux*, New York, Macmillan, 1948.

Meissner, Boris: *Sovjetrussland zwischen Revolution und Restauration* [*Soviet Russia 'twixt Revolution and Restoration*], Köln, 1956.

Melville, Cecil F.: *The Russian Face of Germany*, London, Wishart, 1932.

Moorehead, Alan: *The Russian Revolution*, New York, Harper, 1958.

Nabokov, Vl.: *Nabokov's Dozen*, New York, Doubleday, 1958.

Nikolayevsky, N.: "*Stalin i Ubiistvo Kirova* [Stalin and Kirov's Assassination]," in *Sotzialisticheskii Vestnik* (New York), May, 1956.

Nord, L. A.: "Marshal M. V. Tukhachevsky," in *Vozrozhdenie* (Paris), 1957, Nos. 63-69.

Opishnya, I.: "*Tukhachevsky i Skoblin* [Tukhachevsky and Skoblin]," in *Vozrozhdenie* (Paris), March, 1955.

Orlov, A.: *The Secret History of Stalin's Crimes,* New York, Random House, 1953.

Petrov, V. and E.: *Empire of Fear. Their Own Story,* New York, Praeger, 1956.

Polyansky, V.: "*A. P. Kutiepov i Sovyetzkaya Provokatziya* [A. P. Kutyepov and Soviet Provocation]," in *Yubileinyi Sbornik Obshchestva Gallipoliitzev,* Paris, 1952.

Radek, K. *Der Prozess Gegen Boris Savinkov* [*Boris Savinkov's Trial*], Berlin, 1925.

Rauch, G. von: *A History of Soviet Russia,* London, Thames & Hudson, 1957.

Reilly, S. G.: *Britain's Master Spy or the Adventures of Sydney Reilly,* London, Elkin, Mathews and Marriot, 1931.

Reswick, W.: *I Dreamt Revolution,* Chicago, Regnery, 1952.

Rowan, R. W.: *Terror in Our Time,* New York, Longmans, Green & Co., 1941.

Savinkov, Boris: *Memoires of a Terrorist,* New York, Boni, 1931.

————: *Kon' Voronoï* [*The Black Horse*], Paris, 1924.

————: *Nakanune Novoï Revolyutzii* [*On the Eve of a New Revolution*], Warsaw, 1921.

————: *Posledniye Piss'ma iz Tyur'my* [*Last Letters from Prison*], Moscow, 1926.

————: *Posmertniye Rasskazy i Piss'ma* [*Posthumous Short Stories and Letters*], Moscow, 1926.

————: *Rasskazy* [*Short Stories*], Moscow, 1925.

————: *V Tyur'me* [*In Prison*], Moscow, 1925.

Sayers, M. and Kahn, A.: *The Great Conspiracy. The Secret War Against the Soviet Union,* Boston, Little Brown, 1946.

Schachtmann, M.: *Behind the Moscow Trials,* New York, Pioneer, 1936.

Scheffer, P.: *Sieben Jahre Sovjetunion, 1921-1928* [*Seven Years in the Soviet Union 1921-1928*], Leipzig, Bibliogr. Institut, 1930.

Schellenberg, W.: *The Labyrinth,* New York, Harper, 1956.

Schuman, F. L.: *Soviet Politics at Home and Abroad,* New York, Knopf, 1946.

Semyonov, J.: "*Vtoroï Trust* [A Second Trust]," in *Vozrozhdenie* (Paris), 1935, No. 3720.

Serge, V.: *L'Assassinat Politique et l'U.R.S.S.* [*Political Assassination and the U.S.S.R.*], Paris, Tisné, 1938.

————: *Mémoires d'un Révolutionnaire* [*Memoires of a Revolutionary*], Paris, Editions du Seuil, 1951.

————: *Portrait de Staline* [*A Portrait of Stalin*], Paris, Grasset, 1940.

Sergheyev, A.: "*Zagovory i Mify* [Plots and Myths]," in *Posev* (Limburg), June 4, 1950.

Shulghin, V. V.: "*Posleslovie k 'Triom Stolitzam'* [Postscript to my 'Three Cities']," in *Rossiya i Slavyanstvo* (Paris), October 15, 1927.

————: *Tri Stolitzy. Puteshestviye v Krassnuyu Rossiyu* [*Three Cities. The Story of a Trip into Red Russia*], Berlin, Mednyi Vsadnik, 1927.

Souvarine, B.: *Stalin. A Critical Survey of Bolshevism*, New York, Longmans, Green, 1939.

Soviet Documents on Foreign Policy, I. 1917-1924; II, 1925-1932; III, 1933-1941, ed. by J. Degras, London, Oxford, 1951-1953.

Soviet Russia in the East, 1920-1927, A Documentary Survey, Stanford, Calif., 1957.

Soviet Russia in the West, 1920-1927. A Documentary Survey, Stanford, Calif., 1957.

Stalin, J.: *Sochineniya* [*Works*], Moscow, 1946-1952.

————: *Problems of Leninism*, Moscow, 1945.

Stepun, F. A.: "B. V. Savinkov, Otryvok iz Vospominanii [B. V. Savinkov, An Excerpt from my Reminiscences]," in *Vozrozhdenie* (Paris), 1950, No. 9.

Stewart, Geo.: *The White Armies of Russia*, New York, Macmillan, 1933.

Sudebnyi Otchet Po Dyelu Trotzkistkago-Zinovievskago Terroristicheskago Tzentra [*Official Record of the Proceedings in the Case of the Trotskyite-Zinovyevite Terrorist Center*], Moscow, 1936.

Sudebnyi Otchet Po Dyelu Anti-Sovyetskago Terroristicheskago Tzentra [*Official Record of the Proceedings in the Case of the anti-Soviet Terrorist Center*], Moscow, 1937.

Sudebnyi Otchet Po Dyelu Pravo-Trotzkistskago Bloka [*Official Record of the Proceedings in the Case of the Rightist-Trotskyite Bloc*], Moscow, 1938.

Svanidze, Budu: *My Uncle Joe*, London, 1952.

Svetlanin, A.: *Dal'nevostochnyi Zagovor* [*The Far-Eastern Plot*], Frankfurt am Main, Posev, 1952.

————: "*O Zagovore Tukhachevskago i Zagovorakh Voobshche* [About the Tukhachevsky Plot and About Plots in General]," in *Posev* (Limburg), No. 197.

————: "*Taina Sobytii 1937-1938 gg.* [The Secret of the Events of 1937-1938]," in *Sotzialisticheskii Vestnik* (New York), March 20, 1949.

————: "*Zagovor Tukhachevskago i OKDVA* [The Tukhachevsky Plot and the [Blücher] Separate Red-Banner Far Eastern Army]," in *Posev* (Limburg), No. 196.

Tabouis, Geneviève: *Ils l'ont appelée Cassandre [They Called Her Cassandra]*, New York, 1942.

Tobenkin, E.: "B. Savinkov. The Conversion of the Soviets' Most Spectacular Foe," in *Current History* (London), December, 1924.

Treadgold, D. W.: "The Ideology of the White Movement: Wrangel's 'Leftist Policy from Rightist Hands,'" in *Russian Thought and Politics*, Harvard Slavic Studies Series, Vol. IV, pp. 496-497.

Trevor-Roper, H. R.: *The Last Days of Hitler*, London, Macmillan, 1947.

Trotzky, L.: *La Bureaucratie Stalinienne et l'Assassinat de Kirov [The Stalinist Bureaucracy and Kirov's Assassination]*, Paris, Librairie du Travail, 1935.

————: *The Revolution Betrayed. What Is the Soviet Union and Where Is It Going?*, Garden City, New York, 1937.

————: *The Stalin School of Falsification*, New York, Pioneer, 1937.

Tukhachevsky, M.: *La Marche au-delà de la Vistule [The Advance Beyond the Vistula]*, Moscow, 1923.

————: "Sentinel of Peace. Report to the Central Committee of the CPSU(b), January 15, 1936," Moscow, 1936.

————: *Voyna Klassov [The War of the Classes]*, Moscow, 1921.

Tzurikov, N.: *General A. P. Kutiepov*, Prague, 1937.

"Uralov, A." (pseud. for A. Avtorkhanov): *The Reign of Stalin*, London, Bodley Head, 1953.

"Valtin, Jan" (pseud. for R. J. H. Krebs): *Out of the Night*, London, Heinemann, 1941.

Versonnex, H. de: *"Touchatchevsky,"* in *La Revue Hebdomodaire* (Paris), July, 1937.

Vishnyak, M.: *"Svidetel' Istorii* [A Witness of History]," in *Novoye Russkoye Slovo* (New York), November 11, 1956.

Voitzekhovsky, S. L.: *"Sovyetskiye Sverkh-Azefy* [The Soviet Super-Azefs]," in *Vozrozhdenie* (Paris), 1950, No. 8.

————: *"P. B. Struve v Varshave. Iz Istorii Trusta* [P. B. Struve in Warsaw. From the History of the Trust]," in *idem.*, 1950, No. 9.

"Vraga, R." (pseud. for R. Niezbrzycki): *"Trust,"* in *idem.*, 1950, No. 7.

————: *"Trust i Vnutrennaya Liniya* [The Trust and the Inner Line]," in *idem.*, 1950, No. 11.

————: "Russian Emigration After Twenty Years' Exile," in *Eastern Quarterly* (London), January, 1951, Vol. IV, No. 1.

Weissberg, A.: *The Accused*, New York, Simon & Schuster, 1952.

Wener, M.: "Persons and Personages," in *Living Age* (New York), August, 1936.

Wheeler-Bennett, J. W.: *The Nemesis of Power. The German Army in Politics, 1918-1945*, New York, St. Martin's Press, 1954.

Wilson, E.: *To the Finland Station, A Study in the Writing and Acting of History*, Garden City, N.Y., 1953.

Wolfe, B.: *Khrushchev and Stalin's Ghost*, New York, Praeger, 1957.

————: *Three Who Made a Revolution. A Biographical History*, New York, Dial Press, 1948.

Wolin, S. and Slusser, R.: *The Soviet Secret Police*, New York, Praeger, 1957.

Wollenberg, E.: *"Der Apparat. Stalin's Fünfte Kolonne* [The *Apparat.* Stalin's Fifth Column]," in *Ostprobleme* (Bad Godesberg), 1951, No. 19.

————: *The Red Army*, London, Secker & Warburg, 1942.

Also the back files of the following publications:

L'Ami du Peuple (Paris)
Bolshevik (Moscow)
Bor'ba za Rossiyu (Paris)
Bulleten' Lighy Bor'by za Narodnuyu Svobodu (Paris)
Bulleten' Oppositzii (Paris)
Ce Soir (Paris)
Chassovoy (Brussels, earlier Paris)
Daily Telegraph (London)
L'Echo de Paris (Paris)
Le Figaro (Paris)
Goloss Minuvshago Na Chuzhoy Storonye (Paris)
L'Humanité (Paris)
Huvustadtbladt (Helsinki)
L'Illustration (Paris)
Illyustrirovannaya Rossiya (Paris)
L'Intransigeant (Paris)
Izvestya (Moscow)
Le Journal (Paris)
Krassnaya Zvesda (Moscow)
La Liberté (Paris)
Manchester Guardian (Manchester)
Le Matin (Paris)
Morning Post (London)
Münchener Post (München)
New Leader (New York)
New York Times (New York)
Novoye Russkoye Slovo (New York)

Obshcheye Dyelo (Paris)
Ostprobleme (Bad Godesberg)
Le Petit Parisien (Paris)
Posev (Limburg)
Posledniye Novosti (Paris)
Pravda (Moscow, earlier Leningrad)
Revoliutzionnaya Rossiya (Paris)
Russkaya Mysl' (Paris)
Segodnya (Riga)
Slovo (Riga)
Sotzialisticheskii Vestnik (New York, earlier Paris)
Der Stern (Hamburg)
Times (London)
Uusi Suomi (Helsinki)
Vestnik Obshchestva Gallipoliitzev (Paris)
Volya Rossii (Prague)
Vorwärts (Berlin)
Vozrozhdenie (Paris)
Die Welt (Hamburg)
Za Rossiyu (Paris)

INDEX